Who is an African?

Identity, Citizenship and the Making of the Africa-Nation

Edited by

Jideofor Adibe

Published by
Adonis & Abbey Publishers Ltd
P.O. Box 43418
London
SE11 4XZ

http://www.adonis-abbey.com
Email: editor@adonis-abbey.com

First Edition, May 2009

British Library Cataloguing-in-Publication Data
A catalogue record for this book is available from the British Library

ISBN:9781905068913 (HB)/ 9781906704551(PB)

Who is an African?

Identity, Citizenship and the Making of the Africa-Nation

Edited by

Jideofor Adibe

Dedication

For my Mother, Madam Patricia Nwanyingbo Adibe, who rested in the Lord in 2002. Mama, we miss you every day but we take solace in the knowledge that you are now with our Lord.
For my wife, Ngozi, and children: Adaobi, Udoka and Didi. With all my love

Table of Contents

FOREWORD

I am delighted to be invited to, and have great pleasure in writing the foreword to this important subject matter and topic, viz, the ongoing discussions on "African identity and citizenship" and the current efforts by Africa's leadership to create a "United States of Africa", that will facilitate the construction of unity among the various states and peoples that are designated as Africa and Africans respectively. The question of who is an African is therefore a legitimate one. It is a question that, on face value, appears simple and straightforward. Is it any one born and bred within the geographical area of Africa, of any racial origin – African, Arab, Asian or European? Or should it be purely by a particular racial group? However, as can be seen from the various contributions in this work, answers to that simple question may not after all be that simple as some people designated as Africans may not see themselves as such, while some believe there is a taxonomy of elements that make up an African such that there is a hierarchy of Africans, with some being more African than others.

It can be argued that the problem of identifying who is an African or who the African is, as presented by contributors to this volume, is not significantly different from the problem of identifying who is a Nigerian in Nigeria, the Sierra Leonean in Sierra Leone, the Somalian in Somalia, the Sudanese in Sudan or any other group of people or country in Africa. It is a fact that most of the countries in Africa, as we know them today, are made up of previously independent group of people or ethnic nationalities, which were brought together as nation-states, by the 1885 Berlin Conference and subsequently colonialism. Despite the challenges and difficulties in the nation-building project in Africa, few people will doubt that many of the citizens of these African countries are increasingly coming to see themselves as having a common bond. If we take for an example a case of hypothetical African immigrant shot dead or maltreated in a foreign country, is it uncommon to see citizens of that country come together solidarity protest? This informs us that while it can be said that the nation-building project in various African countries still has a long way to go, it cannot be said to be a complete failure. For instance, is it uncommon to see Cameroonians, Nigerians or South Africans of various ethnic and linguistic groups come together to celebrate the success (or mourn the defeat) of their national football team? This again seems to tell us that the nation-building project in these countries cannot be said to be a complete failure but progressing, even if slowly. It would in fact seem that in almost all African countries, there are increasingly more things that unify the citizens than those that divide them, and it could also be convincingly argued that most of the fissiparous tendencies in many of these countries are in fact becoming weaker, giving way to a more united people and nations.

Can the relative success of the nation building project in various African countries be applied to the various peoples that are called Africans? Yes, I believe it can. Admittedly, almost all countries in Africa today are of colonial creations. Africa was at various times colonised by Arab/Middle East and European powers that introduced new ideas, ideals and systems of government which the African countries adopted and adapted it in their efforts at constructing modern nation states. In Africa, it will appear that the efforts at forging intra-unity within and among the constituent countries did create a conscious Africa and Africans. This does not mean creating an Africa and Africans with a homogeneous worldview. Rather it means that but that despite their differences, Africans of different Africanity, seem to agree for instance on the basic principles of democracy and good governance. I believe Africa is taking a giant stride in the project of making the new African. To me the African unity I envisage is that in which we utilise and use our diversity as strength, and unite to defeat the common challenges of poverty, ignorance, diseases and marginalisation from an increasingly fast-paced corporate world.

Let me end this foreword by associating myself with the views of the editor of this book Dr. Jideofor Adibe that Africa is favoured in the current world conjuncture. In particular I share the sentiments expressed about Barack Obama, the incumbent American President, that Africans require a change of attitude that is post chauvinism for "it is only by being post-racial and reconciler that a Blackman, with an African Muslim father, who was not born into privilege, could emerge President of the most powerful country in the world." I also agree that the emergence of Obama is an additional fillip to the continent's unity project.

I recommend this work to all of us Africans, students of Africa and friends of Africa that truly believe in Africa and African unity. Happy reading!

Rtd Gen (Dr) Yakubu Gowon
Former Nigeria's Head of State, 1966-1975.

Preface

COMPARATIVE AFRICANITY: BLOOD, SOIL AND ANCESTRY

Ali A. Mazrui

September 2009 marks the one hundredth anniversary of the birth of Kwame Nkrumah of Ghana, the great pioneer of post-colonial Pan-Africanism. September 2009 also marks the 40th anniversary of the Libyan revolution and the political ascendancy of Muammar al-Qaddafi, heir to Nkrumah's legacy of continent Pan-Africanism.

By a remarkable coincidence these two anniversaries (Nkrumah's centenary and Qaddafi's fourth decade as revolutionary leader) were implicitly celebrated when Muammar al-Qaddafi was elected the presiding Head of the African Union at a summit meeting in Addis Ababa, Ethiopia, in early 2009. There seems little doubt that both Nkrumah and Qaddafi are historic sons of mother Africa. But are they "Africans" in the same sense of the term? This is where we distinguish between *Africans of the blood* and *Africans of the soil.*

Africans of the blood are defined in racial and genealogical terms. They are identified with the black race. Africans of the soil, on the other hand, are defined in geographical terms. They are identified with the African continent in nationality and ancestral location.

Most Libyans, Egyptians and Tunisians are Africans of the soil, but not necessarily of the blood. Most Diaspora Africans in the United States, the Caribbean, or Brazil are Africans of the blood, but not of the soil. However, most Ghanaians, Nigerians or Ugandans are both Africans of the blood (genealogically belonging to the African race) and Africans of the soil (geographically located in, or belonging to, the African continent).

Who was the first African Secretary-General of the United Nations – Boutros Boutros-Ghali or Kofi Annan? Boutros-Ghali was an African of the soil, but since he was descended from the Copts, Boutros-Ghali was as indigenous to Africa geographically as Kofi Annan. Boutros-Ghali was not an immigrant Arab but was an Arabized descendant of the ancient Pharohnic Egyptians. However, Boutros-Ghali did not qualify as an African of the blood since he was not racially black. Kofi Annan, on the other hand, was the first black Secretary-General of the United Nations from any country. But since he was a black Ghanaian, Kofi Annan was both an African of the blood and of the soil.

It is, however, worth noting that while Boutros Boutros-Ghali and Muammar Qaddafi are Africans of the soil by ancient ancestry, F.W. deKlerk and other white South Africans are Africans of the soil by adoption. This also applies to East Africans of Indian or Pakistani ancestry. They are indeed Africans of the soil by adoption.

What about Barack Obama, the 44th President of the United States of America? Here we need to make one further distinction: the distinction between an *African American* and an *American African*? In the case of an African American the noun is American. And then to the question "What kind of American?", the answer is "an African American". This applies to Colin Powell, Jesse Jackson and other survivors of the Middle Passage.

In the case of an American African, on the other hand, the noun is African. And then to the question "What kind of African?", the answer becomes "an American African". Normally, an American African is still very conscious of his indigenous Africanity, is aware of his immediate continental ancestry, is in contact with relatives in Africa, is bilingual (speaking at least one African language), and is at home with such aspects of indigenous African culture as cuisine (such as fufu for West Africa, matoke for Uganda, sima or ugali for Tanzania, etc.).

Most African Americans, on the other hand, are descendants of the Middle Passage, are not in contact with relatives in Africa, are not native speakers of an African language, and are seldom socialized into African cuisines even when they are Pan-African.

Barack Obama has an intermediate identity between African American and American African. Young Barack Obama did know his Kenyan father; the child last saw the father when Barack was about ten years old. The 44th President of the United States has established contact with the village of his father's birth, and with his Kenyan half-siblings and other African relatives. In this sense, Barack Obama is closer to the identity of American African.

However, the 44th President of the United States has no command of either the Luo language or Kiswahili, and has not been socialized into indigenous Kenyan cuisines. Indeed, he is culturally almost totally American except for his considerable exposure to multiculturalism in both Indonesia and Hawaii. In this sense he is a well-travelled African American, rather than an American African.

If a Diaspora Black like Barack Obama is a bridge between Africans of the blood in Africa and those in the Diaspora, what are the bridges between Africans of the soil of Arab lineage (like Boutros-Ghali and Qaddafi) and Africans of the soil who are black (like Nkrumah and Kofi Annan)? This brings us to the remarkable history of convergence between the Arab people and the African people. When the Arab conquest of Egypt occurred in the 7th century, Egyptians were neither Arab nor Muslim. Their mother tongue was not Arabic, and their religion was not Islam. Today there are more than a hundred million Arab Muslims in North Africa. A new identity has in fact developed – the identity of *Afrabians.*

Geographical Afrabians are Africans of the soil in North Africa who are Arab without intermarriage with Africans of the blood (black Africans). Geneological Afrabians are those who are products of intermarriage between Arabs and black Africans. These include the majority of Northern Sudanese, half of Mauritanians, Swahilized dynastic Afrabian families like the Mazrui of Kenya and Tanzania, and famous Arabs of mixed racial descent like the late President Anwar Sadat of Egypt, whose mother was black.

Ideological Afrabians are Africans of the blood who refuse to recognize the Sahara as a divide, and insist that all people indigenous to Africa (be they Arab or black) are one people. Ideological Afrabians include Kwame Nkrumah of Ghana who insisted on the oneness of the African continent. But by marrying an Egyptian, the lady Fathiyya, their children were genealogical Afrabians.

Cultural Afrabians are usually black Africans who have no Arab blood whatsoever, but are highly Arabized culturally. Many Sudanese (both Northern and Southern) are deeply Arabized in speech and values without being Arab genealogically.

There are also Black Egyptians of the upper Nile and on Nubi Mountains who are steeped in Arab culture but are not products of Arab blood. Berbers of Libya, Algeria, and the rest of the Maghreb might also be regarded as Afrabians. Most of them are bilingual in Arabic and a Berber language, and have assimilated considerable Arab culture.

What about the Hausa and Hausa-Fulani of Northern Nigeria? Indeed, are not the majority of Islamized Africans of the blood (black Muslims) automatically cultural Afrabians? That is a defensible categorization.

Let us now return to the African Union and the election of Muammar Qaddafi as its presiding Head of State. In what sense is the African Union itself an Afrabian institution? How was the torch of Pan-Africanism passed from one Afrabian institution – the Organization of

African Unity – to this new one? And how did Nkrumah as an ideological Afrabian pass on the torch to Qaddafi as a geographical Afrabian?

When the Organization of African Unity (O.A.U.) was formed in Addis Ababa in 1963, Nkrumah was the most important voice for Pan Africanism, Gamal Abdel Nasser regarded Egypt as the vanguard of Afrabia, and Emperor Haile Selassie offered to host the continent-wide Afro-Arab organization. Addis Ababa became the headquarters of a unique experiment in Afro-Arab relations. At that time Qaddafi was unknown.

The primary agenda of the Organization of African Unity (OAU) was, first, to promote the decolonization of the rest of the African continent; second, to protect the boundaries of the newly emerging African states; thirdly, to help promote stability within the postcolonial entities; and fourthly, to struggle against apartheid and white minority governments in Southern Africa. While Arab countries joined forces to fight apartheid in South Africa, African countries became increasingly supportive of the struggles of the Palestinian people. It was a political quid pro quo – Arab support for the effort against apartheid and racism in exchange for African support in the struggle against Zionism and Israeli occupation of Palestinian and other Arab lands. Afrabianism was getting politicized and radicalized.

But the OAU was not only the first institutionalization of trans-Saharan Pan-Africanism. It was also the beginning of the institutionalization of Afrabia. The membership of the OAU included a majority of the population of the Arab world, the bulk of the land under Arab sovereignty, the largest Arab country in population (Egypt), the largest Arab city (Cairo), and arguably the longest-lasting Arab Revolution (Libya).

The forces which created Afrabia across the centuries included the spread of the Arabic language into Africa; the spread of the Islamic religion across Africa; the migration, intermarriage and intermingling between Arab and African peoples across time; trade and economic integration between the Arabs and Africans, and the political penetration of Africa by the Arabs.

But the most comprehensive institutionalization of Afrabia did not occur until the twentieth century when international organizations began to be formed which included both African and Arab members. Such organizations with overlapping Afro-Arab partnership have included the League of Arab States, the Organization of Petroleum Exporting

Countries and the more inclusive Pan-Islamic organizations such as the Organization of the Islamic Conference.

As the twentieth century was coming to an end, and old style colonialism was ending, a new organization was needed with a new agenda for more ambitious regional integration and unification. Could the African continent be converted into a continental free-trade area without tariffs? Could Africa become a full-scale economic community? Could Africa develop a united monetary system, gradually leading to a single currency and a continental central banking system? Could the peer review system lead on to a true Pax Africana – a self pacification system promoting stability and self-policing?

The leadership for this new phase of pan-Africanism was captured by Libya under Muammar al-Qaddafi in a series of initiatives. These included Libyan-hosted meetings prior to the formation of the African Union in 2002, with the new and more ambitious agenda. There was also the drama of the summit meeting of the African Union in Accra in 2007, partly to mark independent Ghana's 50th anniversary, and partly to champion the ambition of rapid unification of African countries, and the creation of a United States of Africa speedily.

The leadership ambition was the passing of the torch from the legacy of Nkrumah to a new legacy of Qaddafi. The openly articulated unification was that of the African peoples. But there was also a silent process of integration – the Afrabian process which was much older than Pan-Africanism. The silent convergence continued between the African peoples and the Arabs, slowly transforming two populations which were once distinct, into a newly integrated force in world affairs. Africans of the soil and Africans of the blood were converging into newer and more comprehensive identities.

Introduction

AFRICA WITHOUT AFRICANS?

Jideofor Adibe

Who is an African? At face value, the answer seems obvious. Surely, everyone knows who the African is, it would seem. But the answer becomes less obvious once other probing qualifiers are added to the question. How is the African identity constructed in the face of the mosaic of identities that people of African ancestry living within and beyond the continent bear? Is Barack Obama and the like African? Do all categorised as Africans or as having an African pedigree perceive themselves as Africans? Are all who perceive themselves as Africans accepted as such? Are there levels of "African-ness", and are some more African than others? Who allots this African-ness, and why? How does African identity interface with other levels of identity and citizenship in Africa?

The above are some of the questions one confronts when trying to academically delineate who is an African. There appears to be three main classificatory schemes in the literature - identification by race, by geography (territoriality) and consciousness (i.e. commitment to Africa, including to whatever the writer/speaker regards as an African culture.

Racial identification

A starting point may be to imagine, what someone generally agreed to be a non-African, say a Caucasian Briton, means when he talks of an 'African'. If a Caucasian British police officer describes the scene of a crime thus: "At the scene of the crime were four Africans and four white boys", what kind of images come to our mind, to differentiate the four 'Africans' from the four white boys? Here it would seem that physical attributes, especially attributes believed to be specifically African or Bantu, would be the primary organising category. If the same police officer changes the description to: "There were four black/negro men and four white boys at the scene of the crime", what sort of imageries come to our mind? Or better put, what sort of imageries do we think he is trying to convey?

We would argue that the use of 'African' is much narrower than the use of 'black' because our hypothetical Caucasian police officer would most likely think of Africans as being different from black Caribbean, Guyanese or African-Americans even though they are all generically called blacks or Negroes. And he is not exactly wrong in thinking that way, for blacks often make conscious distinction among themselves – based on geographical location (.eg Caribbean, Jamaicans, Nigerians etc) or proximity to the dominant Western culture such as the use of 'Black British' (to designate second or more generations born by Africans or blacks from other locations in the UK), etc.

It would therefore seem that when our hypothetical Caucasian police officer used the word 'black', he was trying to convey a broader racial category, extending beyond pure Bantu and skin pigmentation to culture and even the accent with which the non-Caucasians spoke English.

This would seem to imply that while race does matter as an organising category in identifying the African, it would be inadequate in properly delineating, in the Western imagination at least, who is an African from who is black. This problem is compounded by the fact that the system of defining races by skin colour is based on an inaccurate use of one genetic phenotypic difference, when hundreds are actually involved (McCulloch, 2007).

Another problem of using race to define the African is that it would wrongly make all black people Africans. While most blacks obviously share a common bond, including of course that of skin pigmentation, and racial discrimination, does that really make all blacks Africans? Are black Haitians Africans? Would all black Jamaicans be happy to be called Africans? Would all Africans from the continent accept the black Jamaicans or Haitians as Africans on the same level of Africanity as themselves? Another way of putting this is to pose the question: Does the fact that most Caucasian Americans have European ancestry and features make them Europeans? Obviously this is a debatable point. What is not debatable is that an exclusive use of race to delineate the African would banish geography as a factor in categorising who the African is.

Again if we use race alone in the delineation of the African, a legitimate question is raised about non-black with African citizenship, say, the White South Africans, who never knew any other country but South Africa. Are they Africans? And what of the white person, who, despite having lived all his life in the continent, and has African citizenship, does not want to be seen as an African?

In January 2008, the British newspaper, *Guardian Unlimited*, proposed a list of the six best African footballers of all time and ranked the Portuguese hero Eusebio at No. 1, arguing that though he was a Portuguese international, this was only because it was not possible for him to represent his 'native Mozambique'. A blogger, Ayo Akinfe, immediately begged to differ, and challenged any notion that Eusebio was African. He argued that though Eusebio was born in Mozambique, that fact alone was not enough to make him an African: Akinfe (2008) wrote:

> I love Eusebio to death and still vividly recollect those mazy runs of his in the 1966 World Cup and his breathtaking displays for Benfica but the fact remains that he is not an African. Yes, Eusebio was born in Maputo but then so too were Carlos Queiroz, Manchester United's assistant manager, and Abel Xavier, the Portugal and LA Galaxy defender who once played for Middlesbrough, Everton and Liverpool... Accident of birth does not make you an African. Nothing in Eusebio's mannerism, interests, charitable activities or community programmes gives the slightest indication that he is vaguely interested in Africa.

Read between the lines, it would seem that Akinfe is challenging Eusebio's African-ness not only because of his skin colour but also for his not displaying the necessary consciousness of being an African – an issue we shall return to later. The fact the Guardian considered Eusebio an African, while Akinfe, who sees himself as an 'authentic African' (and perhaps is also seen as such by most non-Africans), begged to differ, clearly illustrates the contentious nature of African identity and the ambiguous role of race in delineating who the African is.

Territoriality

On the face of it, a very simple way of delineating an African will be to look at the map of the world and categorise all those who were born in the continent of Africa or who hold the citizenship of one of the countries that make up the continent, or has ancestry in the continent, as African.

This option too has a number of problems. For example, is having the citizenship of an African country sufficient to make one an African? If being born or being a citizen of a country in the geographical expression called Africa is the pre-requisite, what of the millions of illiterate people living in the continent's villages who have never even heard of the word 'African' or 'citizenship'? Again, what of the descendant of African migrants, say second or more generation of parents who migrated from

Africa and who do not hold the citizenship of any African country but feel deeply African? Will they be excluded from being called Africans? If we choose to call all who have 'African' ancestry Africans, how far back in time should we go? And will this not bring back the problem of delineating all blacks as Africans?

Another problem of using geography or territoriality as a basis for identifying the African is that it assumes that all who are citizens of the countries that make up the continent of Africa accept that they are 'Africans'. We do know for sure that not all citizens of the countries in Africa always and in all circumstances accept they are Africans or believe that they share the same level of Africanity with the rest of the peoples of the continent. A clear example of this is the project of pan-Africanism, which in the continent, competes with Pan-Arabism in North Africa. For instance pan-Africanism as a project has had to contend with the division of Africa into north and south of the Sahara - with the "Arab" north, motivated primarily by Arab nationalism and, to a lesser extent, Islamic ideals, drawn more into the vortex of Middle Eastern pan-Arabism rather than the form of Pan-Africanist aspirations favoured by the leaders and intellectuals from sub-Saharan Africa (Snyder, 2003: 103-139). Even within the countries in sub-Saharan Africa, there is often no unanimity among the citizens that they are all Africans on the same level of Africanity. In fact, the late Somali ruler, Siad Barre (1969-1991), was known to have actively discouraged Somalis from seeing themselves as Africans, but rather encouraged them to see themselves more as Arabs. Mohamed Eno (2008) has in fact documented the existence of a form of Apartheid in Somalia against the Bantu Jareer Somalis, who have more Bantu than Arab features.

In several other countries in the sub-Saharan Africa – such as Nigeria, Sudan, Niger and Mauritania – one finds occasional eruptions of tension between segments of the population who see themselves as having more in common with the Arab world than with their fellow citizens. It is also common to hear some Ethiopians and "black" South Africans referring to citizens of other countries of the continent as "Africans" and to themselves as just Ethiopians or South Africans. Travelling to or from the rest of the continent, it is common to hear some "black" South Africans say they are going to or coming from "Africa". Therefore, territoriality cannot be an adequate variable for delineating who the African is.

To further bring home the problem of using territoriality to delineate the African, let us again return to our hypothetical Caucasian police officer. For instance if an Algerian or Egyptian were to be at the scene of the crime, will our hypothetical British officer use the word 'African' to describe those at the scene of the crime? I would suggest they are unlikely. Most likely they would talk about "four Arabs, or Four Middle Easterners or four Egyptians". This immediately underlines the problem of using geography to delineate Africans. Though North Africans geographically belong to Africa, a typical non-African is unlikely, in every day speech, to describe them as Africans. The closest they might get to this description would be to add the prefix "North" to their Africanness, while Ghanaians and Zimbabweans would ordinarily be called Africans without the prefix West or Southern. There will of course remain the question of whether this is because of their skin pigmentation or racial stock or because they come from that part of Africa, where television images and narratives about Africa are different from the familiar stereotypes of hunger, starvation and inter-ethnic tensions. Above all, using territoriality to determine who is an African raises the question of whether identity should be a choice or an imposition.

Consciousness

There are those who believe that 'consciousness' of being an African, or commitment to the cause of Africa, should be the only or main criterion for delineating who the African is. This form of classification is quite popular with the remnants of the African left and those eager to wear the toga of universalism and cosmopolitanism. One Wayne Visser (2005) articulated in his poem, 'Am an African' the sort of sentiments commonly found in the writings or speeches of those who subscribe to this perspective. Visser (2005) wrote:

Am An African

I am an African
Not because I was born there
But because my heart beats with Africa's
I am an African
Not because my skin is black
But because my mind is engaged by Africa
I am an African
Not because I live on its soil
But because my soul is at home in Africa
When Africa weeps for her children
My cheeks are stained with tears
When Africa honours her elders
My head is bowed in respect

When Africa mourns for her victims
My hands are joined in prayer
When Africa celebrates her triumphs
My feet are alive with dancing
I am an African
For her blue skies take my breath away
And my hope for the future is bright
I am an African
For her people greet me as family
And teach me the meaning of community
I am an African
For her wildness quenches my spirit
And brings me closer to the source of life
When the music of Africa beats in the wind
My blood pulses to its rhythm
And I become the essence of sound
When the colours of Africa dazzle in the sun
My senses drink in its rainbow
And I become the palette of nature
When the stories of Africa echo round the fire
My feet walk in its pathways
And I become the footprints of history
I am an African
Because she is the cradle of our birth
And nurtures an ancient wisdom
I am an African
Because she lives in the world's shadow
And bursts with a radiant luminosity
I am an African
Because she is the land of tomorrow
And I recognise her gifts as sacred

Visser's poem echoes Thabo Mbeki's famous 'I am an African' speech: Part of this reads:

> I owe my being to the hills and the valleys, the mountains and the glades, the rivers, the qdeserts, the trees, the flowers, the seas and the ever-changiqng seasons that define the face of our native land. My body has frozen in our frosts and in our latter day snows. It has thawed in the warmth of our sunshine and melted in the heat of the midday sun. The crack and the rumble of the summer thunders, lashed by startling lightening, have been a cause both of trembling and of hope … The dramatic shapes of the [landscape] have … been panels of the set on the natural stage on which we act out the foolish deeds of the theatre of our day. ...

> At times, and in fear, I have wondered whether I should concede equal citizenship of our country to the leopard and the lion, the elephant and the springbok, the hyena, the black mamba and the pestilential mosquito. A human presence among all these, a feature on the face of our native land thus defined, I know that none dare challenge me when I say - I am an African! ...
>
> I am born of the peoples of the continent of Africa. The pain of the violent conflict that the peoples of Liberia, Somalia, the Sudan, Burundi and Algeria is a pain I also bear. The dismal shame of poverty, suffering and human degradation of my continent is a blight that we share. The blight on our happiness that derives from this and from our drift to the periphery of the ordering of human affairs leaves us in a persistent shadow of despair. This is a savage road to which nobody should be condemned. This thing that we have done today, in this small corner of a great continent that has contributed so decisively to the evolution of humanity says that Africa reaffirms that she is continuing her rise from the ashes ...
>
> Whatever the difficulties, Africa shall be at peace!

For Garba Diallo, if you are an African, you will always remain an African. As he puts it:

> One of the core aspects of being an African is to be territorial. No matter how far Africans go and how long they stay away, psychologically they never leave Africa or abandon their African family, friends and age group.... In fact, the more Africans stay away, the more African they become. (Diallo, 2004:15)

Mammo Muchie argues that any construction of African identity must be built on a rejection of essentialism. For him:

> There is no such thing as an essential African character that has been frozen from time immemorial. Africa has always lived in history and through history. Its identity must be expressed through the rejection of racism, ethnicity, parochialism, exclusivity and barbarism. ... Thus an African identity must posit an inclusive, non-essentialist and emancipatory goals (Muchie, 2004:26)

One of the dangers of using consciousness or commitment to the cause of Africa to define an African is that it is so fluid that any one expressing any sort of interest in African affairs could, by this definition, legitimately claim to be an African. Besides, using consciousness to delineate the African could end up de-Africanising a majority of the people who non-Africans will commonly identify as Africans. Does, for instance the village Igbo or Yoruba or Hausa woman in Nigeria have any consciousness of being an African? If, as is commonly believed, such a consciousness is non-existent, or at best insipient, does that then imply that such people are not Africans? If the 'African' most likely to be identified as an African by the outside world does not see himself or herself as an African, and may not even know of the existence of the notion of "African" since the word does not exist in many indigenous African languages, does this tell us anything about the entire notion of African? Does this raise the question of identity and choice? Similarly, is Tony Blair, who as Prime Minister of Britain, said that Africa was a scar on the consciousness of the world, and felt moved enough to set up the Commission for Africa, an African by this definition?

It will seem that a proper definition and delineation of the African will involve the development of a taxonomy of elements used in identifying the African – geography, race, consciousness, place of birth, culture, residence and citizenship. This will of course imply that there are categories of Africans and that yes indeed some are more African (the more of these they possess) than others. This will also seem to suggest that one's African-ness can expand (as when one engages in projects that help to uplift the continent) or contract (as when one relapses into Afro pessimism).

Contributors to this volume have approached the question of Africanity and African identity differently. In "On the Concept of 'We Are All Africans'", Ali Mazrui notes that the notion of 'African' is essentially a colonial construct, pointing out that it was actually colonialism that informed 'Africans' for the first time that they were 'Africans'. He argues that it was in the various colonial schools and enclaves that people from the different nationalities that make up 'Africa' learned for the first time that the rest of the world called the inhabitants of the landmass of which their area formed a part 'Africans'. In another contribution ('Who Are The Africans?'), Mazrui argues that "Europe's greatest service to the people of Africa was not Western civilization, which is under siege; or even Christianity, which is on the defensive. Europe's supreme gift was the gift of African identity, bequeathed without grace or design – but a reality all the same."

Kwesi Prah in "Who is an African?" notes the conflicting emotions stirred by Thabo Mbeki on 8 May 1996, soon after the promulgation of the Constitution for a new post-Apartheid South Africa with his famous "I am an African" speech. Prah observes that that "simple and most obvious affirmation" by Mbeki, who was then the political heir apparent of President Mandela, sent ripples of disconcertion in some circles of South African society, while creating elation and enthusiasm in others. Prah is also critical of an emerging tendency in South Africa to use 'commitment' to define who the African is, and asks which of the major constituencies of the globe ever defines its constituency by "commitment". He contends that to define the African we must pose the question of what "in our experience and collective being defines us in historical and cultural distinction to the rest of humankind?"

After surveying through the minefield of discourses on African identity, Mohamed A. Eno and Omar A. Eno identify at least six different types of Africanity - Africanity by accident of geography, Africanity by birth, Africanity by settlership, Africanity by culture or acculturation, Africanity by ideology and Africanity by pretension or circumstantial Africanity. Steven Friedman examines the notion of 'White Africans" in Africa and blames the tendency to use continental identity to refer to racial category for the refusal of some to "admit white residents of Africa to African-ness". He contends that if we accept that "there is no monolithic African culture, then the white presence could be seen as just one more addition to the cultural mix."

Bankie Forster Bankie in "Arab Slavery of Africans in the Afro-Arab Borderlands – The Sudan Case", Kwesi Prah in "The Politics of Apologetics", Garba Diallo, G. Swart & Monique Theron, Marcel Kitissou and Franco Henwood discuss the co-existence of 'different Africans' and the identity politics constructed from this in the "Borderlands" of Sudan, Mauritania, South Africa, Togo and Nigeria.

Despite the competing narratives and politics of who is an African, a more crucial question is whether an Africa-Nation, (i.e. an Africa, which is not merely a geographical expression but a socio-cultural entity with a common political and economic aspirations) could be fashioned from the current mosaic of competing and contestable African identities. In other words, could Africans, with uncontested identity, sharing similar aspirations, and regarding themselves as Africans who are distinct from other peoples from other regions of the world, emerge from the womb of the current confusion about who is an African?

There have been efforts in the past to create this Africa-Nation and a certain sense of brotherhood among the different Africans. Gamal Nkrumah, Bankie Forster Bankie ("Pan Africa or African Union?"), Issaka K. Souaré & Dossou David Zounmenou, and Helmi Sharawy discuss some of these efforts and give pointers to the possible answers to that crucial question.

Some of the papers in this volume were originally published in the multidisciplinary journal, *African Renaissance,* which I edit. I am grateful to all the contributors. I am also grateful to Professor J Isawa Elaigwu and Ify Mangrover Okonkwo for facilitating the work in other ways.

References

Ayo, Akinfe (2008), "Eusebio is not African" in *guardian.co.uk* , January 20 (http://blogs.guardian.co.uk/sport/2008/01/20/eusebio_is_not_african.html)

Eno, Mohamed (2008): *The Bantu-Jareer Somalis: Unearthing Apartheid in the Horn of Africa* (London, Adonis & Abbey Publishers).

Diallo Garba (2004): "On Being an African", *African Renaissance,* Vol. 1, No. 2, September/October.

Mbeki, Thabo [then Deputy President and later President of South Africa], "I am an African" (speech made on 8 May, 1996, soon after the promulgation of the Constitution for a new post-Apartheid South.).

McCulloch, Richard (2007), "The Races of Humanity' at (http://www.racialcompact.com/racesofhumanity.html <12 December 2008>.

Muchie Mammo (2004), "Many into one Africa, one into many Africans", *African Renaissance,* Vol. 1, No. 2, September/October.

Snyder, Louis L (2003), *The New Nationalism* (New Jersey, Transaction Publishers), pp. 103-139.

Visser, Wayne (2005,) "Am an African" at http://www.waynevisser.com/i_am_an_african.htm 4 November <(20 November 2008).

PART 1

CONCEPTUAL ISSUES: IDENTIFYING THE AFRICAN

Chapter 1

WHO ARE THE AFRICANS?*

Ali A. Mazrui

It was the poet diplomat of Sierra Leone Davidson Nicol, who once wrote:

You are not a country, Africa,
You are a concept
Fashioned in our minds, each to each,
To hide our separate fears,
To dream our separate dreams.

Africa is indeed at once more than a country – and less than one. More than fifty territorial entities with artificial boundaries call themselves "nations."

It is one of the great ironies of modern African history that it took European colonialism to inform Africans that they were Africans. Europe's greatest service to the people of Africa was not Western civilization, which is under siege; or even Christianity, which is on the defensive. Europe's supreme gift was the gift of African identity, bequeathed without grace or design – but a reality all the same.

The pioneer American Africanist, Melville Herskovitz, used to argue that Africa was a geographical fiction. "It is thought of as a separate entity and regarded as a unit to the degree that the map is invested with an authority imposed on it by the mapmakers."[1] In part, the argument here is that climatically the range in Africa is from arid deserts to tropical rain forest; ethnically from the Khoisan to the Semites; linguistically from Yoruba to Kidigo.

Herskovitz referred to that old description of Africa by the Geographer Royal of France in 1656 – that Africa was "a peninsula so large that it comprises the third part, and this the most southerly, of our [European] continent."[2] And a case can certainly be made for the thesis that North Africa is not only a Western extension of the Arabian Peninsula and a northern extension of sub-Saharan Africa; North Africa is also a southern extension of Europe.

But how then did Europe Africanize Africa? In what way is the sense of identity that Africans have as Africans an outgrowth of their historic interaction with Europeans?

In fact, a number of inter-related processes were at work. First and foremost was the triumph of European cartography and mapmaking in the scientific and intellectual history of the world. If Africa invented man in places like Olduvai Gorge, and the Semites invented God in Jerusalem, Mt. Sinai and Mecca, Europe invented the world, at the Greenwich Meridian. It was Europeans who named all the great continents of the world, all the great oceans, many of the great rivers and lakes and most of the countries. Europe positioned the world so that we think of Europe as being above Africa rather than below in the cosmos. Europe timed the world so that the Greenwich meridian chimed the universal hour.

What is more, it was Europeans who usually decided where one continent ended and another began. For Africa, Europeans decided that our continent ended at the Red Sea rather than on the Persian/Arabian Gulf. Europeans may not have invented the name "Africa", but they did play a decisive role in applying it to the continental landmass that we recognize today.

The second process through which Europe Africanized Africa was the process of racism in history. This was particularly marked in the treatment of the Black populations of the continent. The humiliation and degradation of Black Africans across the centuries contributed to their mutual recognition of each other as "fellow Africans".

Andrew Young, when United States Ambassador to the United Nations, once accused the British of having invented racism. Young was at once stimulating and exaggerating. The Anglo-Saxons played a major role in capturing Africans and converting them into commodities for sale on the world market. The maritime and nautical revolution in Europe, and the "discovery" of the "New World", did irreparable damage to Black Africa since it coincided with a new wave of racism. Today one out of every five people of African ancestry lives in the Americas – mostly as ex-slaves.

In Africa itself European racism convinced at least sub-Saharan Africans that one of the most relevant criteria of their Africanity was their skin colour. Until the coming of the Europeans into the sub-Saharan region, Blackness was taken relatively for granted. Fairer skinned Arabs sometimes penetrated the interior of Black Africa, but the Arabs were less segregationist than Europeans and were ready to intermarry with local populations. The primary differentiation between Arab and non-Arab was not skin colour but language and culture. It was Europeans who raised the barrier of pigmentation in Africa.

Related to racism were imperialism and colonization. These generated a sufficient sense of shared African identity for the movement of Pan-Africanism to be born. In the words of Julius K. Nyerere of Tanzania:

> "Africans all over the continent, without a word being spoken either from one individual to another or from one African country to another, looked at the European, looked at one another, and knew that in relation to the European they were one."[3] (Melville J. Herskovits, "Does 'Africa' Exist?" Symposium On Africa (hereafter referred to as Symposium), Wellesley College, Wellesley, Mass., 1960, p. 17.)

Black consciousness south of the Sahara is an aspect of the African identity – but Black consciousness was itself born as a response to European racial arrogance. But if blackness is such an important aspect of Africanity, how real is the Africanness of the Arabs north of the Sahara? In what sense, if any, is Africa truly one continent?

It is worth remembering that the cultural links between North Africa and Africa south of the Sahara did not begin with the Arab conquest of North Africa in the seventh century of the Christian era. For example, Semitic languages in Africa are not limited to Arabic and Hebrew. Amharic, the dominant language of Ethiopia, is Semitic. The language is a custodian of one of Africa's oldest civilizations.

Hausa, the most widespread language in West Africa, is also Semitic-related structurally, as well as being a borrower of a large vocabulary from Arabic. Swahili or (Kiswahili), the most widespread language in Eastern Africa, is not Semitic. But it has borrowed as much from Arabic as the English language has from Latin and French.

Then there is of course the role of Arabic, not only as the dominant tongue of Northern Africa but also as the central language of Islamic worship both north and south of the Sahara.

At the global level the most successful Semitic language is indeed Arabic. But the most important Semitic religion in the world is Christianity, and the most successful Semitic people world-wide are the Jews.

Within Africa, on the other hand, the most successful Semitic people continentally are the Arabs – and their tongue is the most successful Semitic language. What remains to be seen is whether the most successful Semitic religion in Africa will be Islam rather than Christianity.

In the battle for the soul of North Africa, Islam has already won. In the 7th century A.D. Egypt was conquered from Christendom by the Arabs. Apart from the Coptic Church, Christianity has almost disappeared from North Africa today.

South of the Sahara the rivalry between Christianity and Islam has gathered momentum. There are already more Muslims in Nigeria than there are Muslims in any Arab country – including Egypt.[4] In all, the Black Muslim population of Africa is over 100 million. Though unevenly, Islam has spread all the way down to the Cape of Good Hope. Indeed, Islam in the Republic of South Africa is some three hundred years old.

But of course the most powerful force in South Africa is not religion but race. The final act in the racial confrontation was done with the threat of force. In Africa's interaction with Europe, there has been no precedent of white settlers, effectively in control, giving up power to Blacks without a fight. And in South Africa the threat of force compelled the end of Apartheid.

Western economic action did finally convince whites to negotiate – but only under the threat of force. Western sanctions boosted the morale of the oppressed, keeping the day of open armed confrontation delayed just long enough for the white to concede.

Western sanctions were never comprehensive enough to convince the whites to concede Black majority rule; only the threat of racial war forced the end of Apartheid. The US, Britain and the Federal Republic of Germany resisted comprehensive sanctions to the ultimate, but the threat of racial war forced whites to finally give in. I hope it is only a coincidence that the Anglo-Saxons, the Dutch and the Germans have been the worst offenders among Westerners in institutionalized racism. Outside Africa the Anglo-Saxons were the architects of lynching and Jim Crow. The Germans were the architects of Nazism. Within Africa Dutch-speaking Whites were the architects of apartheid. Were these coincidences?

But from an African perspective there is a silver lining. Black South Africans, who are the most underprivileged Blacks of the twentieth century, may well become among the most privileged Blacks of the twenty-first. The Black Untouchables of today in South Africa will be the Black Brahmins of tomorrow.

Black South Africans after the racial war will inherit their birthright – one of the richest parts of the globe. They will also inherit the greatest industrial base in Africa – created by African labour and White expertise. Thirdly, Black South Africans will inherit the nuclear infrastructure which White South Africans have been setting up. Indeed, South Africa under Black rule may well become the world's first Black nuclear power.

The slave trade had once reduced the African to the ultimate underdog. Will nuclear power elevate him back to equality? The nightmare of slavery awaits its final negation by the nightmare of nuclear power. A negation of the negation in a true Hegelian dialectic. *Quo vadis*, Africa?

Notes

1 Melville J. Herskovits, "Does 'Africa' Exist?" Symposium On Africa (hereafter referred to as Symposium), Wellesley College, Wellesley, Mass., 1960, p. 15.

2 Symposium, op. cit., p. 16.

3 Symposium, op. cit., p. 17.

4 Ali A. Mazrui, The Re-invention of Africa: Edward Said, V. Y. Mudimbe, and Beyond, Research in African Literatures, 2005, p.76.

---

* Originally published in: Ricardo Rene Laremont & Tracia Leacock Seghatolislami (eds. 2002): *Africanity Redefined: Collected Essays of Ali A. Mazrui, vol. I,* Trenton, NJ and Asmara, Eritrea: Africa World Press, Inc., 2002 (Series Editor Toyin Falola), pp. 37-41.

Chapter 2

ON THE CONCEPT OF "WE ARE ALL AFRICANS" *

Ali A. Mazrui

Bernard Lewis once grappled with the question "What is a Turk?" and finally put forward, virtually as part of the *definition*, the "sentiment of Turkish identity"—simply thinking of oneself as a Turk.[1] Now the course of world history is being much affected by people who on occasion speak of themselves collectively as "Africans." How important to the definition of an African in politics is the quality of thinking of oneself as an African?

In many respects, Melville Herskovits has maintained that Africa is a geographical fiction. "It is thought of as a separate entity and regarded as a unit to the degree that the map is invested with an authority imposed on it by the map makers."[2] The argument here is presumably that climatically the range in Africa is from arid deserts to tropical forests; ethnically, from the Khoisan to the Semites; linguistically from Amharic to Kidigo. What have all these in common apart from the tyranny of the map maker?

One possible answer is that they have a negative common element: they are alike one to another to the extent that they are collectively different from anything in the outside world. It is perhaps this question-begging assumption which makes President Nkrumah of Ghana insist that "Africa is not, and can never be an extension of Europe."[3] That argument was used against the notion that Algeria was part of France, and it continues to be used against Portuguese "integration" of Angola and Mozambique. In a televised New York debate with Jacques Soustelle when the future of "French" Algeria was still in question, Ghana's Ambassador Alex Quaison-Sackey employed the argument not merely as a variant formulation of the thesis that "Algeria had to be independent of France" but as a piece of evidence in support of that thesis.[4]

Did Quaison-Sackey and his President mean that no nation could—on account of some logical difficulty—overflow across continental boundaries? Was it to be inferred that since, say, the United Arab Republic was at the time an instance of "Africa" (represented by Egypt) overflowing into "Asiatic" Syria, Nkrumah's argument was an implicit prediction of the breakup of that union? And what of Bernard Lewis' Turkey—was it Asia overflowing into Europe or Europe spilling over into the Orient?

It seems more likely that Nkrumah's use of "can never" (in his "Africa ... can never be an extension of Europe") is not one of incapacity but of moral rejection. Europe "can never" *legitimately* extend into Africa, however practical the extension might be empirically.

And yet the element of strict incapacity is not entirely absent from the Ghanaian's exposition of the thesis. It continued to be presented almost like a logical impossibility—the reasoning being something to the effect that if Algeria was part of Africa, and Africa was a separate continent from Europe, then Algeria could not be part of a part of Europe at the same time. The argument sounded persuasive, and continues to sound persuasive in regard to Portugal's "projections" into Africa. But, by itself as an *argument*, it sounds persuasive only if one accepts what Herskovits describes as "the preconceptions that arise from according continental designations a degree of reality they do not possess."[5]

Herskovits himself refers to the description of Africa by the Geographer Royal of France in 1656 as a "peninsula so large that it comprises a third part, and this the most southerly, of our continent."[6] And a case can certainly be made for the thesis that North Africa was in a sense an extension of Southern Europe for a long time—and if the connection with Europe was to an extent broken with the advent of Islam, it was only to turn North Africa into a western extension of the Arabian peninsula and the Fertile Crescent rather than a northern continuation of the area south of the Sahara.

And yet Nkrumah insisted that not even "an accident of history" can "ever succeed in turning an inch of African soil into an extension of any other continent." To him it was self-evident—and "colonialism and imperialism could not and cannot change this basic geographical fact."[7]

The reasoning implicit in this assertion seems to accord greater importance to "geographical facts" than to "accidents of history." Yet the choice of terms could surely be interchanged. To the Frenchman who opposed Nkrumah's thesis, the argument could just as well have been framed in the reverse semantic order that no accident of *geography* could change the basic historical fact that Algeria had had a longer connection with Europe than with, say, the Congo or Tanganyika. Geographical facts are as much "accidents" as historical accidents are "facts." In the politics of Africanism, which aspects are really important?

The very term "Africanism" seems to imply that geography matters more, since "Africa" is a geographic designation. Nkrumah's stand can therefore he taken as further evidence for Max Beloff's argument in another context, that "it is easier to understand the contiguities of geography than the continuities of history."[8]

And yet in regard to Africa the argument cannot rest there. History can be apprehended and felt without being "understood." Indeed, what makes geography important in politics is very often the history behind it. The whole span of historical development may not be relevant. The effect of a period of history is not always to be measured by the number of years it covers. Africa is certainly one instance where a few decades of history led to greater changes than the several centuries that preceded them. One of the changes that these decades have brought about is perhaps a new consciousness of "geographical contiguities" and a new response to them. And so, while acknowledging wide differences in culture, language and ideas between various parts of Africa, Nkrumah could still insist that "the essential fact remains that we are all Africans, and have a common interest in the independence of Africa."[9] That they are "all Africans" may be no more than recognition of a geographical fact: that they have "a common interest in the independence of Africa" is a "continuity" of history.

But is there an implied "therefore" between the two parts of Nkrumah's statement? At first glance it may seem plausible to suppose that if there is some kind of causal relationship between being Africans and being interested in African independence, the latter must follow from the former. This is true, but only partly. The other side of the argument is, paradoxically, that they are "all Africans" because of the common interest in independence; that until a craving for independence was born they were not "Africans" but Ibo, Kikuyu, Balunda, Egyptian, Somali and Zulu. In other words, if Nkrumah's "We are all Africans" is an assertion of a self-conscious collectivity, then the collectivity is as much an effect as a cause of the self-consciousness.

Taking the argument a stage further, the craving for independence presupposes, of course, an absence of independence, [10] *i.e.*, in this instance, the advent of the colonization of Africa. Are we then to conclude that it was colonization which made it possible for Nkrumah to say "We are all Africans"? And if so, what has happened to Nkrumah's repeated argument that the process of colonization had included "the policy of divide and rule?"

The two arguments are not impossible to reconcile. Certainly Julius Nyerere seemed to subscribe to both. In his furious letter to *The Times* (London) just before he resigned, he accused the paper's news-reportage of trying to drive a wedge between "the Government and the people of Tanganyika on the one hand and the people of Kenya on the other." And, like a true nationalist, he wanted to "state quite categorically that the time for the policy of divide and rule has passed."[11] Yet Nyerere had been known to argue in a way which suggested that if the imperialists divided Africa (as a policy) in order to rule, they also united it (in effect) by the very act of ruling. At a symposium at Wellesley College almost two years earlier Nyerere had emphasised that "the sentiment of Africa," the sense of fellowship between Africans, was "something which came from outside." He said: "One need not go into the history of colonization of Africa, but that colonization had one significant result. A sentiment was created on the African continent—a sentiment of oneness."[12]

Carried to its logical conclusion this says that it took colonialism to inform Africans that they were Africans. I do not mean this merely in the sense that in colonial schools young Bakongo, Taita and Ewe suddenly learned that the rest of the world had a collective name for the inhabitants of the landmass of which their area formed a part—though this was certainly one medium by which Africans were informed by colonialism that they were Africans. A more important medium was the reaction against colonialism leading, as it did, to a new awareness of the "geographical contiguities" mentioned above, and the new responses that this called out. The result was felt even by the Arab North—so that a new type of Egyptian told his countrymen:

> ...we cannot, in any way, stand aside, even if we wish to, from the sanguinary and dreadful struggle now raging in the heart of the continent between five million whites and two hundred million Africans. We cannot do so for one principal and clear reason: we ourselves are in Africa.[13]

Perhaps for the first time in that country's history a ruler of Egypt was taking a stand to awaken his countrymen to an implication of the "geographical fact" that they too were "in Africa." Almost as emphatically as his Ghanaian counterpart, the Egyptian President was to commit himself to the policy of "We are all Africans."

But was the Egyptian an African in the same sense that Nkrumah was one? The answer must be a qualified "No." To the extent that they were both from within a continent that underwent some form of colonial rule, and to the extent that this gave them a certain sense of fellow feeling, the Egyptian and Nkrumah could both be regarded as "Africans." But while the Egyptian was an African only in the sense that Nehru was an Asian, Nkrumah was an African in a more significant meaning. To put it another way, Nasser was an Egyptian in a deeper sense historically than Nkrumah was a Ghanaian, but he was an African in a shallower sense emotionally than Nkrumah was an African. The continental feeling built up by colonialism was more emphatic in Africa south of the Sahara than it ever was either north of the Sahara or in Asia. The particularly marked artificiality of the sub-Saharan "nations," even when compared with those in Asia or North Africa, is certainly an important part of the explanation. The question then arises, from what is this importance derived?

One approach to the answer is to examine the individual side-effects of this sub-Saharan artificiality. Among these were the collective labels that the colonial powers had to give to the multiplicity of tribes within each territory. The British administrator in India, for example, did not have to call Indians "Asians." When he did not call them Hindus or Muslims, Gujerati or Punjabi, he lumped them together as "Indians." Such sentiment of oneness as this created was therefore limited to the Indian sub-continent instead of encompassing the entire Asian continent.[14] There was, to be sure, a degree of fellow feeling with other Asians. But this led to very little talk in Asia about a "United States of Asia," realistic or not. Nor was there the same degree of conviction behind any inchoate sense of belonging to the "same" race on a continental scale. As Lord Hailey observed, the spirit of Asianism had not "involved the emergence of a concept of pan-Asianism in the East."[15]

In sub-Saharan Africa, however, there was often no territorially exclusive term to designate the indigenous inhabitants in a given territory—at least, not when these were being distinguished from the immigrant races. In India an exclusive club could have a sign "No Indians admitted." In Tanganyika or Kenya it would not have been racially specific to say "No Tanganyikans" or "No Kenyans" since these terms had little natural ethnic content.[16] The term "African" seems to have gained currency in some instances as a euphemism for the term "native." When the Legislative Council came into the multi-racial territories of East Africa, the seats for the races were allocated in continentalistic terms—"African" seats, "European" seats and, after the Indian partition, "Asian" seats.

Thus, to use Nyerere's rhetoric, "Africans, all over the continent, without a word being spoken either from one individual to another or from one African country to another, looked at the European, looked at one another, and knew that in relation to the European they were one".[17] In relation to another continent, this continent was one: this was the logic of the situation.

Nevertheless, he was putting it too strongly when he talked of Africans "all over the continent." For where the "nations" were not entirely artificial it was possible for the colonial powers to think of and describe the natives as "Somalis" and "Sudanese" without resorting to the all-encompassing "Africans." And to the extent that the narrower terms did not emphasize affinity with the rest of the continent, the "spirit of Africanism" of the Somalis or the Sudanese is not of the same depth as that of the "Tanganyikans." Indeed, this applies even to those natural nations within artificial ones, like the Buganda of Uganda. The point to remember is that where colonial boundaries approximate very closely to ethnic ones, and where there is a degree of homogeneity within the boundaries to give the concept of "nation" some substance over and above the mere existence of legal boundaries on the map, there is less of a pull toward identity with what Nyerere calls "Africans all over the continent." As Lord Hailey put it in connection with some such homogeneous, if especially small, territories, "Africanism is seen there mainly in terms of the maintenance of the national identity of the indigenous community concerned."[18]

It nonetheless holds that if, as Herskovits claims, Africa is "a geographical fiction," Tanganyika and Ghana are greater fictions. As an English settler in Africa wrote:

> The administration of some of these artificial divisions has made a practice of trying to foster a synthetic patriotism towards "Tanganyika" or the "Gold Coast". . . . These loyalties to a wholly artificial and unrealistic administrative boundary…tend to obscure and undermine the underlying sense of oneness across the continent which I have heard expressed in the constantly reiterated phrase "We Africans."[19]

But if the feeling of "We Tanganyikans" is beginning to undermine the feeling of "We Africans," for how long can we continue to think of the latter as less "synthetic" than the former? If Nigerians are developing a greater loyalty to "Nigeria" than to "Africa," for how long can it be maintained that they are less Nigerians than they are Africans? It is all very well, one might argue, for the sympathizers of African unity to lament that

> ...the youthful generation of Africans. . . have seen in school colored maps of Africa . . . all the forty divisions clearly demarcated by thick black lines; and it is hard for them to remember that such concepts as "Nigeria" or "Tanganyika" are of very recent origin and are wholly artificial.[20]

But if a "youthful generation" finds it hard to remember that a fiction is a fiction, for how long can it remain so?

Here we come to the different levels of what has come to be known as "African nationalism." In 1944 a British Colonial Office Advisory Committee on Education in the colonies drew attention to the finding that travel and contact with other nationalities had given rise among Africans to a "dawning realization of themselves as Africans, even as 'nationals' of a territory like Northern Rhodesia, playing a part in world affairs."[21] It was, in other words, a consciousness not only of being "Africans" but also of being Africans from a particular territory. The term "African nationalism" very often crowds out other forms of nationalism. It is used to denote any form of nationalism *in* Africa, involving *Africans*—the nationalism that looks inward territorially, like that of Nigerians after independence; the nationalism that looks inward tribally, like that of the Kikuyu in the 1940s and 1950s; and the nationalism that looks outward continentally or regionally and envisions the submergence of the colonial units into a larger creation.

When, however, a distinction *is* made between these different meanings, the tendency is to think of the narrower territorial or tribal nationalisms as being in some sense "less nationalistic" than the wider continentalistic brand. The Nigerian who is for exclusively Nigerian interests thus becomes less of a "real Nationalist" than an Nkrumah or a Touré who seems prepared to sell his country's sovereignty for a vision of continental unity.[22]

Perhaps here the contrast with Europe is particularly striking. The rebellion against dynastic empires in Europe was, in a sense, a rebellion against large, multi-ethnic or multilingual states—a rebellion which could not easily be reconciled with pan-Europeanism. And even today that Englishman is nationalistic who is opposed to giving up the sovereignty of England for the sake of a united Europe. Why then is the particularist Nigerian less of a nationalist than the pan-African Nkrumah?

Both in Africa in its recent history and in Europe in the wake of "self-determination" after World War I, nationalism had denoted a commitment to what Nkrumah has described as "the application of . . . the right of a people to rule themselves."[23] This is just another way of expressing opposition to foreign rule in moral terms—and in an idiom that African nationalism inherited from European nationalisms. Where Africa parts company with Europe is on the crucial issue of what is a "foreigner."[24] In Europe the "foreign" ruler was generally himself a European. To have rebelled against him and then subscribed to the idea of "uniting" with him in a pan-European spirit was politically illogical.

In the case of the continental brand of African nationalism this difficulty does not arise since the "foreign" ruler is a ruler from outside the continent altogether. It is therefore quite consistently "nationalistic" to win independence for Ghana, set out to build it as a nation, create a sense of patriotism toward it, and at the same time declare an intention to submerge its "national" identity within a giant state on a continental or sub-continental scale. But even if this is conceded to be consistently nationalistic, what could make it a more justifiable definition of "the real nationalist" than the particularism of the Nigerian who refuses to give up his Nigerian "identity"?

One answer might be that the Nigerian is resigning himself to the arbitrary frontiers imposed by colonialism and therefore deserves to be regarded as less of a nationalist. This line of reasoning sometimes goes to the extent of implying that the creation of a "United States of Africa" would not be something entirely new but rather in effect a return to things as they were before the advent of divisive colonialism. The same Nyerere who said at Wellesley College that colonization gave birth to African fellowship told the Royal Commonwealth Society that it was *pre*-colonial African history which demanded that "African unity must have priority over all other associations"[25]—as if the colonial period had interrupted a fellowship that went far back before it.

The argument here had virtually become "We were all Africans until colonialism split us into Tanganyikans, Kenyans and Nigerians." It is certainly true that they could not have been Nigerians and Tanganyikans before the advent of colonialism, since colonialism created Nigeria and Tanganyika. The logical jump is in the assertion that they must "therefore" have previously been just "Africans." Nor is it a simple case of the very word "African" being itself *non*-African in its inception, however true that may be. Rather, it is a case of the inhabitants of the continent having known other, often *narrower* group classifications than the "Tanganyikans" and "Nigerians" of post-colonial days.

And yet there is a persistent reluctance in the continentalistic type of African nationalism to acquiesce in the map drawn up at Berlin in 1884.[26] Indeed, the Berlin Conference which partitioned Africa served as the inspiration of the first All-Africa people's conference held in Accra in December 1958. One observer maintained at the time that the connection between the two conferences occurred to the Chairman of the Accra Conference, Mr. Tom Mboya.[27] Mboya's slogan "Europeans, scram out of Africa" was meant not only to echo the phrase "European scramble for Africa" but also amounted to a demand that Europeans should pull out now, so that Africans could set about putting Africa "back together again."

Any one, then, who did not subscribe to this vision of putting Africa back together again was something short of a true African nationalist. There might be differences of opinion over how far into the future this aim was to be pushed, and over the form and pattern in which Africa was to be put together. But a considerable consensus had developed at least on the point that African unity is possible only when the European ruler has "scrammed out" of the continent as a whole. In the words of Sékou Touré, "the liberty of Africa is indivisible."[28]

This doctrine of indivisibility is persistent in the language of nationalism in Africa. In part it arises out of the same factors, which led the colonial powers to apply the broad term "African" to indigenous inhabitants of different parts of the continent. In one sense the African nationalist has to think of Africa as "indivisible" because the rest of the world tends to think of it as such. At least outside Africanists' circles, it is frequent enough to hear an atrocity in the Congo being stretched in significance and deemed a reflection not merely on Congolese but also on African capacity for, say, self-discipline. In the face of such generalizations, actual or anticipated, a nationalist from Ghana may decide that if he cannot defend himself by pointing out that he is not Congolese, he might as well defend himself by defending the Congolese—by discovering exclusively "external" causes for the troubles of that country.

At this level then, the African image of their own indivisibility is a reflection of the image of Africa that the outside world has tended to hold—going back to the days when Africans were classified together as "all backward" or "all primitive," with little regard for the enormous variations of social and political development in different parts of the continent. It is significant that the reflection has become more real than the original before the mirror of time—and empty European generalizations like "They are all Africans" are becoming less empty as the Africans themselves, in fellowship, affirm that so they are indeed.

But the doctrine of African indivisibility has intellectual as well as psychological roots; and the New World has certainly played a part in this. It was, for example, from Abraham Lincoln, as well as from John Stuart Mill, that Julius Nyerere says he learned of Western notions of institutionalized democracy.[29] And yet Nyerere himself was not educated in America. Clearer traces of American influence are to be discerned in those African nationalists who did spend formative years in the United States—the most famous of these being Azikiwe of Nigeria, Nkrumah of Ghana and Banda of Nyasaland. Pan-Africanism has then a root in the New World not only because Afro-Americans like DuBois and Garvey launched it onto a world stage but also because many even of the African fathers of Pan-Africanism were themselves exposed to elements in American political thought.

It is, of course, dangerous to single out specific ideas in African thought and trace them to the New World. But one can at least hazard an estimate and even point to certain American thinkers who were especially influential. American writers today sometimes give the impression of putting Thomas Jefferson first as a persistent intellectual force in the world.[30] In doing so they are in danger of projecting their own estimate of important American thinkers onto the rest of the world. Actually, for every African who has heard of Thomas Jefferson, probably several knew of Abraham Lincoln—even if only as the liberator of Negro slaves in his country. Some may well have acquainted themselves with the kind of arguments Lincoln used in support of that liberation—especially, that the Union could not "permanently endure half slave and half free." This was, in fact, a classic formulation of the doctrine of the indivisibility of freedom; and it has been echoed down the generations since. In 1899 the American Anti-Imperialist League was already extending Lincoln's ideas to colonialism at large and asking America not to betray Lincoln by persisting in colonizing the Philippines.[31] By 1947 an African leader, Nnamdi Azikiwe, was arguing in West Virginia that "one half of the world cannot be democratic and the other half undemocratic"[32]—and the conclusion to be drawn was that the colonies must be liberated.

By 1962, America which had dramatized that argument nationally by a Civil War a century ago was being asked by an old defender of white settlers in Africa, Mrs. Elspeth Huxley, to make it clear to the now independent African governments that their countries could not, "any more than others, contract out of the rule that freedom is indivisible." [33] In regard to the position of the white settlers—of whose rights she had long been champion in opposition both to Margery Perham[34] and to African aspirations—the colonial wheel had come just about full circle.

But if the Africans were now betraying the ideal of an indivisible freedom, what had their struggle been all about?

The question can best be answered by first examining what any nationalism is all about. Frederick Hertz once defined national consciousness as "the combined striving for unity, liberty, individuality and prestige."[35] Need these four aspirations be of equal weight? Must liberty, for example, be as important as, say, prestige to any people with a national consciousness? Can the precise combination of the different elements vary in importance not only within the "consciousness" of a single nationalist but also between one nationalist and another?

This opens up the relevance of the particular circumstances which give rise to national consciousness. If there have been occasions of what John Stuart Mill might describe as "collective humiliation,"[36] it would make a difference what form the humiliation took. Did it just deal a blow to a people's "prestige"—as by, say, beating them in a space race to the moon? Did it go further and actually deprive them of their "liberty"? Did it "divide" them in order to do so? On the answers to such questions would rest the aspirations of such a people within their national consciousness, and indeed their very aptitude for realizing them.

For example, one of the major differences between English-speaking and French-speaking Africans is that the latter have been the more culturally creative of the two. It has been pointed out often enough that Leopold Senghor of Senegal was a poet, Keita Fodéba of Guinea a producer of ballets, Bernard Dadié of the Ivory Coast a novelist and Cofi Gadeau a playwright, before they held office in their respective states. One reason advanced to explain this is that the Africans who were ruled by France were more exposed than their British counterparts to "collective humiliation" in the cultural field. Their creativeness was thus a response to the assimilationist assumption that African culture was inferior to that of France.[37]

And yet, curiously enough, far less talk of "our British heritage" is heard among English-speaking Africans than of "our French cultural background" among at least the Brazzaville group of former French subjects. The latter's rebellion against French cultural arrogance has not really taken the form of a determined attempt to tear away from the French influence—in spite of Senghor's homage to *Négritude*. Theirs, in fact, is less a rebellion than the paradox of rebellious emulation. While Nkrumah and Nyerere would at least like to believe that such a thing as "African Socialism" is fundamentally indigenous, Senghor prefers to talk in the more rational but less nationalistic terms of a "socialism based on the seminal cultural values of both Africa and Europe."[38] This approach, even if more persuasive, surely constitutes a lesser degree of insistence on the distinctiveness of an African personality. Sékou Touré is in many ways unrepresentative of the French-speakers—and it was perhaps because of his stronger Africanism that at his meeting with Senghor in 1962 on the question of settling African differences he was informed once again of Senghor's belief that Africa should be "open to all the pollen of the earth and to all the fertilizing contributions of the various civilizations and continents."[39] The reason for Senghor's insistence is that to him the concept of "We are all Africans" is, if equated with what he calls "continentalism," a form of autarchy—and "like all autarchies it denies the interdependence of peoples. ..."[40]

On such occasions Senghor comes dangerously near to joining those "cosmopolitans" whom Rousseau once accused of trying to "justify their love of their country by their love of the human race and make a boast of loving the entire world in order to enjoy the privilege of loving no one."[41] Presumably it would then be the English-speaking Nkrumah with whom the nationalistic Rousseau would be in sympathy. In Rousseau's terms, Nkrumah at least justifies his love for Ghana by his love of the African rather than the human race. And even when he makes a boast of loving the entire world, it is but to love a continent. "We are all Africans—and the rest of the world is not," is the essence of his outlook.

Yet it is possible to exaggerate the difference between these two African views. No one acquainted with the varied sides of Senghor's philosophy can doubt that he, too, has a deep emotional attachment to his own race. To say that he and Nkrumah differ only as to the means for achieving a common end would be not only platitudinous but also somewhat inaccurate, unless that end is given a broad name like "Africa's assertion of herself." The two African outlooks would still differ in their interpretations of what would constitute such an assertion.

Nevertheless, agreement even on broad objectives must be deemed significant for the future course of African history. It remains now to examine the impulse behind those objectives and the nature of the quest.

What is the central aspiration in the national consciousness of the emerging African?

The language of African nationalism in recent times has tended to suggest that the central aspiration was liberty, indivisible or not. Single word slogans like *Uhuru, Kwacha* and "Free-Dom" have emphasized this. So has the understandable conceptual framework which makes "anti-colonialism" a demand primarily for "liberation"—and proceeds from there to the precarious conclusion that the basic motivation behind African nationalism is a desire for "freedom." That African freedom is immensely important to the African nationalists is, of course, beyond doubt. But it is not to be hastily assumed that the average African really shares Lord Acton's conception of liberty, not as a means to a higher political end but as itself the highest political end. The average African does not rate liberty even in the sense of "independence" so high. Instead, there are higher political ends that such liberty is, as a means or prerequisite, needed for.

One alternative end which might suggest itself is equality. And it is certainly an end now obscured in all the chanting of "independence" in the remaining colonies and "freedom from neo-colonialism" in the countries already sovereign. Even in Kenya, which has only just emerged from being a "White Man's Country," the cry for equality has all but disappeared from the vocabulary of the African nationalist. The days when *Pan-Africa* could carry an article by a Kenya nationalist under the heading of "Kenya Today: Equality is Our Slogan"[42] seem to have really receded into history.

All the same it must be emphasized that nationalism in Africa is still more egalitarian than libertarian in its ultimate aspirations. This is not to underestimate the logical complications in any attempt to disentangle the concepts of equality and of liberty—complications that may be suggested by recalling that the first Declaration of Independence from British colonial rule opened with the premise that "all men are created equal." And yet disentangling the two concepts can surely be carried at least to the extent of suggesting that whereas the Americans proclaimed "equality" in pursuit of independence, the African nationalists have now sought independence in pursuit of equality. Indeed, the development of African nationalism is a progressive metamorphosis of what would be acceptable as an adequate expression of racial equality.

In that development can be traced a transition from the notion that "freedom is indivisible" to the notion that "equality is indivisible"—that until all Africans are regarded as the equals of Europeans, no African can be sure that he is accepted as an equal. To substitute Tom Mboya's phraseology, "as long as any part of Africa remains under European rule, we do not feel that Africans will be regarded in the right way."[43] What this means is that "the manumission of mother Africa from the foreign yoke"[44] is essential not only for its own sake but also for elevating the African in the eyes of the world—and in African eyes too. The underlying logic of this belief is that the slave needs his freedom to be the equal of free men, as well as to exercise it.

On closer analysis, however, the African quest combines the aspiration of equality with those two other nationalistic aspirations which Hertz described as "individuality and prestige." The obvious designation for the combination is "dignity"—a word even more imprecise than "equality." Perhaps it is useful to coin a term like "dignitarianism" for such a movement, and then give it some precision by definition. It can, for example, be defined to *exclude* the nationalism that takes its minimal or strictly "human" dignity for granted and only seeks to reunite, say, Germans with fellow-Germans across an artificial border. African examples of such unification-minded nationalisms include the Bakongo, confident of themselves in relation to their neighbors, but seeking to unite with fellow-Bakongo. Then there are the Ewe, still restive at division. In their cases "dignity" has been a vague incidental to the central aspiration of reunification—no matter how often it was used as a rallying slogan.

Sub-classifications are possible within the dignitarian forms of nationalism. There is the nationalism that seeks to protect its "dignity" from some impending danger, real or imaginary. Examples are the nationalism of the Afrikaaners of South Africa and, in a different context, that of the immigrant elite in Liberia and of the Amharic aristocracy in Ethiopia. These peoples have had no doubt about their own "dignity" as they have seen it. Their recent preoccupation, in varying degrees of intensity, has been with how to ensure its continuation. This then is protective dignitarianism.

The nationalism of re-unification like that of the Arabs, or even of the Bakongo, can be dignitarian if unity is envisaged as a means of *recovering* some lost dignity in a glorious past. Here again it is a question of degree of emphasis rather than of the complete absence of this or that aspiration. As Thomas Hodgkin put it, "since Byron reminded the Greeks of Sappho and Marathon every nationalist myth has included this element of past greatness."[45] But Hodgkin goes on to note that although "no Western European seriously questioned the fact that there had been periods in the past when Arab and Indian civilizations, owing little to European stimulus, flowered . . . the case of the peoples of Africa is different."[46] For them it is not a simple case of recovering a dignity which every one concedes they once had. It may indeed be an attempt to recover their own respect for themselves, but it is also an endeavor to win for the first time the respect of others. Self-respect and respect by others, difficult to separate as they usually are, are in the Africans' case even more so. Theirs then is an assertive rather than strictly "restorative" dignitarianism—the kind that impelled Jomo Kenyatta early in 1962 to advise the Europeans of Kenya to learn for the first time to address the African as *Bwana.*

And when, out of similar convictions, Premier Obote on the achievement of Uganda's independence refused to extend his country's recognition either to South Africa or, in spite of the Commonwealth link, to the Federation of Rhodesia and Nyasaland, that old Lincolnian notion of an indivisible freedom had found its ultimate maturity in the concept that the dignity of man was indivisible.[47] On such a level, the African nationalist of whatever shade of Africanism, becomes Rousseau's "cosmopolitan"—rising from the emotion of "We are all Africans" to the aspiration of "We are all men."

The emotion is likely to persist for as long as the aspiration is no more than an aspiration. Nationalism feeds on ambition, and ambition feeds on "conflict" or competition with others. The ambition is the creation of a respected image of *Bwana* Mwafrika,[48] and the conflict is with the forces in the way. And so there will remain, even now that independence has been substantially achieved, an area of life within which Africans may continue to feel that they are, in Lumumba's phrase, "brothers in race, brothers in conflict."[49] To the question whether they are brothers because of "race" or because of the "conflict," it can only be said that the two merge together and become virtually indistinguishable.

Notes

1 *The Emergence of Modern Turkey* (Oxford University Press, 1961). See especially his Introduction: The Sources of Turkish Civilization, pp. 1-17.

2 Melville J. Herskovits, "Does 'Africa' Exist?" *Symposium On Africa* (hereafter referred to as *Symposium),* Wellesley College, Wellesley, Mass., 1960, p. 15.

3 Speech to the 15th Session of the United Nations General Assembly, 23 September 1960. Publication of the Permanent Mission of Ghana to the United Nations, p. 9.

4 See NBC Script of "The Nation's Future," December 3, 1960, N.B.C. Television Debates.

5 *Symposium, op. cit.*, p. 16.

6 *Ibid.*

7 Speech to 15th Session of U.N. General Assembly, *op. cit.*, p. 9.

8 "The Prospects for Atlantic Union," *The Times* (London), February 2, 1962.

9 Preface, *I Speak of Freedom* (London: Heinemann, 1961), p. xiii.

10 A distinguished African philosopher argued at a meeting in Oxford recently a state of independence was a state of nature—and one to be "gained" only because it had been lost, certainly not as something new.

11 *The Times,* January 19, 1962.

12 "Africa's Place in the World," *Symposium, op. cit.*, p. 149. For brief analysis of his argument see my article "Why Does an African Feel African?", *The Times* (London), February 17, 1962, reproduced in Canada in *The Globe and Mail,* February 22, 1962.

13 Gamal Abdul Nasser, *The Philosophy of the Revolution* (Economica English edition, Buffalo, 1959), p. 74. A discussion of the limits of Nasser's role in Africa occurs in my article in *African Affairs* (Journal of the Royal Institute of African Affairs, 1963) entitled "Africa and the Egyptian's Four Circles."

14 Indeed, that the Indians considered one another "fellow Indians" at all was, to a great extent, an outcome of their, shared colonial experience too. But fellow *Asians* was much too sophisticated. As Iain Lang observed in a review in *The Sunday Times* (London, February 25, 1962) "If you were to tell a Punjabi peasant or a Malay fisherman that he was an Asian he would be most unlikely to know what you were talking about." Roy Sherwood (*Peace News*, London, March 1962) even moralises on the subject, saying: "A regrettable survival of colonialist thinking is the lumping together of all the non-white peoples of the Indian and Pacific Oceans under the comprehensive term 'Asians'." The phenomenon is discussed in Michael Edwardes' *Asia in the Balance* (A Penguin Special), 1962. No less significant,

however, was the phenomenon of "Asian" jubilation over the 1905 Japanese victory over Russia.

15 *An African Survey, Revised 1956* (Oxford University Press, 1957), p. 252.

16 Such clubs or hotels could, of course, carry either the double-negative sign of "No non-Europeans admitted" or the sign "Europeans only." But a country like South Africa would present complications since Japanese, though geographically "non-Europeans," were legally "white." Official South African terminology prefers to call their black citizens "Bantu," but Albert Luthuli, in his Nobel Prize lecture, asserted his own preference for the term "African." Kenya certainly needed also a proper name for the "blacks" more acceptable than "natives." Nor was the stratification in Kenya simply between "White" and "non-White." For example, three scales of pay used to prevail—"European," "Asian" and "African"—just as three types of lavatories, schools and the like were provided. Even further subdivisions were observed in some instances, but these are less relevant to this discussion.

17 *Symposium, op. cit.*, p. 149.

18 *An African Survey, op. cit.*, p. 255. The small High Commission territories are indeed extreme examples of this, but this only puts them at one end of the scale.

19 Frank Johnson, "United States of Africa." *Pan-Africa*, Vol. 1, No. 6 (June 1947). See esp. pp. 3-4. The journal included at the time among its "Associate and Contributing Editors" Kwame Nkrumah and Jomo Kenyatta.

20 Frank Johnson (reproduction of above article), *Voice of Africa*, Vol. 1, No. 4 (Accra, April, 1961).

21 *Education in African Society*, Colonial No.186, 1944, p. 55.

22 A strong, radically nationalist trend has existed within at least the younger generation of Nigerians. Following the 1962 Commonwealth Prime Ministers' Conference speculation in Britain started as to why the Nigerian Government, with all its pragmatism, rejected out of hand a proposal for associate membership in the E.E.C. Walter Schwarz, speaking on the European Service of the British Broadcasting Corporation in October, 1962, suggested that "Nigeria's Government, always open to attack from its own youth for being too lukewarm about its nationalism, simply finds it politically impossible

to lag behind Ghana on this issue." See also my article, "African Attitudes to the EEC," *International Affairs* (London, January, 1963). Visiting newsmen to Nigeria once discovered at a special meeting with young Nigerians at Nsukka that most of the youth were strongly in favour of Nkrumah's brand of militant African nationalism, without by any means necessarily coupling it with hero-worship for Nkrumah. One reference to this meeting appeared in the *New York Times*, March 3, 1962. Of course, the radicalism of youth is not peculiar to African countries; but young people are a stronger pressure group in the new states than in some of the older ones.

23 Speech to 15th Session of General Assembly, *op. cit.*

24 See my article "Edmund Burke and Reflections on the Revolution in the Congo," *Comparative Studies in Society and History*, January, 1963.

25 *Commonwealth Journal* (London, Royal Commonwealth Society), Vol. 4, No. 6 (November-December, 1961), p. 254.

26 There is some ambivalence about this. It is permissible, at least as an ideal, to unite two *complete* countries. But a change of frontiers that would, say, make Ghana bigger and Togo smaller, and still leave two countries independent, is unacceptable to most Africans. In such a case, most Africans would agree with the U.N. representative of the Ivory Coast who put forward the policy of accepting the territorial limits obtaining at the time of independence at least "in order to avoid internecine wars which might jeopardize the independence just acquired with such difficulty." (UN Document A/PV.1043, October 27, 1961). The Brazzaville group is clearly unenthusiastic about any radical or immediate unification measures; but this distinction between changing colonial frontiers by complete integration and changing them by partial annexation would be accepted by many of even the most radical Pan-Africanists.

27 Edwin S. Morisby, "Politics of African Unity: No longer Tail to the Asian Dog?," *Manchester Guardian*, January 2, 1959.

28 "Africa's Destiny," *Africa Speaks*, eds. James Duffy and Robert A. Manners (Princeton, 1961), p. 35.

29 "... the idea of government as an institution began to take hold of some African 'agitators' such as myself, who had been reading Abraham Lincoln and John Stuart Mill . . . ."—Nyerere, "The African and Democracy," *Africa $peaks, op. cit.*, p. 33.

30 Saul K. Padover makes a somewhat different claim—that a great interest in Jefferson had emerged abroad after a long period of ignorance. See his " 'Jefferson Still Survives . . .' ", *New York Times Magazine,* April 8, 1962, p. 28.

31 "We hold with Abraham Lincoln, that '...When the white man governs himself, that is self-government, but when he governs himself and also governs another man, that is more than self-government—that is despotism.'...'Those who deny freedom to others deserve it not for themselves, and under a just God cannot long retain it'."—Platform of the American Anti-Imperialist League, October 17, 1899, reprinted in *Great Issues in American History,* ed. Richard Hofstadter (New York, Vintage Books, 1961), vol. II, p. 203.

32 Zik's speech to graduates of Storer College, Harpers Ferry, West Virginia, on the occasion of his receiving the honorary degree of Doctor of Literature, June 2, 1947. See *ZIK* (Cambridge University Press, 1961), p. 83.

33 "Africa Struggles with Democracy," *New York Times Magazine,* January 21, 1962. p. 10.

34 Elspeth Huxley's correspondence with Margery Perham was published as a book, *Race and Politics in Kenya* (London, Faber and Faber, 1944), with an introduction by Lord Lugard. Eighteen years later, when it was a question of white settlers' rights as against the British Government rather than of their rights as against the Africans, the two women were at last in agreement. "Having often disagreed over Kenya's affairs," they said in their joint letter to *The Times* (London, July 5, 1962) "we now find ourselves in harmony about one issue—the claims of the European farmers for compensation"—from the British Government.

35 *Nationality in History and Politics* (New York, Oxford University Press, 1944), pp. 12-13.

36 *Representative Government,* ed. R. B. McCallum (Oxford, Basil Blackwell, 1946), p. 291.

37 Thomas Hodgkin and Ruth Schachter, "French-Speaking West Africa in Transition," *International Conciliation,* No. 528 (May, 1960), p.387.

38 "West Africa in Evolution," *Foreign Affairs,* Vol. 39 (January, 1961), p. 244.

39 See *Africa 1962,* No. 15, July 27, 1962, p. 4.

40 "West Africa in Evolution," *op. cit.*, p. 243.

41 *Contrat Social* (1st version). See C. E. Vaughan, *The Political Writings* of *J. J. Rousseau* (Cambridge, 1915), vol. I, p. 453.

42 *Pan-Africa*, Vol. 1, No. 6, June, 1947, p. 7. *White Man's Country* is the title of a famous book by Elspeth Huxley about Lord Delamere's Kenya. At the time Mrs. Huxley was convinced that there was not even such a thing as an "African," and she was therefore something of a precursor of Herskovits. As late as 1950 she was being taken to task by an 'African' in these terms: "On the evidence of the many varied ethnic groups which exist in Africa, she (Mrs. Huxley) asserted that there was no such thing as an African. This assertion was made during a radio debate with Leonard Woolf. One wonders why an entity that did not exist had to be debated." Dr. S. D. Cudjoe, *Aids to African Autonomy* (London, The College Press, 1950), p. 23.

43 Reported in *Mombasa Times* (Kenya), January 11, 1962.

44 The phrase is from Dr. Azikiwe's message to President Nkrumah on the occasion of Ghana's fifth anniversary as an independent state. See *The Times* (London), March 7, 1962.

45 *Nationalism in Colonial Africa* (London, Frederick Muller, 1956), p. 172.

46 *Ibid.*

47 Obote's stand on the Federation of Rhodesia and Nyasaland was the more interesting because, while he refused to recognise the present Government of the Federation, he was nevertheless against the Federation's dissolution—a stand which put him almost in a class by himself among African nationalists.

48 This means more than "Mr. African"; it has deeper connotations of respect. On its own the Swahili word *Bwana* can loosely be translated as "Sir." On October 14, 1961, Jomo Kenyatta said: "Non-Africans who still want to be called 'Bwana' should pack up and go, but others who are prepared to live under our flag are invited to remain." On January 28, 1962, the price of being welcome in Kenya was raised a little higher. It was no longer enough that the immigrant should cease to expect "Bwana" for *himself*: "I want Europeans, Asians and Arabs to learn to call Africans 'Bwana.' Those who agree to do so are free to stay," said Kenyatta. *The Times* (London) aired a controversy—with distinguished Africanists taking part—on what Kenyatta really meant by his demand. *The Sunday Times* (London) carried a controversial article by Tom Stacey on June 3, 1962, on the subject. By that time

Kenyatta himself had explained that he was demanding respect rather than servility from the Kenya European. The quest for this "respected image of *Bwana Mwafrika*" can conflict with "freedom" in some sense. See my article "Consent, Colonialism and Sovereignty," *Political Studies*, Vol. 11, No. 1 (February, 1963).

49 In his address to his compatriots on the occasion of the Congo's independence. Like many another African nationalist, he would have addressed the rest of the continent in similar terms. A translation of the speech is reproduced under the title "The Independence of the Congo" in *Africa Speaks, op. cit*. The phrase occurs on page 93.

---

* First Published in *Enterprise Magazine*. Jo'burg. May 1998.

Chapter 3

WHO IS AN AFRICAN? *

Kwesi Kwaa Prah

Introduction

When on May the 8th, 1996, soon after the promulgation of the constitution for a new post-Apartheid South Africa, Thabo Mbeki, then political heir apparent of President Mandela, made a speech in the Constitutional Assembly, in which he affirmed that "I am an African". This simple and most obvious affirmation sent ripples of disconcertion in some circles of South African society, while creating elation and enthusiasm in others.

What was significant was that, this patent fact of being an African, for some reason, for a leader of the stature of Mbeki, who was the prospective President to boot, was for too many people a threatening fact, something not to be said, something to be denied by silence; something South Africa was not yet ready for; something nightmarish, something which for those who in the past had been successfully fed on the myth of the "*swarte gevaar*" was a signifying message which produces a knee-jerk reaction and sends alarm bells ringing.

Those who were elated and enthusiastic were overwhelmingly African. Coming out with "I am an African" for them meant that Mbeki had backbone and was prepared to present his Africaness with pride, no fear, and no shame.

Nowhere else in sub-Saharan Africa would the statement "I am an African" trigger the sort of reactions that it set into motion in South Africa. Indeed, for the rest of Africa, to state "I am an African" would amount to stating so much the obvious, that people would wonder what is wrong with the leader. Has he or she lost his or her marbles? The African character of the rest of sub-Saharan Africa has never been denied. The problem we have here in South Africa is that, the African character of the society has been so suppressed and oppressed that to reveal it in any shape or form is "subversive". This is the point about apartheid, which denied Africans citizenship in their own country and pushed them into

Bantustans. The existence of Bantustans ensured the currency of the myth that Africans are not a majority in South Africa.

Being African

If the fact of being an African is so contentious in Africa, so also is the question, who is an African? I am aware of the fact that, there is a school of thought, especially popular in South Africa, which defines the African as anybody "committed to Africa". To this school, I ask, what is this commitment? What does it amount to? How is it to be measured? Is an African peasant committed to Africa? Was Mobutu Sese Seko committed to Africa? Was Moise Tshombe not an African? Was Cecil Rhodes in his commitment to African projects of various sorts therefore an African? Which of the major peoples of this globe defines its constituency on the basis of "commitment"?

The question "who is an African" is important. It is particularly so, for those who want to see a united Africa. Over ten years ago I raised this question as part of on-going debates on Pan-Africanism on this continent and the African diaspora. For the purposes of this article, the relevant part of the argument which I have made in greater length in my book *Beyond the Colour Line* (Vivlia Publishers/Africa World Press) is that:

"In many parts of Africa, people who do not regard themselves as Africans are regarded as such by Africans. Being African is virtually equated with citizenship. I think this is often deliberate and wicked. As I have often insisted, if everybody is an African, then nobody is an African. I am not suggesting anything chauvinistic. I have never been an inward-looking essentially xenophobic mind, and do not at present intend to become that. I am only too aware of the equality and commonality of humankind. Needless to say, we have this century been witness to too much evil and crimes against humanity by xenophobic minds, and fascist social systems, to entertain in all sanity such warped ideas. But history demands of us that, we stand up and be counted, that we define for ourselves clearly on the basis of African history and culture, as a strand in the history of humankind. What in our experience and collective being defines us in historical and cultural distinction to the rest of humankind? What is our contribution to human history, and the making of the culture of homo-sapiens today and yesterday? What makes us Africans?.

The racial definition of an African is flawed. It is unscientific and hence untenable. No serious mind today would use the race concept in any way except as an instrument for poetic imagery. What I am saying is that no group of people has been "pure" from time immemorial. Notions of purity belong to the language of fascists and the rubbish-bin of science. But before my observations are misunderstood let me take the argument into another direction. Most Africans are black, but not all Africans are black, and not all blacks have African cultural and historical roots. Jews range from blond to black. Another example, Arabs also do. I am not denying the fact that this continent is the cradle of the African and as far as we know today the birthplace of homo- sapiens. There are many groups in Africa today which are not African, do not describe themselves as African or wish to be so regarded, peoples whose cultures and histories are linked and derived from extra-African sources. Needless to say, they are full citizens and must always remain full and equal citizens in all respects to the Africans amongst whom they live, and I dare say apartheid and caste systems of any kind should not be tolerated, since we seek ultimately the freedom of humanity, and the untrammelled social intercourse of all the peoples of this earth.

The cultures of these minorities who live amongst us have helped in the enrichment and cosmopolitanization of social life and tastes in large areas of Africa. Some of these groups may in due course of time and history come to regard themselves as African. All peoples have a right to their culture and its usage. But cultures are not stagnant or fixed entities. Cultural change is a permanent feature of all societies. No human group has from time immemorial been hermetically sealed, culturally or otherwise. Diffusion, interpenetration and mixing are the real substances of the historical process, but at every given historical conjuncture, people are formed by the existent culture they produce and reproduce. But cultures are created and also wither. When cultures die, the people whose culture declines and falls, do not necessarily physically die, they become other people. Often they are absorbed by more dominant cultures.

Obviously, there is constantly a world culture in creation. This universal cultural fund is shared literally by all people. The phenomenology of a global village underscores this point. It is a cultural fund to which we all in principle contribute, but in practice, it is the dominant or hegemonic cultures of the world, which determine active cultural development in this sphere. There are many, particularly among westerners, who too easily and rather ethnocentrically, equate universal culture with western culture. In a world of competing cultures, growth, prosperity and cultural advancement is a factor of economic and political power. This is why, for example in the case of South Africa, under Afrikaner National party rule, the language of the Afrikaner, Afrikaans, which had started as a *patois* was developed and rapidly elevated to a language of modern science and technology, and forced on to the rest of the population.

Culture, history, attachment to these and consciousness of identity, and not skin colour, primarily defines the African. The fact that most Africans or people of African historical and cultural descent are black is only one characteristic, a bonus that generalizes and typifies Africans. And indeed, I dare say, for us, in the absence of a strong unifying religion or single language, colour has become an easy and fortunate identifying attribute of most people who regard themselves as African. Thus while others have used our colour to distinguish us for oppression and denigration, it is at the same time one of the most fortunate coincidences which identifies a people whose cultures have over centuries been woefully shattered by the oppressors. While in recent centuries slavery by Europe and the Arab world has hung heavily on African history, Africans have existed long before these periods, and cannot be defined as a people mainly on the basis of this experience. Definitionally, being African is not simply or essentially a reaction to the history of oppression. It includes this, but also stands before and transcends this history. Major features of the nations of humankind include commonality of religion, geography, language, and mythology. But in no instance are all these features present, or present to the same extent."

It is also important to remember that, the African identity (like all identities) is not a closed phenomenon cast in stone. It is a changing condition with evolving terms and conditions of reference. What remains the touchstone in this evolutionary process is that, the emerging understandings of Africanness must be emancipatory for Africans and the rest of humanity.

---

* This was first published in *The American Political Science Review*, Vol. LVII, No. 1 (March), 1963, pp. 88-97.

Chapter 4

SURVEYING THROUGH THE NARRATIVES OF AFRICAN IDENTITY

Mohamed A. Eno & Omar A. Eno

Introduction

Any question about identity, whatever that might be, is complex, particularly when the various social scientists define it each according to the tutelage of their particular discipline. This means that the formation of identity itself entails intricacies. Members of one nation or society may not agree on the interpretation of what symbol should really constitute their identity or what it should be based on. As a result of the inherent conundrum, identity becomes a variable which is a property of conscience and also of conscious imagination; an entity laden with fluidity since there exists not one identity for a person but many identities with the function of each one of them carefully calculated on the premise of convenience in a certain context, class and clan. The complexity, however, seems to increase as its application is adjusted and readjusted from individual identity to that of collective distinctiveness shared by a group. The latter type also stretches the complication as it is shifted from family unit, one clan, race, or nation to another. Consequently, African citizenship becomes as intricate to explain as African identity is indefinite to define. The cumbersomeness in the definition invites more questions than there can be an agreement on their answers and qualifications.

Immigration too, whether voluntary or forced, has taken its toll on the formation of African identity. It has created a major phenomenon in the tracing of a workable description for an African identity that could respond to the versatile categories of ethnicities, individuals with degrees of Africanity and of races that would want to identify themselves with Africa while being of a Diasporic culture in another continent. These realities open the door for the dynamics of African Diasporism which have emerged as what can be called a deliberate hybrid of African migration into various parts of the world and vice versa. Underlying this reality is another phenomenon by which the entire setup of African identity is constructed or reconstructed in order not to lose touch with

African citizenship. Therefore, this essay discusses aspects of African identity in general and how the degree of identity may vary within the same country, as in the example of Somalia, which consists of a segment of people who consider themselves as Arab descendants and an opposing one of African indigenous stock such as the Bantu-Jareer.1

The method used for this essay is mainly sources recorded in previous studies but relevant to this essay as well as secondary data collected from various written literatures by Somali and non-Somali scholars of renown. While some of those authors are oriental scholars who studied Somalia from the locus of a homogenous society of Arab origin, the other section consists of revisionists who contradicted that long-enduring perception of homogeneity and nomadic pastoralism with a more viable thesis of heterogeneity, multi-ethnicity, and multi-culturality; hence an identity confusion of a Somalia that lingers undeterminably between Arabness and Africanness.

What constitutes an identity?

Some categories and hermeneutics of Africanity

As a continent, Africa holds together a diversity of ethnic groups and races that are further classified and even often sub-classified into a multitude of smaller clan entities that share some kind of kinship, common values, social beliefs, cultures and ethno-political structures. Adediran (1999) concurs with us by contending that if "...a collection of people share a common, self applied appellation, have a sense and share belief in a common heritage then for all intents and purposes they should be regarded as an ethnic group (pp 42-49)." Lovejoy (2000: 10) emphasized, "...ethnicity is not a thing to be discovered by a test conducted either by historians today or by people in the past who applied ethnic categories to themselves or to others. Ethnic identification involved and involves reinterpretation and re-invention of the present and the past." (For more about ethnicity see Unger and Conley 1996; Diouf 1998; Gomez 1998)

In some countries including Somalia, these ties are tightly knit and are more structured than in other countries, varying between rural and urban societies. But all the peoples in the continent may claim African identity in one way or the other depending on the reasons adduced for that claim. The following are some (though not exhaustive) types of Africanity or Africanness as we may find on the continent:

a) Africanity by accident of geography: This group consists of those who happened to be in Africa without their wish to be there; individuals who found themselves living in the continent by virtue of circumstances beyond their control.

b) Africanity by birth: Someone who was born in Africa regardless of his/her race or ethnic group, or even political ideology or cultural doctrine.

c) Africanity by settlership: These are citizens of colonial regimes who arrived as prospectors, whose governments allocated them expropriated land from the African indigenes. This group became settlers and decided to live in the continent after independence, either continuing to exploit African land and manpower or opting to sell 'their' land and property to other Africans before venturing into other activities.

d) Africanity by culture or acculturation: Someone who may not be an African by ethnicity but who has lived in the continent long enough as to have adopted the way of life, culture and tradition of the average African.

e) Africanity by ideology: Someone who may or may not be of African blood or ethnic background, but whose understanding and sentiment for Africanity is based on African thought, values, ideology and other sentiments of intuitive desire to be part of the African world.

f) Africanity by pretension or circumstantial Africanity: This group comprises of individuals or societies who use African identity as and when it suits them for their specific purposes; in other words, circumstantial Africans. Members of this group are not pleased to be identified with Negritude or blackness, be it by values, ideology, culture, ethnicity or any other quality except by 'the accident' of existing on the continent. This is close in nature to the type mentioned in (a) above.

Diversity of the African Identity

According to Appiah (1992:37) before diversity took its course, all people originated from one source, that's why "[t]here is no doubt that all human beings descend from an original population (probably, as it happens, in Africa), and that from there people radiated out to cover the habitable globe." Despite Appiah's contention, classification in one way or the other of the people on the continent is possible. As such, we may have diversified groups composed of:

a) African Negroid stock: Black Africans of sub-Saharan regions made up of the Negro inhabitants of the continent;

b) Afro-Asiatic Stock: This breed consists of those whose ancestors came to Africa from parts of Asia, mainly India, whether in search of better opportunities for survival or with the colonial regimes as junior administrative staff or as technicians or skilled people. This group may not necessarily have contractual marriage with the African indigenes but, due to long residence in the continent, have qualified to use the African segment of their identity, although at times we may call them 'Asians';

c) Afro-European stock: This indicates those diverse Europeans who came to Africa as a result of colonialism or other reasons but who later determined to remain in their respective African countries as citizens; or the offspring of African and European marriage or concubinary;

d) Afro-Arab stock: Descendents of Arabian immigrants or those born to African and Arabian parents who made the continent their home regardless of their original or ancestral home country;

e) An Arab stock of light skin pigmentation that maintains mainly an Arab-Islamic culture. This type of African identity is dominant in the Northern part of the continent and is also visible in the Sudan and some parts of East Africa.

Based on the above classifications, identity is as phenomenal as it is fluid. What is actually bona fide about identity is its symbolization of societies, the uniqueness with which it qualifies a group as distinct from other societies. Rennie states that "[i]dentities are basic to the classification of societies" (P.163). This classification of distinctness is not a factor that is isolated but one which embeds beliefs and other cultural or historical experiences (or both) which the members of a certain society value much as their way of life. The thesis here seems to support the perception that "ideology includes a value component" (p163) that is dearly sacrosanct to any given group of people that shares a certain commonality.

To some degree, we agree with Peil and Oyeneye (1998:5) about people becoming part of a society "by birth", though we also believe other methods and narratives exist in other societies (Schlee 1994; Helander 2000; M. Eno 2008). But, is this a sufficient qualification for one to be accepted as such, even when one does not appreciate his being part of the ideals and values that inform the norm and socio-cultural beliefs of that society?

One of the conundrums of identity is that, as a tool, it can be traded in a magnitude of ways and situations, as and when it becomes applicable, and as such at times laden with undertones of ideology. Observing identity from a sociological point of view, Giddens (2002:29) postulates:

> The concept of identity in sociology is a multi-faceted one, and can be approached in a number of ways. Broadly speaking, identity relates to the understandings people hold about who they are and what is meaningful to them. These understandings are formed in relation to certain attributes that hold priority over other sources of meaning.

Controversial and complex as the qualification to, and for Africanness, remains, more disagreement may even emerge from the more conservative nationalists who might still live with a grudge caused by the untended wounds colonialism has caused to generations of Africans. One of the most excruciating pains of these unhealed wounds, among others, is the psychological as well as material damage, which the white man has caused in the appropriation of land, the most precious property of the African peasant. As prominent Kenyan scholar Ngugi wa Thiong'o (1983:26) elaborates:

> The white settler came early in the country and he immediately controlled the heart of the economy by appropriating the best part of the land to himself...The white settler was told that this would be a white man's country, and he was able to use his political power to consolidate his economic position. He forced black men into labour gangs, working for him in the 'White Highland.' "

Discussing a similar situation but focusing on the Somali context , Omar Eno (2004) weaves his lengthy writing about Italy's exploitation of the indigenous Bantu population. He narrates how the appropriation scheme resulted in "...the establishment of immense Italian plantations, which were acquired by confiscating the indigenous arable land between the two rivers Juba and Shebelle" (p143). (See also Ahmed Q. Ali 2004)

According to wa Thiong'o so "massive was the land given to people like Delamere and Grogan" (p27) that in order to realize the goal of the settler scheme "violence was used to thwart the cause of justice" (p29). In the long run, it was the common consciousness of the peasantry that waged the long hard struggle to regain its economic source from the white man. The result was the consolidation of segments of tribal-'nations' into a broader identity of one nation.

Nation as identity

Not very unlike the conundrum that surrounds the definition and interpretation of identity, the explication of the term 'nation' is also contentious, particularly from our African perspective. Owing to its large ethnic diversity and loyalty to a specific geographical territory, the pre-colonial African society was composed of ethnic polities with independent structured leaderships. So, as it emerged, the concept of the wider nation demarcated by colonial territorial boundaries, as we see them today, has appeared as an outcome of the need for a consolidated effort in waging a collective rebellion against European colonialism. Therefore, to a considerable degree, there exists an ethnic/tribal[2] nation that is very immediate to an individual member of an ethnic group whose territorial and genealogical distinctiveness is measured against the other ethnic groups that surround their tribal borderlines. Very often, more integrity and individual sacrifices are ascribed to the tribal/ethnic group one subscribes to than to the 'peripheral nation' that was born as a result of colonialism. In Walker Connor's (1994) perception, the essence of what is called a nation is one that remains intangible. Indeed it is a kind of solidarity that is embedded in a communal belief, a norm that holds a highly cherished social 'self' driven by strong psychological force that informs distinctness of the group concerned. As Nasong'o (2008:24), drawing from Connor puts it, "when analyzing a socio-political situation, what ultimately matters is not what is, but what people believe." Connor, however, seems to agree with Anderson (1983) that the concept of nation or nationhood, in reality, binds together political communities which are imagined.

Gellner (1925-1995) contends that such ideas as nation-state, nation and nationalism have sprung into life as a result of 'modern civilization', which also came as an offspring of the industrial revolution. Somehow, Gellner (1983) tends to believe that "in traditional societies the concept of nationalism was not much known about", or adhered to as such. But Anthony Smith challenges Gellner's perception by noting the existence of a cohesive relationship between nation and earlier societies, since the idea of nation seems to have firm connections with what was earlier seen or described as ethnic group – society based on common pedigree or genealogical forefather, cultural identity and as a group that identifies itself with a given geographical territory. Smith's view is interpretable to the ethnic-based societies of Africa, which Somalia remains a good example.

Complexity of Somali Identity: who is an African?

There is nowhere the issue of identity takes more queer dimensions than in Somali society, a matter that Mohamed Eno calls "identity confusion" as compared to identity formation. When carefully examined, the Somali identity has sustained itself in turbulent existence between:

a) Long enduring claim of Arabness by which the community seeks superiority over Negritude/Africanity; and
b) That of Africanity which the nomadic Somalis look down upon as depreciated humans of inferior quality, and as a result of which Indigenous Negroes (Bantu/Jareer) are degraded and victimized.

The Arabness of this Horn of Africa people is an identity, which was well orchestrated by the Somali people themselves and narrated to foreign scholars who came to the country to study the theme of Somali origin. In an outstanding work in the country, Luling (2002:82) noted: "The genealogy of every Somali can be traced back to a single ancestor, the legendary Hiil. Hiil in his turn is said to be descended from the Quraysh, the lineage of the prophet."

Another British anthropologist, I. M. Lewis (1955) has noted of the Somali-Arab alliance and writes: "Somali tribes have often become powerful through alliance with immigrant Arab Sheiks, of whom in retrospect they consider themselves the descendants" (p14). Lewis goes further to name specific nomadic clans who attached themselves to Arabian forefathers and writes, "the Darod family of tribes traces descent from an immigrant Arab culture-hero" (p18). He also describes the Isak in northern Somalia as "traditionally the descendents of an Arab Sheik" (p23). Likewise, the Hawiye who trace their genealogy from an Arabian ancestor do not want to be left out of the Arabian connection.

This Somali-Arab identity was recently revisited constructively and academically disputed by a number of scholars. One of them, sociologist Abdi Kusow (1995:83) questions the veracity of the tradition because, according to him, the "early Arab immigrants who arrived before the 16th century were mainly disjoined individual families who came as a result of economic and political pressure within their homelands" (p83) and therefore had neither a proof of nobility nor the significance in number to overwhelm statistically their indigenous hosts (Mohamed Eno 2008).

Notwithstanding the apparent scholarly suspicion, the myth of Somali origin from an Arab pedigree was sustained by lack of examination into Somali genealogy. The argument was often avoided as a taboo whose investigation amounted to a betrayal of the oral traditions. One Somali intellectual and writer, Ali Mouse Iye (2008:81-82), who encountered that scenario comments:

> I thus learned a difficult lesson: nobody, not even scholars, can question in writing, the founding myths of the Somalis. In other words, I was accused of being unfair and unfaithful to my oral culture, by challenging in writing the authenticity of a cherished legend, and by transforming and ensconcing my heretic view in writing, giving it the veneer of scriptural truth.

From another critical perspective, Somali egalitarianism and pastoral democracy became dismayed at Kusow's revelation of "increasing identity assertions of previously suppressed social identities" (xiii) thence debunking an oft-hidden identity crisis within the society (See also M. Eno 2008; Eno & Eno - forthcoming). The said "assertions" undermine the purported ethno-cultural homogeneity while yet standing in favor of a Somalia that constitutes multi-ethnic communities of diverse ancestral identities i.e. Africans, Persians, Arabs and so on, but under various social strata framed by the nomads. It is the appearance of the voices of these 'suppressed social identities' that somehow partly shook the balance off the homogeneity concept which, as a consequence, paved the way for the disquieting of the revisionist scholars who overturned the earlier narrative about Somalia from its mendacious and untested homogeneity and cultural nomadism to one of multi-ethnic reality constructed on the pillars of cultural diversity.

Taking an untraditional course about Somali identity, Besteman (1995:43) argues, "Somalia can no longer be represented as a 'nation of nomads' or 'a pastoral democracy'" thus connoting the existence of identities and cultures other than Somali-'Arab' and pastoral nomadism. After a keen observation of the interplay between the Somali communities and the undesirable socio-ethnic status of the Bantu Jareer indigenes, Besteman elaborates, "the ambiguity of their status as Somali and non-Somali at the same time has perhaps facilitated their representation as a distinct and unified social group within Somali society" (p44). She challenges early writers of Somali homogeneity and cultural nomadism by laying open the distinctive identities of the two groups: "people who are jareer are considered more 'African,' as distinct from Somalis, who are considered more 'Arabic'" (p47-48). (For more about Jareer – Jileec Somalis read Omar Eno "The Jareer Factor in Somali History: Emphasis on Ethnicity, Slavery, Stigma, and Plantation Economy (1840-2000); Forthcoming PhD Dissertation).

In one of his contentious and most read works on Somalia, Ali J. Ahmed (1995) censures orientalist scholars for their part in purporting the core Arab element in Somali genealogy. The same concern, as Ali (1995:141) writes, was raised by a Washington Post reporter who describes the country as "Poor Somalia – not enough Arab and not enough African." An analysis of the reporter's well-articulated but taunting phrase, informs a kind of derogation which, in our opinion, does not look down on either Africanness or Arabness in their rightful entities, but the dilemma that harbors anything short of any of them i.e. being in-between and, therefore, impure. But to reach a specific goal in an unavoidable situation, a Somali may instantly swerve from his Arab identity to that of Africanity: a) If s/he encounters discrimination or identity denial from that group; b) If the African identity serves to achieve a goal at a specific time and place.

Our argument, focusing on this peculiar characteristic of the Somali, appears to be supported by several researchers who studied Somalis. In a very recent study, Kroner (2007) reveals how Somalis configured with Africanity under a circumstance of oppression and discrimination:

> The negative attitude of their host country's population leads the Somalis to form a new group identity versus the Egyptian/Arabs while in other countries I heard quite often that at least some Somalis have Arab ancestors and they differentiate themselves from Africans. So said Said Omar, 'The Somali people who say that they have Arab ancestors don't know what they are talking about. We are Africans!' He goes on to state that 'the Arabs are the biggest racists, they are worse than Apartheid. They despise us because we are black.' In the case of the Somalis in Egypt, due to multiple forms of discrimination they embrace an African identity (p56).

Although Kroner quotes her respondent as saying "They despise us because we are black" and that in Egypt the Somalis "...embrace an African identity"; a close analysis of Kroner's work also shows how Somalis resort to the very identity (Africanness) they despise and denigrate in their own country, as was elaborated in Ahmed and in

Besteman above. But such embrace was made possible only after encountering "multitude forms of discrimination."

Somalia's genealogical connection to Arab ancestry has a long history among scholars, oral historians and traditionists, all of whom encountered at one stage or the other how Somalis ..."differentiate themselves from Africans" (Kroner, p56). As a further elaboration of our contention about the Somalis' superiority complex over Africans, and for that matter over Negritude, we may quote a verse from the poetry work of popular Somali bard Ali Dhuux in despise of the black African citizen:

Annaku caddaankaanu la loolannaa
Madowgu ma Ciseyno

Translation:

We compete with the white man, (and therefore)
Deem no respect for the Blackman/black race

Ali Dhuux's remark reminds us of Jafferson, cited in Appiah (1992), who "...argued in his *Notes on the State of Virginia,* that the Anglo-Saxon people were superior to blacks in the endowments both of body and mind..." (p49). On the other hand, while some of those born in Africa are distancing themselves from Africanity, others of African ethnic background but born in other continents, are more attached to Africa. For instance, Du Bois cited in Appiah (1992:41) affirms that

> "Africa is of course my fatherland. Yet neither my father nor my father's father ever saw Africa or knew its meaning or cared over much for it. My mother's folk were closer and yet their direct connection, in culture and race, became tenuous; still my tie to Africa is strong."

Another historical incident was reported in *The East African Standard* (1930) after Somalis waged a strong protest against the "status under the law of the Colony of the Natives of Africa" which classified them as Africans. Rather than being classified as Africans, the Somalis preferred that "they should be recognized as Asiatics" regardless of the higher tax they would be imposed in the latter category, as long as they were recognized for their Arab identity!

Claims of Somali homogeneity and Arab identity, led to the suppression of the identity of the African stock among the community; the specific group scholars describe as 'the aborigines', 'indigenes', 'Negroid stock', 'Zenj', 'Jareer', 'Bantu', or as 'residues of the

Bantu/Sabaki speaking tribes of Shungwaya.' (See Cerulli 1957 -- 1964, Nurse 1980; Allen 1983; Luling 2002; Eno & Eno 2007).

Despite his paradigmatic portrayal of Somalia as an homogenous society of pastoral democracy, I.M. Lewis hints at the diversity of the people in this African peninsula in his citation of Puccioni as the latter discusses another category of people consisting of "...despised people of possible Negroid origin with whom the other Wangial (*Somalis*) do not intermarry" (p40) (Emphasis added). Lewis elaborates the category of the "despised people" as the indigenous Bantu stock consisting "...of original nuclei of pre-Cushitic Negroid inhabitants" (p41). The era in Lewis' context traces these events back to a time when "[m]ost of the country, certainly the southern part, was peopled by Negroes" who were not slaves as mentioned in the mythical tradition of the self-ennobled Somali nomads, but as people "who seem to have constituted the aboriginal population" (p45).

The narrative here clearly displays the identity divide between the people; one group yearning for identification with Arabness and the other celebrating the pride of its African Negritude. In a radical essay by a Somali scholar, Ahmed (1995:141) comments on the Arab–African identity divide, taking SAMO (Somali African Muki Organization) as an example, the movement that advocates for justice and equal rights for the oppressed Bantu-Somalis in contrast to the organizations of the predominant Somali (Arab) nomadic groups. He wrote:

"By including 'African' in its name, the organization bares a hidden secret in Somali society. Supporters of the movement belong to the segment of the Somali society who are often given the derogatory epithet of Jareer (kinky hair)".

In one instance, Ahmed describes the Bantu – Jareer people as a " group that has among other reasons been victimized for their physical features" (p142) and their identification with Negritude and/or Africanity. After noting the perplexity of identity within a single nation, with Somalia being a case in hand, we may cross to the other side of the African identity in the enterprise of Pan-Africanism.

Pan-Africanism

How to define the constituents of African identity may be problematic in the context of Pan-Africanism. Here we have to consider certain realities about the dynamics of African identity.

Although there are many ways to identify one's ethnic "identity," it's even more complex and confusing when some segments of the "African" society tend to not only refrain from identifying themselves with other African ethnic entities but in fact disdain Africanism. Indeed, Somalia and some other nations in the African continent opted to identify themselves as Asiatic-Arab rather than Africans, not simply from the perspective of identity per se, but also from a socio-psychological belief that the former is superior to the latter. Based on such attitude and thinking, several so-called Africans perceive that being an African is a derogative identity.

It is worth reminiscing that several individuals (including scholars) from certain Northern African countries, the Sudan and Somalia, whom we (separately and together) encountered in discussions on race and identity on various occasions in Africa, Europe, Asia and in America, preferred to identify themselves *first* with their Arabian identity (for which they had a right to) than with their African citizenship. By this paradigm, ethnicity seems to be more of a priority than the national geographical identity. But, among the aforementioned countries, the dilemma rests with Somalia and Sudan who are ethnically black but categorize themselves *first* as Arabite stock.

To begin with, we assume the answer to the questions: *what should constitute Africanity*, or, *who should qualify to be an African?* - should not summarily evade the other inevitable segment of the question: *who should determine the qualities of Africanness and/or qualifiers for Africanity?* These types of questions need to be adequately exhausted particularly in considering the various aspects of the multi-raciality and multi-ethnicity of the communities living on the continent. Relevant also is the question: *Should Africanity be determined on the premise of ethnicity or in terms of language or culture or ideology?* Even if the philosophy of Pan-Africanism materializes, how will the language or languages that will be Africa's identity through its medium of communication be determined among the diverse ethnic national and regional languages that are already in (or have shown) rivalry with one another? Robert July (1992:29) highlights this tendency about Africa of "whether an accurate assessment is best achieved by racial or by linguistic qualification."

Although Lipset holds the notion that whereas in European or Canadian society nation is tied to community and that ideological commitment is what holds the nation of America together; the situation of Africa is quite different where ethnicity and segmentary tribal entities predominantly characterize the society. A multi-ethnic Africa ushers in another reality about Africa; that of linguistic perplexity which will heave a burden in the scheming of a politically as well as socially consolidated

African continent. As we have seen in the process of formulating a national identity, a type of national language was used effectively to connect with people and mobilize them (Wright 2004). Contrarily, in the wider sense of establishing a common African identity that is workable, the primary obstacle may be the adoption of a common vehicle of communication that also reflects Africa by identity.

Therefore, whatever the political orientation or economic strategies, a question will remain as to whether one or more African languages will be adopted as a symbol of African identity and as a vehicle of communication, or whether a European (colonial/imperial) language will take this function as a medium of communication (as it is today) to the disadvantage of African identity and unity. The linguistic aspect of the question needs to be appropriately addressed considering the significance of language as a representative of a *certain* culture and as such an *identity* of a group and not the other/s.

The linguistic domain has increased recently compared to the ethnic or racial mirror from which Africa was usually seen. Like the ethnic complexity, July notes the linguistic paradigm as "a technique that indeed eliminates certain complications, but unfortunately introduces others" (p20). On the other hand, even if the uphill task of formulating the qualifiers of African identity is painstakingly elaborated and agreed upon -- whether ideologically- or physiologically-based -- the determination of which African language to adopt will remain a puzzle since linguistic rivalry poses a serious problem to the African societies at the clan or tribal levels within many nations. This reality prefigures a concern, especially when world class African scholars like Ahmed (1996) reveal that in many African countries, including Somalia, "...the kind of language used is in contention" (p2). The solemn reason for this anxiety denotes another more dominant factor in contemporary African society as language shapes "the socio-political and economic definitions of the nation" (p3). (For more about the problem of languages in Africa see Bokamba 1992; Mazrui and Mazrui 1995; M. Eno 2005, 2008)

Zeal and over-ambition to create a more unified, more cohesive Africa to function as the states of the European Union or the US may expose what Winston Churchill would call (2002:756) "a situation both immeasurable and laden with doom" to a continent and people already politically and economically vulnerable, ravaged by disease, war, corruption and resource mismanagement; factors that contributed significantly to the continental brain drain and the creation of an immense population of African Diaspora scattered in the various corners of the world. These, together with other external forces, including the legacy of slavery and colonialism, have reduced Africa to a position of "...a troubled continent, bubbling with conflicting forces and tribal, personal, and national rivalries" (Palmer and Perkins, p502).

Notwithstanding our contention with Davidson (1955:233) about Africa's being "united by a common acceptance of despair" because of Africa's struggle against colonialism and its effects rather than acceptance of it, we seem to agree with his suggestion of the continent being "united by a common surge of hope," a hope which, in our opinion, holds a vision and ideology for unification, while yet struggling "to realize in practice the African political aspirations."

Looking at the African scene from another perspective, and reviewing Lippman's statement that "the true constituent members of the international order of the future," which indeed Africa is an entity, "are communities of states," an amalgamation of the holders of African identity under a single banner may contribute in many respects to the world societies, while simultaneously bearing in mind the fact that not all these African identities have emerged from the same historical experience or socio-political orientation.

However, it may not yet be too late for Africa to learn from previous discrepancies related to the formations of institutions and counter-institutions which one after the other became unproductive and in fact collapsed due to what Palmer and Perkins suggest as "rivalries among the leaders of the new African states and by conflicting interests and orientation" (p585). Some reminiscent examples are: Conference of Independent African States (CIAS); and The Proclamation of the Casablanca Group, which has not lived up to expectations.

Conclusion

Quoting Collins and Porras (1997:40) Ramphele (2001) writes, "One of the most important steps you can take in building a visionary company is not action, but a shift in perspective." We seem to endorse this notion of "a shift in perspective" for Africa to participate in the global economy as well as political power play. But in order to achieve worthwhile results of an effective "shift in perspective" the scheme should first of all lay its foundation firmly at the national level. A unified African ideological stance as well as identity-consciousness (and not ethno-centrism) can not be realized when a certain segment of the sons and daughters of Africa depreciate their black identity and the values of African consciousness just to a symbol of inferiority. We concur with Ramphele that "A shift in perspective is surely needed to liberate those trapped by this stigma" (p68). Accordingly, until and unless we learn to be intrinsically proud of who we are, and the ideological doctrine for which we stand, Africans are bound to lose touch with the reality of their identity.

One step towards making 'a shift in perspective' is, as Ramphele suggests, "...to confront the legacy of inferiority and superiority complexes" (p68). It is necessary that some of us first of all overcome the evils of psychological torture such as stereotyping and its affluent product – prejudice -against one another. In other words, Africa has to take the initiative of addressing at the national level all sorts of ill-will caused by the "particular culprit" (Steele 1992:68) called stigma. In the circumstance where in the same country one section of the society craves for a non-African identity and another suffers marginalization, degradation and victimization owing to its African identity, the answer to the question of *who is an African* acquires a certain sense of urgency. Or, put in another way: *who is more African?* Whatever the perspective, mutual co-existence is eventually what everyone will want the continent to achieve, rather than the formation of pseudo-identities and genealogical lineages of inexplicable origin.

References

Adediran, B. (1999) "Yoruba Ethnic Groups? A Review of the Problem of Ethnic Identification" in Paul Lovejoy. (Ed) The African Diaspora (course Reading Kit). Pp. 442-49.

Ahmed, A. J. (1995) "Daybreak is Near: Won't You Become Sour?" In Ali J. Ahmed (ed.) The Invention of Somalia. Red Sea Press.

Ahmed, A. J. (1996) Daybreak is Near: Literature, Clans and the Nation-State in Somalia. Red Sea Press.

Ali, A. Q. (2004) "Land Rush in Somalia" in Abdi M. Kusow (ed.) Putting the Cart before the Horse: Contested Narratives and the Crisis of the Nation-State in Somalia. The Red Sea Press.

Allen, J. de Vere, (1983) "Shungwaya, the Mijikenda and the Traditions. International Journal of African Historical Studies; vol (16)3, pp455-485.

Anderson, B. (1983) Imagined Communities: Reflections on the Origins and Spread of Nationalism. New York: Verso.

Appiah, K. A. (1992) In my Father's House: Africa in the Philosophy of Culture. New York: Oxford University Press.

Besteman, C. 1995. "The Invention of Gosha: Slavery, Colonialism and Stigma in Somali History" in Ali J. Ahmed, ed., The Invention of Somalia, Red sea Press.

Bokamba, E. G. (1992) "The Africanization of English" in Braj B. Kachru (ed.) The Other Language: English across Cultures. Urbana and Chicago: The University of Illinois Press.

Cerulli, E. (1957) "Il Libro degli Zenji" in Somali, Scritti vari Editi ed inediti (3 vols. Roma.

Collins, J. and Porras, J. (1997) Built to Last. New York: Harper Business

Connor, W. (1994) Ethno-nationalism: The Quest for Understanding. Princeton, NJ: Princeton University Press.

Davidson, B. (1955) *The African Awakening*. London.

Diouf, S. (1998) Servants of Allah: African Muslims Enslaved in the America. New York University Press.

Eno, M. A. (2005) "What are the main causes of the predicament in the acquisition of ESL in Somalia?" MA Dissertation, University of Sunderland.

_____(2008) The Bantu – Jareer Somalis: Unearthing Apartheid in the Horn of Africa. London: Adonis and Abbey Publishers Ltd.

Eno, O. A. "Landless Landlords and Landed Tenants" in Abdi M. Kusow (Ed), Putting the Cart before the Horse: Contested Narratives and the Crisis of the Nation-State in Somalia. NJ: The Red Sea Press.

Eno, O A. and Mohamed A. Eno (2007) "The Making of a Modern Diaspora: The Resettlement Process of the Somali Bantu Refugees in the United States" in Toyin Falola and Niyi Afolabi (eds.) African Minorities in the New World. Routledge, Taylor and Francis Group.

_____(Forthcoming) "A Tale of Two Minorities: Contrasting the Somali Bantu and Gaboye Communities of Somalia" in Michael Mabanaso and Chima Korieh (Eds.) Minorities and the State in Africa. Routledge

Eno, O. A. (Forthcoming) "The Jareer Factor in Somali History: Emphasis on Ethnicity, Slavery, Stigma, and Plantation Economy (1840-2000)" PhD Dissertation.

Gellner, E. (1983) Nations and Nationalism; Oxford: Blackwell

Giddens, A. (2002) Sociology; 4th edition. Polity

Gomez, M. (1998) Exchanging Our Country Marks. The University of North Carolina Press.

Helander, B. (2000) "The Hubeer in the Land of Plenty: Land, labor and vulnerability among a southern Somali clan" in Catherine Besteman and Lee Cassanelli (eds.) The Struggle for Land in Southern Somalia: The War Behind the war. London: HAAN Associates.

Iye, A. M. (2008) "Reflections on the Literatures of the Horn of Africa: The Case of Somali Literature" in Ali J. Ahmed (ed.) The Road Less Traveled: Reflections on the Literatures of the Horn of Africa. Red Sea Press.

July, R. (1992) A History of the African People; 4th edition; Nairobi: EAEP

Kroner, G-K. (2007) "Transit or Dead End? The Somali Diaspora in Egypt" in Abdi M. Kusow and Stephanie Bjork (eds.) From Mogadishu to Dixon: The Somali Diaspora in Global Context; NJ: Red Sea Press.

Kusow, A. M. (1995) "The Somali Origin: Myth or Reality" in Ali J. Ahmed (ed.) The Invention of Somalia. Lawrenceville: NJ. The Red Sea Press

Kusow, A. M. (2004) "Preface" in Abdi M. Kusow (ed.) Putting the Cart before the Horse: Contested Nationalism and the Crisis of the Nation State in Somalia. Red Sea Press.

Lewis, I.M. (1955) Peoples of the Horn of Africa: Somali, Afar and Saho. London: International African institute.

Lipset, S. M. 1990, Continental Divide: The Values and Institutions of the United States and Canada. London: Routledge.)

Lovejoy, P. E. (2000) "Identifying Enslaved Africans in the African Diaspora" in Paul E. Lovejoy (ed.) Identity in the Shadow of Slavery. London and New York: Continuum.

Luling, V. (2002) Somali Sultanate: The Geledi City-State Over 150 Years. Haan Associates.

Mazrui, A. A. and Alamin M. Mazrui (1995) Swahili State and Society: The Political Economy of an African Language. Nairobi: East African Educational Publishers.

Nurse, D. (1980) "Shungwaya and the Bantu of Somalia: Some Linguistic Evidence" in Hussein M. Adam and Charles L. Geshekter (eds.) Proceedings of the First International Congress on Somali Studies; Chico CA: Scholars Press.

Peil, M. and Oyeneye, O. (1998) Consensus, Conflict and Change; Nairobi: EAEP Ltd.

Ramphele, M. "Combating Racism in South Africa: Redress/Remedies" in Hamilton et al (eds.) Beyond Racism: Race and Inequality in Brazil, South Africa and the United States. Lynne Rienner Publishers.

Rennie, J.K. "Ideology and State Formation: Political and Communal Ideologies among the Southeastern Shona 1500—1890" in Ahmed I. Salim (ed.) State Formation in East Africa. Heinemann Educational Books.

Schlee, G. (1994) Identities on the Move: Clanship and Pastoralism in Northern Kenya. Nairobi: Gideon S. Were Press.

Steele, C. (1992) "Race and the Shooting of Black Americans" Atlantic Monthly (April):68-76.

Ungar, S. and T. Conley (eds.), (1996). Identity Papers: Contested Nationhood in Twentieth-Century France. Minneapolis, London: University of Minnesota Press.

Wa Thiong'o, N. (1983) Homecoming. Lawrence Hill and Company Publishers Inc. Reprint.

Wright, S. (2004) Language Policy and Language Planning. Palgrave Macmillan.

Notes

1 Please take note that the names Bantu and Jareer will be used in this chapter interchangeably because both names refer to the same people.

2 Although these days the word tribe is often used by many, it was historically introduced by European colonialists to Africa. For the purpose of this chapter and from an anthropological and sociological perspective we are safe to use the word "tribe." Prior to the arrival of Europeans, Africans used words such as kinship, clanship, endogamy, etc.

Chapter 5

BELONGING OF ANOTHER TYPE: WHITENESS AND AFRICAN IDENTITY

Steven Friedman

Can one be a citizen of a country but not its continent? A while ago, I shared a platform in Germany with the black editor of one of our South African newspapers. At question time, a Zimbabwean member of the audience raised his hand and, when recognised, said: "I wish to ask a question to my African brother". I replied," which one?" This triggered a lengthy argument over whether a white South African was, indeed, an African – much of it initiated by my co-panellist who assured me that, as a white South African, I would always be a compatriot, but never an African.

Beyond Absurdity

At first glance, the argument is absurd. How can one be a British citizen but not a European? Or an Indian citizen but not an Asian? On reflection, however, it is possible to see what was bothering him. Continental identities are not always simply about where people happen to live: "European", "African" and "Asian" tend to be used not only to describe where people make their home, but their racial and cultural identity. Part of the editor's reaction may be explained, for example, by the fact that white racism in South Africa (and presumably in other countries on the continent which experienced white minority rule) was once justified by its proponents not as a system in which whites enjoyed rights at the expense of blacks, but in which "Europeans" did so at the expense of "non-Europeans": some discriminatory signs would proclaim that the facility was reserved for "Europeans only". Further afield, African-Americans, of course, may never ever have visited Africa, while Britain's "Asian community" includes people who are British enough to be elected to that country's Parliament and, who, similarly, may never have got round to travelling to Asia. In both cases, it is race, not continent of residence, which is being used to define the person.

This tendency to use continental identity to refer to racial category makes a refusal to simply admit white residents of Africa to African-ness more understandable. It could also be argued that the cultural identities of white residents of Africa may not be particularly African: white South Africans often tend to derive their models and inspirations - whether in politics or the arts or in their views on economic organisation – from Europe or North America. In the South African context, there is another reason for reticence: "white Africanness" has been used at times as an excuse for behaviour which suggests that identity is being used purely as a convenience. Thus the apartheid government, particularly in its reformist period, was known to insist on its Africanness in an attempt to relieve diplomatic pressure: it was, it insisted, an African government like any other and so ought not to be singled out for special treatment. To do so, was to discriminate against Africa's white inhabitants. While the continent and the world were clearly not fooled, for some, this did discredit the notion of white African identity. Some on the continent might also feel that major white-owned South African companies rely on Africanness as a route to commercial advantage but find no other use for it as they happily list on the London Stock Exchange while flaunting their Africanness south of the Sahara.

Given this context, a tendency by black African intellectuals, particularly in Southern Africa where the white settler presence has been most evident, to insist that authentic Africanness is beyond the reach of Africa's whites, is more understandable.

Beyond Essentialism?

But, while this background may help us to understand why some see a white African as a contradiction in terms, it does not necessarily justify this claim. Firstly, the view that whites, because of their European roots, lack an insight into African culture misses the point that the continent is not culturally homogenous – there is no single African culture. The most obvious reason for insisting on this is the cultural difference between the countries of the Maghreb on the one hand, sub-Saharan Africa on the other. But even within the sub-Saharan section, there is significant variation. Just as there are cultural differences between French and German people, or Koreans and Indians, so is there between Africa's many identities. If there is no monolithic African culture, then the white presence could be seen as just one more addition to the cultural mix.

One implication is that excluding whites (or anyone else on the continent) from Africanness is likely to do little to enrich African identity.

On the contrary, excluding new manifestations of this identity closes off the possibility that new forms will emerge continually, enriching the whole. Secondly and similarly, African cultures are not hermetically sealed from those of Europe or other parts of the world, notably America. The colonial experience has obviously left significant cultural traces – the Anglophone-Francophone-Lusophone distinction, for example. But the influence continues: we are all wont to point out the impact of the United States and of Northern culture more generally on Africa (and, indeed, everywhere else).

This influence could, of course, be dismissed as a product of dominance, of the extent to which those with power are able to impose their culture on others. In this view, it is an aberration, or at least a consequence of circumstances, which Africans should be seeking to challenge, not to celebrate. Certainly, there are aspects of this influence, which can be seen as a form of domination. But not all of it can be dismissed in this way.

Only those cultures which have been able to erect physical barriers to foreign penetration have managed to seal off external influence and then only for a time. Nor is cultural isolation a blessing. Albania before the end of the Cold War was often cited as a society which had succeeded in cordoning itself off from foreign influence: but it is hardly a role model: indeed, all the evidence suggests that the effect of isolation was overwhelmingly to retard its development – culturally as well as in all other spheres. Cultures do not suffer when they are exposed to external influences – they become richer and stronger.

If, therefore, white Africans are subject to European and North American influence, so too are black Africans. While the extent may differ, this is no difference in principle and, therefore, not a sound basis for a distinction.

Next, while whites using Africanness for convenience may be a justifiable source of irritation, who is to decide whether people are "entitled" to an identity because they are sincere about embracing it? And what standards should they apply? Deciding who is sincerely living out their identity is largely arbitrary and can be a cloak for dreadful human rights abuses since people can be excluded from a political community because their identity is not "genuine". Excluding whites from an African identity because we are "only using it for convenience" is, therefore, a slippery slope, enabling some to decide who is African and who not.

Certainly, it is important to encourage whites to feel rooted in this continent, to feel that their future is bound up in Africa's. But it does not necessarily follow that this should determine whether people are allowed an African identity.

The idea that those who choose to be Africans are indeed so, is in fact deeply rooted in Pan-Africanist thinking, at least in the way in which it has manifested itself in South Africa. Thus the clearest statement of white eligibility for Africanness comes here from the Pan Africanist Congress of Azania, which insists that it is: "Inspired by the belief that all citizens in South Africa who identify themselves with Africa and her indigenous people are African".[1]

This can be read in two ways.

It could be interpreted to mean that African identity is not unconditional, that some sort of test is required to determine whether the would-be African really does identify. This runs into the objection made earlier – that an insistence that someone, somewhere, will determine the degree to which the relevant individual identifies with Africa and her people is to make identity dependent on an arbitrary decision by someone other than the person seeking that identity.

But the formulation can be read in another way – to say that anyone who chooses to identify themselves as African should be accepted as African. This implies that it makes no sense to set up criteria to determine identity in the first place and that people should be encouraged to define who they are.

Choosing Who We Are

What precisely is lost if identity is seen as purely self-defining, if anyone is African if they choose to define themselves as African?

The obvious objection is that people who do not deserve to be African will be admitted. But how does one deserve Africanness – or, indeed, any other identity? There might be an argument for this at the rhetorical level. But only there.

The point can be made by drawing an analogy with race.

To insist that people born into a racial group ought not to be identified with it is a rhetorical flourish which might serve to make a political point. Thus, South Africa's Black Consciousness movement would, under apartheid, denounce blacks who collaborated with the regime or were seen not to be sufficiently assertive in their black identity as "non-whites". By implication, blackness was a status, which needed to be earned. But the term was quite clearly meant to make a point, not to describe reality: no-one in the movement seriously believed that "non-whites" were not black - they were using a rhetorical flourish to say that some blacks ought to be prouder of who they were and more willing to fight for it.

In the same vein, it could be appropriate to argue that white Africans ought to do more to identify with the continent and to deepen their roots in it. It might even be appropriate for those who feel strongly about this to insist that these would-be Africans still have a way to go before they deserve the identity to which they are said to aspire. But this would operate at the level of political debate only: to insist that white Africans should do more to earn their Africanness is not to deny that they are, indeed, African.

There are, in effect, two kinds of objections to the notion that whites born in Africa are African. In the first case, there is something essential about being African which has been transmitted through many generations. Those who look different and have arrived here via other parts of the world might be accepted as fellow citizens, but never as Africans. The second insists that Africanness is attainable by outsiders but is not automatically acquired.

One is essentialist, the other is not. Both, however, discriminate between "acceptable" forms of African identity and others.

Ironically, Africans have been among the planet's most consistent victims of this sort of thinking, which denies people the right to frame their own identity and to expect others to respect that. Only an approach which allows all of us, white Africans included, to choose our own identities, is likely to enrich African identity by allowing the full spectrum of its expression to be seen and heard.

Notes

1 See 'Pan Africanist Congress' http://www.suntimes.co.za/online/election/parties/paca.htm

---

* This article was originally published in the September/October 2004 edition of the journal *African Renaissance*

PART 2

AFRICAN IDENTITIES AND CO-EXISTENCE: EXAMPLES

Chapter 6

ARAB SLAVERY OF AFRICANS IN THE AFRO-ARAB BORDERLANDS – THE SUDAN CASE *

Bankie Forster Bankie

Slavery has existed in all the ancient civilizations of Asia, Africa, Europe and pre-Columbian America. It had been recognized and accepted by the Abrahamic religions- Judaism, Christianity and Islam (Prah 2005). Africans do not need to feel particular shame for practising slavery amongst themselves.

Africans on the continent did sell their kith and kin into slavery. Such practices happened all over the world. For instance today human trafficking is monitored. Indigenous slave practices went on in Africa and still do. However these indigenous slave practices are not commercialized and barbarous as practiced under Arab or European leadership. By and large slaves married into the host community and lost that identity in the new family. As Prah states with both Arab and European slavery, Africans were not the machines, but the cogs in a process whose outcome was unknown to them. The denial of their languages and cultures in effect denationalized the Africans turning them into Arabs.

Arab-led slavery of Africans is an issue that both Africans and Arabs frequently treat as a matter to be hushed-up because of the embarrassing reaction it generates. It is a historical reality which differentiates the fate and the aspirations of Africans on the one hand and Arabs on the other, in their different attempts to achieve African unity and Arab unity respectively. Both Pan-Africanism and Pan-Arabism, if pursued democratically, would assist in the emancipation and development of the two peoples. At the heart of the complex Afro-Arab relationship are the realities of racism and forced Arabisation / Islamisation. The Durban United Nations World Conference on Racism of 2001 chose to avoid racism in Afro-Arab relations. It did humanity a disservice. It took Darfur to bring the issues of racism and forced Arabisation / Islamisation to global focus. Racism is a reality of life in the Borderlands of the Africa, in places such as Sudan, Niger, and Mali etc. Akbar Mohamed, the African

American spiritual leader, is quoted at page 53 of the Amman Seminar (1983) Report on Afro-Arab relations as follows:

> ....Akbar Mohamed, in a lecture delivered at the Institute for African Studies in Cairo, argued that there is still some subconscious racism on the part of the Arabs toward the Africans, that slavery is very strongly exploited in Africa against the Arabs, and that the Arabs do not try to discuss this issue with the Africans.

While the truth is uncomfortable, it is impossible to move forward towards historical reconciliation through "holocaust denial" or by "collective amnesia". Denying the truth of what Helmi Sharawy of the Arab Research Centre for Arab-African Studies and Documentation (ARAASD) Cairo, Egypt calls the "ambiguous relations' of the Afro-Arab cultural interchange in the Borderlands, will not assist reconciliation. For more than a thousand years the Sahara has been the melting point of the two cultures. Slavery was generalized in the Borderlands, stretching from Mauritania on the Atlantic, eastwards through the Sahel to Sudan on the Red Sea, with slaves being captured from black Africa and taken, often on foot, northwards through the Sahel into Arabia and out of Africa. Whereas the trans-Atlantic slave trade has been the focus of the on-going struggle for reparations Adwok Nyaba states that Arab enslavement of Africans, has either been ignored, minimized or completely rejected on false account that the Arabs either were 'brothers in Islam' equally colonized and oppressed by the West or participated in the decolonization struggles of the African people. In the history of Africa there have been two major hegemonic interventions. The first was by the Arabs starting in the 8th century AD, and the second was via the European expansion, which was consolidated in the 19th century. Whereas the European penetration subsequently partially withdrew leaving in place neo-colonial entities after the according of independence, the Arab presence was characterized by the denationalization / Arabisation of the people and a sustained campaign to annex territory, islamise and practice slavery. This process is seen today in Libya, Mali, Niger, Chad, Sudan, Mauritania, in the area called the Afro-Arab Borderlands (Prah 2001).

From the proceedings of the UNESCO Symposium held in Cairo 28 January to 3 February 1974 on the Peopling of Ancient Egypt at page 45 it is stated that archaeological studies indicate that trade between Sudan and Egypt was taking place as early as 4000 BC or earlier and that the trade in gold and slaves was thriving between 700 and 400 BC. Adwok states that slavery of black people in the Nile Basin began in earnest with the defeat of the Mamelukes of Egypt by the Ottoman Empire in 1517 and that the commodification and merchandisation of the slaves route down the Nile to Southern Europe, Arabia, Persia and China is traced to the first quarter of the nineteenth century. Africa has a Western Diaspora, in the Caribbean, Europe and in the Americas, and an Eastern Diaspora, which is less known by those living in the Western hemisphere. The Eastern Diaspora includes North Africa and points east of Africa, in the Gulf States, Arabia, the Middle East and Asia. Hunwick states in Joseph Harris' edited text 'Global dimensions of the African Diaspora' (1993) that movement of slaves along the Nile to the Red Sea, the Indian Ocean, Persian Gulf and India probably accounted for the uprooting of 'as many Africans from their society as did the transatlantic trade'.

Arabia has ambiguous views about the role of the Western Diaspora in Africa. At page 42 of the Report on the Amman Seminar of 1983 on Afro-Arab relations convened by the Centre for Arab Unity Studies and the Arab Thought Forum, Yusuf Fadi Hasan states:-

The African Nationalist movement was a secular one. It was started by black Americans as a reaction to racial discrimination and its call for African unity centred around negritude. After the 1945 Manchester Conference the movement transferred to Africa but was kept out of North Africa, and it seems that the role of African Muslims was limited from the outset.

Hasan on the same page, states the preference of some, such as Senghor, to see the unity of Black Africa first before the establishment of cooperation with Arab Africa.

Under Arab slavery men were castrated and the women were used as sex-machines, so that over generations the off-spring of the enslaved women merged into general Arab society, albeit into an inferior caste-type class of sub-species. Today we have slave descendants across the Sahara, such as the Harantines in Mauritania, to the ebony blacks in Arabia. This is because the slaves were so many that the slavers could not ethnically dilute them into *café au lai*t. Castration and male culling was and is practiced.

Mekuria Bulcha (Bulcha 2003) estimates that over 17 million Africans were sold to the Middle East and Asia between the sixth and twentieth centuries. In Bulcha's view the distinction between western and Islamic slavery is largely figurative. Both arrangements involved violence and cruelty as well as the devaluation of humanity. Africans in the Middle East and Asia remain 'a disjointed Diaspora', although records indicate a persistent desire amongst them (in the Eastern Diaspora) to repatriate.

Arab slavery is still on-going in Africa in the Afro-Arab Borderlands. Much of the attention to contemporary Arab slavery of Africans focuses on Sudan and Mauritania but from Mali, Algeria, Niger, Libya and Chad filter through reports about slave practices. Afro-Arab relations will remain distorted so long as Arabia considers Black Africa a civilization vacuum and so long as Africans in general remain indifferent. To change such perceptions, developed over a millennia, poses challenges for all, which should be met rather than avoided. Arabia needs to confront the historical dimensions of slavery rather than pretending its non-existence.

Yusuf Fadi Hasan in his contribution on the historical roots of Afro-Arab relations in the Report on the Amman Seminar of 1983 on Afro-Arab relations at page 35 refers to the Arab cultural, social and spiritual homogeneity pushing southwards in Sudan, eroding African cultures. This relentless push southwards of Islam and Arabisation is what we witness today in Darfur with the Janjaweed attacks on the African sedentary farmers. This is a spatial pattern in the Sahel in general.

The subject of Arab slavery of Africans is one, which many, including the African states, would prefer to have buried and about which there is an unspoken understanding that Africans should remain silent, including Nkrumah. The practice has existed 1400 years, but both Africans and Arabs in general, for different reasons, exhibit insensitivity to it. Muslim academics, both Arab and African, shy away from the Arab slave trade. Islamic leaders are profoundly defensive on the issue. In the proceedings of the Cairo symposium of 1974 it is recognized that blacks peopled Sudan 'since very ancient times'. MacGaffey (1961) is quoted, writing on North Sudan, that black people came down the Nile and entered Nubia. He calls these people 'invaders'. They mixed with the 'Hamitic' people of the desert. MacGaffey refers to 'endemic struggles between riparian Negro populations and desert dwellers'. There exists, we are told, a contrary thesis of the Egyptian historian, A. Batrawi, of waves of immigrants entering into Sudan from the North.

Civilization was centred in the Nile Delta where irrigation allowed for food surpluses and thus food security, for the development of a powerful civilization. So the civilizations of the Sudan were attributed by Adams (1949) to successive waves of immigrants from the north. The same symposium refers to those living in the Nile valley south of the tenth parallel as different from those living northwards. These people, it is stated, due to climatic conditions did not move northwards. These people (i.e. Southerners) were described as being 'without history' and of interest only to anthropologists. The south as far as Egypt and the colonialists were concerned, was peopled by savages.

Ronald Segal in his book 'Islam's Black Slaves: The Other Diaspora', explains that the Islamic slave trade began some eight centuries before the Atlantic trade and was conducted on a different scale providing slaves more often for domestic – including sex – and military service. In the Arab-led slave system, some slaves achieved positions of authority, a few became rulers. In Segal's view, because of specific spiritual teachings, Islam was generally more humane than the west in its treatment of slaves and in its willingness to bestow manumission, although the process of captivity, subjugation and transportation was extremely cruel. Segal looks at the appeal of Islam to African-American communities and the denial by some black Muslim leaders like Louis Farrakan of the continued existence of African slavery and oppression in contemporary Mauritania and Sudan. An interesting point made by Segal in an interview was that 'whereas the gender ratio of slaves in the Atlantic trade was two males to every female; in the Islamic trade, it was two females to every male' It needs to be noted that the Arab slave trade concentrated particularly on children. The Arabs focused and still do on children, because children are easier to re-educate and Arabise. They are also easier to capture and transport to Arabia. The significance of the title of Segal's book is that it brings to the attention of the North American audience that there is another African Diaspora, in this instance – the Eastern Diaspora, where more slaves were trafficked than to the Western hemisphere.

With Islam and slavery came the Arabisation of the African. Yusuf Fadi Hasan at page 56 of the Amman Report states:

> I could not separate Islam from Arabism. The former is the vehicle for the latter. Furthermore, Islam is the spiritual base of Arab culture.

The significance of this, which is generally on view in the Borderlands, is that Islam as an expansionist spiritual trend comes clothed in Arab culture, so much so that the two are inseparable. So that if Islamic fundamentalism is expanding its influence in Africa, so is Arabism, conversely, in this process, African nationalism in general is in retreat except in South Sudan. This is an issue African leadership, be it at the level of the African Union, or individual states, is unable to address and which Africans in general, must expose. The Arab conquest of North Africa and parts of the Nile Valley spread their influence throughout the

Sahel in the seventh century and planted confusion in the minds of Africans. In the Sudan more than anywhere else, profession of Islam and speaking the Arabic language made one an Arab. Many African ethnic communities in Sudan such as Borgo, Berti amd Maali fell victim to this deception. In the 1960s these zealous African Muslims were used to fight the Southern Sudanese. The relentless struggle of the Southern Sudanese against oppression, including enslavement by northerners, has spread to other marginalized and peripheral peoples in the west, centre and east of Sudan. When the first war ended in Sudan with South Sudan winning a measure of self-rule through the Addis Ababa Agreement of 1972, this left in the cold the Arabised Africans who had fought on behalf of the Arab dominated northern political elite in Khartoum in the name of national unity. The current genocide in the Darfur region of Western Sudan, where the Khartoum government has used a tactic of ethnic cleansing by arming an Arab nomad militia, the Janjaweed, to attack African farmlands, pushing Africans off their land, continues the Arab push southwards, which is part of the Arab national expansionist project dating back centuries supported by the Arab League, which has seen Africans pushed southwards from the Mediterranean coast into the arid Sahara area. Arabia in general characterizes events in Darfur as 'tribal feuds'. Concerning this Prah stated (2004) ' It needs to be said without fear or favour that Africans cannot accept a slow encroachment of their national areas by the Arab world'. Adwok Nyaba speaking in Durban at the United Nations Conference Against Racism, Racial Discrimination, Xenophobia and Related Intolerance (Prah 2004) states that the war in the Sudan:

> 'Is also a war of resistance – African resistance in the Sudan against de-Africanization at the hands of Arabs. The war indeed is the continuation of the Afro-Arab conflict that commenced fourteen centuries ago when the Arabs set foot on the African soil.'

On the issue of reparations for Arab-led slavery in Africa, the thesis of Adwok Nyaba presented at the Conference on Arab-Led Slavery of Africans, convened on the 22nd February 2003 in Johannesburg, by the Centre for Advanced Studies of African Society (CASAS), Cape Town, South Africa and the Drammeh Institute of New York, USA, is that reparations is a political issue with a legal objective, requiring mobilization and common purpose. A Final Declaration was published, as well as the proceedings of the Conference. Conference endorsed reparations and called for a civilization dialogue between the Arab and

African nations. The World Conference Against Racism and its NGO Forum added their voices to those seeking reparations for African slavery. There are no legal rules governing the law of reparations. The study of other such initiatives indicates first extensive legal posturing creating a powerful moral climate supporting reparations, thus shaping public opinion – as the primary stage in the campaign for reparations.

The demand for economic reparations is based on slavery, genocide and the merciless systematic killing of Sudanese people in an attempt to push them off their lands, to obtain their natural resources. As Prof. Sidney Harring states in his brief 'German Reparations to the Herero Nation: An assertion of Herero Nationhood in the path of Namibian Development'

> 'It would be both a futile and dishonorable discourse to venture into any kind of a comparative analysis of genocide ..... genocide is genocide ..... Modern international law of reparations is dominated by extensive Jewish claims for reparations against Germany and other countries, but this is not the limit of reparations claims.'

A case is pending against the Japanese for reparations for Korean 'comfort women', forced into prostitution by the Japanese army. Other European claims, including that of the Romani people, raised by other peoples subjected to mass extermination in concentration camps, have failed. Where there have been successes, these represent important advances in human rights law.

The Ovaherero claim for reparations prepared by Sidney Harring gave careful attention to the existing international law of reparations. Such a claim is preceded by a general inquiry into the appropriateness of reparations as a political and legal remedy for the damage caused by slavery, war and internal strife before proceeding to political mobilization, to raise consciousness. A study of the Sudan situation concluded that reparations is the appropriate remedy for the human rights abuse suffered by the people of the Sudan.

As Harring says, if situations (such as in the Sudan) are 'reasonably analogous to existing reparations claims, to dismiss them out of hand must turn on considerations that can only be called racist'. Harring goes on to say that if such claims are well grounded legally, then broader policy issues may be implicated and must be heard, for there exists no consistent legal basis for any of the modern reparations regimes.

The concept of reparations, is rooted in natural law, the common law and international law, for it is an equitable principle that the beneficiary of an ill–gotten gain, for instance crude petroleum, should make restitution, both out of contrition and goodwill, but also to restore the victim to some part of their previous life.

Harring states that 'within the modern world, liberal democracies have used the language of reparations in making voluntary payments through various statutory regimes to their own indigenous or minority populations' – most often such settlements are ultimately political – done by Parliaments and Governments.

In the Sudan case it was reported by Prof. Abdel Ghaffar M. Ahmed, former Executive Secretary of the Organisation for Social Science Research in Eastern and Southern African (OSSREA), by his e-mail of the 21st January 2003, that since May 2001, a group of Sudanese, invited by OSSREA, having discussed the issue of slavery, came up with the suggestion that an apology was at the time in order. According to Prof. Abdel Ghaffar, that position was then taken up by members of the Opposition in the Sudan. This position was reflected in a statement made by Saddiq El Mahdi in mid January 2003, as reported in Al Ahram newspaper in Cairo, Egypt.

The United Nations Conference Against Racism (WCAR) held in Durban in 2001, was part of the growing movement for reparations, for the enslavement of Africans and for colonialism in general. The Declaration of the NGO Forum of the World Conference Against Racism held in Durban dated 3 September 2001, makes specific reference to the on-going enslavement of Sudanese (e.g. trans Saharan and trans Indian Ocean) which it categorises as 'crimes against humanity' (para 73). The Programme of Action of the NGO Forum supports reparations as redress in such instances. The NGO Plan of Action urged Sudan, amongst others, to abolish slavery and give reparations to the victims of slavery (para 235). The Plan demanded Arab nations amongst others, which participated and benefited from slavery, establish an international compensatory mechanism for the victims of these crimes against humanity.

The Declaration of the United Nations World Conference Against Racism, of September 2001, held in Durban, calls on states concerned to prevent such practices as slavery (para 99) and to pay reparations (para 100). States such as the Sudan were urged to set up Tribunals (para 165) in such instances and to enact relevant laws (para 166).

The Word Conference Against Racism and its NGO Forum have added to the growing demand for reparations for African slavery. Already there exists legal documentation on this issue. In 1993 in Nigeria a Pan-African meeting on reparations, chaired by Ambassador Dudley Thompson was convened. As Harring states the current discourse on African economic recovery is premised on the understanding of a quid pro-quo from the developed countries to Africa for the past super-exploitation of Africans. Also the thirteenth and fourteenth amendments to the United States Constitution provide moral and legal credibility to the case for reparations for African slavery and 'for the devastation of colonialism, primarily involving blacks still living on the African continent'.

The issue of quantum in the legal claim for reparations is a delicate matter, requiring more attention. Legal claims in general require the setting of damages. The 'costs' of colonialism and slavery in the Borderlands might be described as 'incalculable' – thus presenting a barrier to these claims. Also there exists no absolute law on the limitation of reparation claims. Harring goes on to state:-

For policy reasons, it makes no sense to limit reparations for genocide to the actual victims: they are most often dead, and that is precisely the nature of the evil of genocide and, for the same reasons, it makes no sense to require that some modern state represent the interests of a victimized people'.

There exists no formal legal rules governing the law of reparations. Based in the experience of other reparation regimes, extensive public and legal posturing, creating a powerful moral climate supporting reparations and thus shaping public opinion is the primary stage for the realization of reparations.

The Bridgetown Protocol, being the official report from the Afrikans and Afrikans Descendants World Conference Against Racism held in Bridgetown, Barbados 2-6 October 2002 (see part IV, para D concerning Mauritania and Sudan), addressed the issue of slavery in the Sudan. On the 22nd February 2003, the Centre for Advanced Studies of African Society (CASAS) in Cape Town, South Africa in conjunction with the Drammeh Institute in New York, USA convened in Johannesburg, a Conference on Arab-led slavery of Africans. The Declaration emanating from this Conference explained the trajectory of the contemporary movement for reparations for Arab-led slavery

The Declaration referred to the Universal Declaration on Human Rights of December 1948, the United Nations Declaration on the Elimination of All Forms of Racial Discrimination of November 1963 and the International Convention on the Elimination of All Forms of Racial Discrimination of December 1965, which came into force in January 1969.

Reference was made to other consensual meetings around the issue of racism including the United Nations World Conference and NGO Forum Against Racism, both held in Durban.

The Johannesburg Conference studied in depth the issue of Arab-led and Ottoman slavery in the Northern Borderlands of the African Nation, being the area where Africa meets Arabia running from Mauritania on the Atlantic Ocean in the west through the Sahel to Sudan on the Red Sea in the east. By way of clarification,in this context, the African Nation is defined as Africa south of the Sahara, plus the Eastern and Western Diasporas. The Johannesburg Declaration amongst others called for apologies for slavery and reparations from the Arabs to the Africans. It accused Arab societies of genocide particularly in the Sudan. It also accused such societies of ethnocide of African people through forced cultural Arabization processes. The African Union was required to address the issue of the slavery of Africans in the Afro-Arab Borderlands.

The Aweil and Twic communities of northern Bahr El Ghazal, in the Sudan, the members of which originally met in Oxford, United Kingdom on 6th July 2003, issued their Oxford Declaration on demands for investigations, prevention, prosecution and reparations for the crimes of slavery and genocide and other crimes against humanity against the Aweil and Twic of northern Bahr El Ghazal in south Sudan. The Declaration called on people in the Sudan, Africa, the African Diaspora and throughout the world to consider the Declaration for:-

Fair and appropriate investigation, prevention, prosecution and reparations for the crimes which have been or are being committed against the humanity of the peoples of Aweil and Twic of northern Bahr El Ghazal and others in war afflicted Sudan.

The object of this presentation is to bring to light the reality of Arab-led slavery of Africans, a reality which is unknown to the generality of Africans at home and abroad, largely due to the fact that since self-government African leaders have not informed their people of the realities of other Africans in the Borderlands. The paper does not seek to compare the Arab and western exploitation of Africans, such comparisons are odious. What affects one African affects all. Gone are the days when those living in peace in one part of the African world, can be indifferent about the goings on elsewhere in that world. The sooner the leaders wake up to this reality, the better it will be for all.

The truth of the matter is that such Afro-Arab solidarity that exists after the Bandung Conference, was build on false premise that the power relations were equal. The fact is that Arabia had a preferential relationship with Europe (e.g. Anglo-Egyptian Joint Administration of Sudan, which opposed black South Sudan). Egypt is the dominant influence as far as Sudan is concerned. Whereas Egypt is interested in the free flow of the Nile, according to Reeves (2001) Egypt would prefer a vassal state in Sudan and thus had an interest in an unstable Sudan. The south of Sudan serves as a buffer between black Africa and Arabia. According to Reeves for Egypt the maintenance of the status quo in Sudan takes precedence over Egypt's alliance with the United States on the Israel / Palestine issue. It was the Israeli-Palestinian issue, which complicated the West's relation with Arabia. Africa in third world solidarity went along with Arabia, but was relegated to the position of a junior partner, who was not consulted and taken for granted. Thus the Palestinian Liberation Organization (PLO) did not hesitate to side with Khartoum in its fight with the south. On the future of the Borderlands in general, today despite apparent shifts the west in general and Egypt prefer the maintenance of the status quo and the continued marginalization of the black Africans, to an uncertain future.

Such an unhealthy disequilibrium in Afro-Arab relations was not assisted by the first crop of leaders in Africa in the 1960, who chose to overlook the realities of history. Their errors of judgment haunt us today, in places such as Darfur and Mauritania, where the contempt and the lack of human respect is self evident.

What is happening is not the exploitation of religion or slavery to settle scores, but to advance the possibility of a civilizational dialogue, it is in the interest of both parties to face the past and the future in honesty, without self-righteousness and the pointing of fingers. The facts are there for all to see. Matters have proceeded a pace since the 1983 Seminar on Afro-Arab relations which took place in Amman, Jordan and its proceedings read today as an exercise in window-dressing and self-deception at which the African voice was not heard; a monologue as in the past, which portends ill for the future, if the other voice in 'the dialogue' is not addressed. This voice is not that of west, east or southern Africans, but that of those Africans living in the Borderlands of the African nation, where Africa meets Arabia, in places such as Darfur.

Conclusion

To conclude, herewith a citation from page 62 of the book the 'Arabs and Africa', being the report of the Amman Seminar edited by Khair El-din Haseeb, which quotes from Dunstan M. Wai's 'African-Arab relations in a universe of conflict: An African perspective' at pages 2-3 and 22-32, as follows:

> ....D.M. Wai argue(s) that twelve centuries of relations between sub-Saharan Africa and Middle Eastern Arabs were not altogether harmonious. The Arabs infiltrated Africa, enslaved its people, imposed Islam on them and educated them, but until now the Africans have not connected by infiltrating the Arab region....Wai argues that the Arabs and Africans have hardly anything in common and that their value systems stemmed from quite different social and environmental systems and are thus far apart.

Wai's observations cannot be mitigated by Egyptian support for African liberation in the short Nasserite period (1952-79), which support was abandoned in 1979 with the signing of the Egyptian-Israeli peace treaty. It is true comparatively that Europeans sought first to control the man and thereafter his land. This they did via their Christian missionaries and the Bible. However whereas Euro-African relations date only from one to five centuries, Afro-Arab relations are millennial and their influence qualitatively and quantitatively is more significant. By virtue of the writing of African languages in Arabic script – Ajami – Arabism penetrates the souls of those who live in the Borderlands more profoundly than Euro-Christianity did in, for instance, southern Africa. In both instances Africans are captive to extra-African influences.

Islam has given the world outstanding examples of international fraternity among peoples. This has been a point of attraction. Some of its spiritual content is sublime to an extent transcending class, tribe and race. However it has, in Africa, been unable to submit itself to autocritique. Possibly due to racism it overreached itself. Whereas Christianity has rooted itself in modern Africa, Islam has remained feudal, in want of renewal. Then in the contemporary period the new strain of fundamentalism is being introduced encouraging further rigidity, whereas reformism from an African perspective would be more appropriate. Increasingly amongst the westernized African urban elite Islam, fundamentalism and terror are seen as interconnected and a threat and an encroachment, which does not mean that governments constituted by these elite will meet the challenge posed by encroaching Islamic fundamentalism. On the contrary these elites are likely to concede 'defeat' without a fight, in the face of such confrontation in the Borderlands, and to pretend no threat exists.

The reflections of the Amman Conference of 1983 failed to anticipate the rise of violent Islamic fundamentalism, a consequence of the frustrations arising from the inconclusive Arab-Israeli conflict. African and Arab nationalism are in conflict, indeed African nationalism has long been on defensive posture vis-à-vis its Arab counterpart. This reality, plus the pressures of fundamentalism and Arabisation pose a direct challenge to African leadership. Prah (2004) is correct when he states that whereas Pan-Africanism and Pan-Arabism run historically parallel they are separate and that whereas the Arabs have their Arab League Africans aspire and will realise their own structure.

References

Bulcha, M. (2003). *The Red Sea Slave Trade: Captives' Treatment in the Slave Markets and Islamic Societies in the Middle East*. Paper delivered 22 February 2003, at the Conference on Arab-Led Slavery of Africans, Johannesburg.

El-Din Haseeb, K (1985). *'The Arabs and Africa'*. London, published by CroomHelm.

Harring. S (2002). *'The legal, claim for German reparations to the Herero nation' on http://academic.udayton.edu/race/06hrights/GeoRegions/Africa/Namibia01.htm*

Excerpted from: Sidney Harring, German Reparations to the Herero Nation: an Assertion of Herero Nationhood in the Path of Namibian Development, 104 West Virginia Law Review 393-497, 393-398, 401-410 (Winter 2002)

Nyaba, P.A. (2003). *Righting the Past Wrongs Against the African People: Time for Arab Restitution for the Nile Valley, Red Sea and Indian Ocean Slave Trade*. Paper delivered 22 February 2003, at the Conference on Arab-Led Slavery of Africans, Johannesburg.

Nyaba, P.A. (2003). *Self-Determination, Reparations for Arab-led Slavery in the Sudan, and the Afro-Arab Dialogue*. Unpublished paper.

Prah,K.K. (2001). *'Race, discrimination, slavery, nationalism and citizenship in the Afro-Arab borderlands'*. Frankfurt. Published in EPD, Entwicklungs-Politic.

Prah, K.K. (2004) *'Towards a Strategic Geopolitic Vison of Afro-Arab Relations'*,

Paper delivered at African Union meeting of experts, Addis Ababa, unpublished.

Prah, K.K. (2005). ,' *Confronting Arab-Led slavery of Africans'* in'*Reflections on Arab-led slavery of Africans'.* Cape Town.

Published by CASAS

Reeves, E. (2001). *'Egypt and the peace process for Sudan: unjustified Obstructionism',* published in the Sudan Democratic Gazette.

Segal, R. (2001). Interviewed by Suzy Hansen, Salon Media Group. dir.salon.com/books/int/2001/04/05/segal/index.html.

Sharawy, H (1999). *Arab Culture and African Culture Ambiguous Relations.* Tunis. Published by ALESCO.

United Nations Educational, Scientific and Cultural Organization-UNESCO (1978) '***The*** *Peopling of ancient Egypt and the deciphering of the meroitic script'*, Paris, published by UNESCO.

---

* Originally published in African Renaissance Vol.1 No.1 May/June 2004, pp78-81

Chapter 7

THE POLITICS OF APOLOGETICS: GENOCIDE DENIAL IN DARFUR

Kwesi Kwaa Prah

In the aftermath of the collapse of Nazi Germany in 1945, the singularly heinous crimes of Herr Hitler and his followers were subjected to global and detailed scrutiny. The genocidal campaign against European Jewry, which he and his hordes flagitiously described as the "final solution", was brought to the wider notice of humanity as the atrocities in and out of the Nazi death camps, (the *Vernichtungslager* and *Todeslagers*) under Hitler's equally mephistophelean disciple Heinrich Himmler, came to light. It was at this time that the inane excuse by many Germans that "*wir haben nicht gewust*" (we did not know) caught the world's attention. Many Germans were claiming that while the devilry was going on they, like the legendary hapless three monkeys, saw nothing, spoke nothing and heard nothing. In our pronouncements about the devilry that is going on in Darfur, we need to be careful not to put ourselves in a position where somewhere along the road we offer similarly lame explanations. Even more crucial is the need to avoid providing by word and deed comfort and succour to the perpetrators of evil in Darfur.

We have seen the genocidal barbarism that Rwanda descended into in 1994, when between 500,000 and 800,000 people were butchered in three months. This genocide was mostly carried out by two extremist Hutu militia groups, the *Interahamwe* and the *Impuzamugambi*, during a period of about 3 months from April 6 through mid-July 1994. Since the 1960s, the brutal carnage of the Angolan war, the Liberian war, the Sierra Leonean killing fields, the Casamance imbroglio, wars in Guinea, Mozambique, Uganda, Guinea Bissau, the incessant slaughter in both the Congos, the Sudanese wars, the Chadian civil wars, the Tuareg wars, the Central African Republic, the Nigerian civil war, war and the collapse of the Somali state as we knew it, the Eritrean and Ethiopian wars and other internecine conflicts have left Africans benumbed and traumatized, with little and sporadic respite from intermittent but continued blood-letting.

With weak democratic institutionalization, tin-pot dictatorships and warlordism, the immediate future of Africa and Africans look bleak.

We appreciate the fact that in all wars, all the contending parties claim God to be on their side. None invoke the devil's name in their support. In South Africa, the *Truth and Reconciliation* process revealed some atrocities committed by the insurgents. But, it would be grossly disingenuous to suggest that in either scope or intent, those that were fighting the racist government committed crimes anywhere near equality to the fiendish villainy of the Apartheid regime. As Herr Hitler's war drew to an ignominous close the greatest fear of German citizens in the face of Soviet military advances was treatment at the hands of Soviet forces who had suffered about 20 million dead (military and civilian) and through these colossal sacrifices had broken the back of the Nazi war machine. In Darfur, we know that the insurgents have also been responsible for atrocities, but the moral standing of the perpetrators and the resistance are worlds apart, and the scale of the atrocities are incomparable.

We can go on, *ad infinitum,* to debate whether or not the tragedy of Darfur has reached genocidal proportions; whether it is a counter-insurgency and an insurgency; whether it is a civil war or not a civil war; whether it is as brutal as the Iraqi case; whether the numbers of people that have been killed in Darfur are anywhere near the numbers that have been killed in Iraq – the bottom line would be that, these two scenarios represent enormous tragedies in our times and deserve the attention and anger of humanity against those that are responsible for them.

The Bush administration started the tragic misadventure in Iraq with lies about weapons of mass destruction (WMD), which were never there. But the grounds for this misadventure had long been in preparation. In February 1998, Bill Clinton argued that; "what if Saddam fails to comply (with UN sanctions), or we take some ambiguous third route which gives him yet more time to develop this (WMD) programme? He will conclude that the international community has lost its will... [that] he can go right on, and do more to rebuild an arsenal of devastating destruction. And some day, I guarantee you, he'll use this arsenal." On October 31, 1998, Clinton signed the Iraq Liberation Act, which stated that; "it should be the policy of the United States to support efforts to remove the regime headed by Saddam Hussein from power". And, in that same year, 1998, the US Congress authorized President Clinton to "...use US armed forces pursuant to UN Security Council Resolution (UNSCR) 678 to achieve implementation of UNSCRs 660—667." In December 1998, Clinton's

National Security Council Advisor Sandy Berger's view was that "for the last eight years, American policy towards Iraq has been based on the tangible threat that Saddam poses to our security.... That threat is clear ...." What has so far been little appreciated is the fact that control of oil resources formed an important, but little discussed, reason for the Bush intervention to topple former US protégé Saddam Hussein. The American public knows better now and will know more in the future about the Bush administration's unspoken and hidden war aims. Iraq is everyday on world television. The bombings and dreadful gore are unfailingly harrowing.

Darfur has for long been a little known place in Africa. Now, for the past 4 years, it has been thrust into the forefront of our imagination. People have slowly come to learn about the contradictions and conflicts of the Afro-Arab borderlands. The contestation and conflict between pastoralists and sedentary cultivators runs roughly parallel to Arab and African in Darfur, between an Islamist tradition from the north-east and a tradition from West Africa, between African language-speakers and those who prefer or rely on Arabic and Arabic customs. Islam found a footing there in the 16th century, and took on the more mystical, Sufi forms common to other parts of sub-Saharan Africa. The most impoverished are the African groups. These latter also form the social bases of the insurgency. What needs here to be categorically stated is that, competition over resources does not necessarily lead to war and/or genocide. It is the way such competition and other allied problems are resolved which is ultimately determinant and decisive. If democratic and culturally tolerant policies are advanced, it is possible to avoid conflict.

Mamdani's Darfur

Over the past 3 – 4 years Mamdani has written two articles which confuse issues and intentionally or unintentionally throw dust in our eyes with regards to what is happening in Darfur and whether or not we can describe it as genocide. The first article I saw appeared in the collection of the 2004 Editorials from *Pambazuka News*.1 The second article has recently been put out in the March 2007 issue of the *London Review of Books*.2 My attention was drawn to the second article by a young colleague who asked in an email; "I don't know why Mamdani has been going on as a denialist of the racist genocide in Darfur. Please direct me to any readings which may enlighten me on this matter." Mamdani indulges in technicist sophistry, tiptoeing nimbly around the real issues in Darfur and effectively providing solace to the Khartoum regime.

Mamdani's implicit audience in both papers is the American public, and he directs a great deal of his attention to outlining how above all *New York Times* columnist Nicholas Kristof "often identified as a lone crusader on the issue" of Darfur has succeeded in spreading a false alarm about genocide in Darfur. He effectively establishes an eloquent and bruising debate between himself and Kristof about "naming." But in all this, he makes controversial assertions some of which we want to examine here.

In the first paper, Mamdani asks; "How Can We Name the Darfur Crisis?" Indeed, this is the title of the paper. In the second paper, the title becomes "The Politics of Naming: Genocide, Civil War, Insurgency." The two papers in fact cover almost the same ground, but in the recent paper, he attempts to ineffectually beef up his evidence. He also discusses Iraq more fully. However, with the introduction of the Iraq tragedy into the discussion he tries to shift and dilute the argument and focus of his whole discourse from what he wants to say about Darfur; that genocide is not taking place, and takes to pyhrric semantics about genocide. It is a position, an argument, stated in passive mood.

The question could be asked more actively, "what is happening in Darfur." That is more direct and avoids much of the obfuscation and intellectual ducking and diving that we read in these two papers. Mamdani assembles a wealth of facts, but he does not see his way successfully out with a synthesis. In my estimation, this is partly the result of his methodological drift towards post-modernism. One cannot quarrel with many of Mamdani's facts and some of the historically attestable substance of his argument. It is his judgment and the way he draws inferences between these facts that his selection of saliency fails him.

It is an ironic lesson that, Gen. Bashir and his dictatorship will find comfort, reading Mamdani. They have committed no genocide, although about a third of the population of groups like the Fur, Messalit, Zaghawa, Birgid, Daju, Berti, Tama, Tunjur and others have been forcibly through a deliberate combination of torture, rape, gunfire and aerial bombardment, by aircraft and helicopter gunships, been dislocated from their homes and villages and forced to flee across the border to the miserable safety of cross-border refugee camps in Chad. The murderous Janjaweed are now also operating in Chad. There are 200,000 in these cross-border (Chad) refugee camps. Estimates are that between 220,000 and 300,000 people have lost their lives since early 2003 from this campaign of state-sponsored terror. Of a former Darfur population of about 6 million, 2 million are now in surrealistically overcrowded refugee camps. The

Sudanese government is using ethnic cleansing and forced displacement as a counter-insurgency strategy. It is useful to recall that, "ethnic cleansing" as a descriptive phrase was a euphemism used by Slobodan Milosevic to describe the mass killings in the former Yugoslavia.

The phenomenon is hardly new. Goody reminds us that, this is how the Anglo-Saxons emptied most of England of Celts, pushing them to the western extremities of the island. That was also how the Latins moved north into once German lands. From the sixteenth century onwards, European expansion involved the constant transfer, confinement or destruction of so-called "primitive" peoples throughout the Americas, in Australia, South Africa, or the Antilles. Again and again, indigenous populations were reduced to "ethnic minorities". Since the Second World War, three devastating operations of ethnic cleansing have historically been registered in the Mediterranean, Middle East and the Indian subcontinent; the partition of India, the creation of Israel in the late 1940s and the division of Cyprus in 1974.[3]

Both the sustained brutal carnage of Iraq and the slaughter in Darfur are horrific realities of our times. There is strong similarity with respect to the main protagonists in the cycle of violence. Much of what Mamdani says here about the similarities are acceptable. In Iraq, since the American invasion and the end of the conventional war to overthrow Saddam Hussein, an insurgency against the coalition of invasion forces and the current Iraqi US-backed government has emerged and is growing by the day. The main butchers in Iraq now are the vigilantes, sectarian militia and paramilitaries pitching Shia against Sunni, and vice versa. In Darfur, the vigilantes, sectarian militia, and paramilitaries are Arabized or Arab groups. The Sudanese government is supporting these groups with weapons and aerial bombardment to effect scorched earth policies of ethnic cleansing. In a recent article in the *Al Ahram Weekly*, Gamal Nkrumah quoting Sudanese First Vice-President Salva Kiir (a Southern Sudanese), writes that; "Khartoum's proxy militia, the ethnic Arab Janjaweed are wreaking havoc on the hapless indigenous non-Arab population of Darfur. Furthermore, the Sudanese President's failure to hold his cronies accountable for trashing his country's international reputation by defying the international community's wish to deploy UN troops has exacerbated the situation."4

Understanding Darfur

In order to understand what is going on in Darfur and much of the Afro-Arab borderlands we need to take a broad historical view of the situation. It must be remembered that Arabs first entered the African continent almost 1400 years ago. The first Arabs to enter Africa were early followers of the Prophet Mohammed who sought refuge in Christian Ethiopia in what is often called "the first *hejra*" in 615 A.D. A quarter of a century later, in 639 A.D. many more the Arabs under the military command of Amr ibn al-As, by fire and sword, pushed their way into Egypt during the great movement of expansion of the lands of the Caliphate. This was during the caliphate of Umar b. al-Khattab. By the end of the 7th century, the territory of the Caliphate in Africa had expanded westwards to the Atlantic, covering what are now the countries of the Mahgreb; Libya, Tunisia, Algeria, and Morocco. By fair or foul means, today, Arabs and Arabized Africans occupy about a third of the African continent and the processes of the Arabization of Africans continue. Darfur and much of the Sudan are squarely located in the frontline and vortex of this process. It is an expansionist process, which Africans must address. Is this acceptable? My view is that it must be halted. Africans are happy to be what they are. Arabization is unacceptable.

Mamdani asks; "Is Darfur genocide that has happened and must be punished? Or, is it genocide that could happen and must be prevented?" He argues the latter. The basic weakness in this thinking is that an ahistorical and undialectical assumption has been made in the understanding of genocide. The point is that, genocide is not only an event, indeed it is rarely simply so. It is more significantly a process. What I mean is that, we are not going to wake up from one day to the next and find that overnight, we have moved from a pre-genocidal to a genocidal reality. Genocide is almost always a consequence of an approach to warfare. Once the foundations and direction of a genocidal route have been put in place, baring seriously mitigating circumstances or major reverses on the war-front, genocide is fairly consequential. The question we must ask is, is there a genocidal process underway in Darfur? What are the politics and ideology of the insurgency and counter-insurgency with respect to the phenomenology of genocide? When we understand the ideology of the counter-insurgency we can ascertain if the intention and process is genocidal or not.

In an article, which appeared in the *Washington Post* on June 30th, 2004, Emily Wax writing from El Geneina tells the story of three young women who walked into a scrubby field just outside their refugee camp in West Darfur. "They had gone out to collect straw .... They recalled thinking that the Arab militiamen who were attacking African tribes at night would still be asleep. But six men grabbed them, yelling Arabic slurs such as *'zurga'* and *'abid,'* meaning 'black' and 'slave.' Then the men raped them, beat them and left them on the ground, they said. They grabbed my donkey and my straw and said, 'Black girl, you are too dark. You are like a dog. We want to make a light baby,' said Sawela Suliman, 22, showing slashes from where a whip had struck her thighs as her father held up a police and health report with details of the attack. They said, 'You get out of this area and leave the child when it's made.'" It is important to note that this was not an isolated incident. The mind and thinking behind such cruel and barbaric acts are telling. Years ago, Joseph Oduho, one of the founders of the Sudan African National Union in the South, drew my attention to the fact that the military principle of *"ibid yektul abid"* (killing a slave with a slave), has history in the Sudan and was frequently heard during the First Civil War (1956 – 1972).

Emily Wax's testimony continues with the revelation that, ".... interviews with two dozen women at camps, schools and health centers in two provincial capitals in Darfur yielded consistent reports that the Arab Janjaweed militias were carrying out waves of attacks targeting African women. "The victims and others said the rapes seemed to be a systematic campaign to humiliate the women, their husbands and fathers, and to weaken tribal ethnic lines. The pattern is so clear because they are doing it in such a massive way and always saying the same thing," said an international aid worker who is involved in health care. She and other international aid officials spoke on condition of anonymity, saying they feared reprisals or delays of permits that might hamper their operations .... She showed a list of victims from Rokero, a town outside of Jebel Marra in central Darfur where 400 women said they were raped by the Janjaweed. "It's systematic," the aid worker said. "Everyone knows how the father carries the lineage in the culture. They want more Arab babies to take the land. The scary thing is that I don't think we realize the extent of how widespread this is yet." Another high-ranking international aid worker said: "These rapes are built on tribal tensions and orchestrated to create a dynamic where the African tribal groups are destroyed. It's hard to believe that they tell them they want to make Arab babies, but it's true. It's systematic, and these cases are what made me believe that it is part of ethnic cleansing and that they are doing it in a massive way." ... In El Fasher, the capital of North Darfur, about 200 miles east of El Geneina, "Aisha Arzak Mohammad Adam, 22, described a rape by militiamen. They said, 'Dog, you have sex with me,' Adam, who was receiving medical treatment at the Abu Shouk camp, said through a female interpreter that she was raped 10 days ago and has been suffering from stomach cramps and bleeding. They said, 'The government gave me permission to rape you. This is not your land anymore, *abid*, go.'"5

In another report, we are informed that; "When describing attacks, refugees often referred to Government of Sudan (GOS) soldiers and Janjaweed militias as a unified group; as one refugee stated, 'The soldiers and Janjaweed, always they are together.' The primary victims have been non-Arab residents of Darfur. Numerous credible reports corroborate the use of racial and ethnic epithets by both the Janjaweed and GOS military personnel; 'Kill the slaves; Kill the slaves!' and 'We have orders to kill all the blacks' are common. One refugee reported a militia member stating, 'We kill all blacks and even kill our cattle when they have black calves.' Numerous refugee accounts point to mass abductions, including persons driven away in GOS vehicles, but respondents usually do not know the abductees' fate. A few respondents indicated personal knowledge of mass executions and gravesites."[6]

Several observers and concerned parties have indicated that the tenets of the counter-insurgency include the view that the Islam of the insurgents is inferior or ideologically deficient at the mass base of society. Islam in Darfur, for the majority, is more of West African inspiration than of immediately easterly derivation. Daoud Ibrahim Salih, a refugee from Darfur and a founding board member and president of the *Damanga Coalition for Freedom and Democracy*, a group that developed from exiled Darfurian refugees in Cairo expresses himself thus; "We, the Darfurians, did not commit any crimes, just that we are African," …... "We are very ordinary people, as you can see from the pictures…Today, genocide is happening, right now while we are speaking, for my people in Darfur." …. "We did not take Islam in the full package, which means assimilation and Arabization …. Second, they want to take the land, because Darfur is a huge area…That's why all of the Arabic countries are supporting Sudan's government."7 Apophthegmatically, Daoud Ibrahim Salih summarizes the position thus; "To stop genocide means to stop Arabization, to stop genocide means to stop assimilations, to stop genocide in Darfur means to stop the dividing of Africa."8 The then United Nations Secretary General, Kofi Annan, in characteristic understatement, in guarded and diplomatic style, described the Darfur situation as "bordering on genocide."

Mamdani successfully calls into question Kristof's extravagant and fabulous numbers, and also summons to witness Obasanjo and Ntsebeza. Obasanjo's utterances feature in both the 2004 and 2007 articles. Obasanjo in 2004, at a time he was chair of the African Union (AU) and involved in delicate negotiations between the Khartoum regime and the Fur insurgents had said that, "before you can say that this is genocide or ethnic cleansing, we will have to have a definite decision and plan and programme of a government to wipe out a particular group of people, then we will be talking about genocide, ethnic cleansing. What we know is not that. What we know is that there was an uprising, rebellion, and the government armed another group of people to stop that rebellion. That's what we know. That does not amount to genocide from our own reckoning. It amounts to of course conflict. It amounts to violence." What Mamdani fails to add is that, in an address at the headquarters of the African Union (AU) in Addis Ababa, the Ethiopian capital, on Tuesday, 10th October, 2006, Obasanjo, then President of the largest contributing country to the AU's protection force in Darfur - set out the need for the AU to hand over to the United Nations there, while retaining its African composition. "It is not in the interest of Sudan nor in the interest of Africa, nor indeed in the interest of the world, for us all to stand by, fold our hands and see genocide in Darfur." Soon after the Darfur crisis exploded on the world scene, Ntsebeza, the well-known South African jurist, in work commissioned by the UN Security Council had not at that stage found explicit grounds for declaring genocidal acts or intent in Darfur.

In his, *Darfur: The Ambiguous Genocide,* Gerard Prunier informs us that, the real logic of the war is related to a word which Nazism, the demise of colonialism and the development of scientific anthropology have marginalized into intellectual exile and political opprobrium: the word "race". "...in the 1980s Colonel Gaddafi and Prime Minister Sadiq al-Mahdi gave an answer: Darfur was poor and backward because it was insufficiently Arabized. It had missed out in the great adhesion to the Muslim *umma* because its Islam was primitive and insufficiently Arabic. ...The situation was pregnant with the potential for enormous destruction because it fitted only too well within the broader context of racial prejudice in the Sudan."9 Prunier points out that, during the 1980s, Gaddafi as self-appointed leader and modern prophet of the Arab world distributed vast quantities of arms in Darfur, his plan was to get rid of Africans and replace them with Arabs. It is the same Gaddafi who said at a press conference in Amman at an Arab League summit (7th October, 2000) meeting that, "two-thirds of Arabs live in Africa and the remaining third must join the other two in Africa." Mamdani is worried about the fact that an important contention of the international campaign against the Sudanese government and its proxy militias is that, "the ongoing genocide is racial: 'Arabs' are trying to eliminate 'Africans'", but his objections cannot stand up against such evidence as produced here.

Arabization and the Assimilation of Africans

Arabization has been the historical instrument for the expansion of the Arab culture and Arab political world on the African continent. From the earliest times, the acculturation of conquered peoples, trading partners and the spread of Islam, became the motor for Arab expansion in Africa. In many parts of the world, Islam has not led to Arabization. This is the case with Iran, Pakistan, India, Afghanistan, the countries of Central Asia, Turkey, and parts of China, Malaysia, Indonesia, the Philippines and some other areas of the world. Local cultural traditions have prevailed in spite of the penetrative influences of Islam.

For many Messalit, Fur, Birgit and Zaghawa the Islamic acquired religion sits astride an older African religious system. There is therefore often combinations of indigenous pre-Islamic traits and at other times Africanized and nativized Islam. The popularity of these is what the Janjaweed see as a stumbling block to greater Arabization. Like the Yezidi Kurds, the Fur practice in effect a religion, which is an eclectic mix of indigenous African pre-Islamic traditions and usages, and Islamic ones. But the injunction that "Arabic is the language of the God" has historically seduced many to bend to the sweep of Arabization and Arabism. Today the Nubians are about 3 million in Egypt, a country of 70 million people. In the Sudan, the Nubians are very many more. Large sections of the Nubians, in both Egypt and the Sudan, have over centuries been Arabized, but in recent years a strong Africanist recollective tradition is societally firming in Egypt in tandem with similar processes in the Sudan as a whole; among the Beja around Kasalla, the Blue Nile region, the South Sudan, Nuba and Darfur. The noose is closing around what the Sudan Peoples Liberation Movement in its early years described as "the Khartoum clique."

From the onset of the post-colonial era in the Sudan, Arabization has been an avowed political offering of the political elite. Both military and civilian regimes the Sudan has seen for the past half-century have upheld the policy of Arabization. It is inherently a racist policy. Mamdani bemoans those he describes as "demonizing Arabs". It would have been useful to be explicit and explain this. If he is suggesting that those who are fighting Arabization and the international campaign against genocide in Darfur are Arab demonizers, then he has nailed clearly his flag to his mast. The ideology of the war on the side of the counter-insurgency is Arabist. There are many Africans on the continent and in the Diaspora who reject Arabization, who have no sympathy with the idea of changing Africans into Arabs, who are happy to be Africans and who do not want to be something else. They in fact have that right. Other minorities in the Arab world till today speak in increasing volume about the non-Arab character and otherness of their communities. They include Syriac, Moronites, Chaldeans, Assyrians, Kurds, Turkomen and Berber communities.

Many African intellectuals also took note of Osama bin Laden's threats about Darfur. In 2006, He called for Islamist militants to prepare for a "long war against the Crusader plunderers in western Sudan." What such thinking cannot truly face is that both sides in the Darfur war are made up of Muslims, Arab Muslims and African Muslims. But, the African Muslims are regarded by their Arab fellow-inhabitants as heretics. Most of us cannot support big-power intervention in the area, in whatever shape or form, but the AU in combination with the UN is, if well coordinated, acceptable. Many Africans are still waiting to hear, loud and clearly, Arab criticism of Sudanese government policy in Darfur. It is remarkable that the silence of members of the League of Arab States is so resounding.

The idea of assimilation and Arabization of Africans comes to us in many guises. Ali Mazrui's rendition of it made in September 2004 in an interview with an Arab media house, reads as follows, "I do believe that the African People and the Arab People are, at the moment, two people in the process of becoming one. So the process has been underway for centuries and they will, one day, be virtually indistinguishable, but at the moment it is a continuum, rather than a dichotomy."[10]

An ethnic group is a group with a sense of common identity based on history, cultural affinities and solidarities of identification. Members of an ethnic group tend to identify with one another, or are so identified by others, on the basis of a boundary that distinguishes them from other groups. This boundary may take any of a number of forms - racial, cultural, linguistic, economic, religious, political - or differing combinations of these factors. Ethnic boundaries are frequently more or less permeable. Of all the factors, which define an ethnic group, the racial factor is the least significant. Race is in anthropological usage an ascribed/biological category; all the other factors are achieved categories. These latter are cultural. It is the cultural factor (understood to include language, traits and customary usages), which is the most important. It is nurture not nature which defines ethnicity. Ethnicity therefore largely overlaps with the notion of a cultural group. Mamdani is mistaken when he writes that; "The various tribes that have been the object of attacks and killings (chiefly the Fur, Messalit and Zaghawa tribes) do not appear to make up ethnic groups distinct from the ethnic groups to which persons or militias that attack them belong. They speak the same language (Arabic) and embrace the same religion (Muslim)." This is factually simply not correct. Arab ethnicities here include, the Baggara or Shuwa Arabs, Taisha, Rezeigat, Habbaniya, Beni Halba and others. In multi-lingual Africa, most people speak several languages. The fact that I speak English does not make me an Englishman. Arabic in the Sudan is a hegemonic language, and in places like Darfur most people would know Arabic, but that does not make them Arabs. The Janjaweed are ethnically Arab militias armed and supported by the Sudanese government. Yes, they embrace the same religion, but the Arabs of the Sudan regard the Islam of the Africans as inferior.

Mamdani writes that; "the dynamic of civil war in Sudan has fed on multiple sources: first, the post-independence monopoly of power enjoyed by a tiny "Arabized" elite from the riverine north of Khartoum, a monopoly that has bred growing resistance among the majority, marginalized populations in the south, east and west of the country; second, the rebel movements which have in their turn bred ambitious leaders unwilling to enter into power-sharing arrangements as a prelude to peace; and, finally, external forces that continue to encourage those who are interested in retaining or obtaining a monopoly of power." He is correct in identifying the root cause of the conflict as the monopoly of power by what Garang often described as the "Khartoum clique." But why is Mamdani after saying that this clique has monopolized and marginalized the populations of the south, east and west, then go on to say that the insurgents, the overwhelming majority in the east, south and west, should share power with what in his own words are "a tiny Arabized elite from the riverine north of Khartoum." In democracies power rests with the majority. The English say, "you cannot have your cake and eat it."

He then goes on to say that, "the dynamic of peace, by contrast, has fed on a series of power-sharing arrangements, first in the south and then in the east. This process has been intermittent in Darfur. African Union-organized negotiations have been successful in forging a power-sharing arrangement, but only for that arrangement to fall apart time and again. A large part of the explanation, as I suggested earlier, lies in the international context of the War on Terror, which favours parties who are averse to taking risks for peace. To reinforce the peace process must be the first commitment of all those interested in Darfur." No, to reinforce the peace process the democratic rights of the majorities need to be acknowledged and respected. The simple reason why African Union organized arrangements have time and again fallen apart is that as Abel Alier years ago wrote about the post-colonial ruling class in Sudan they have made an easy habit of dishonouring agreements.[11] They fear the implications of democracy in the Sudan.

Apparently one of the most irksome facts about the Darfur international campaign in Mamdani's view is that "the conflict in Darfur is highly politicized, and so is the international campaign. One of the campaign's constant refrains has been that the ongoing genocide is racial: 'Arabs' are trying to eliminate 'Africans'. But both 'Arab' and 'African' have several meanings in Sudan. There have been at least three meanings of 'Arab'. Locally, 'Arab' was a pejorative reference to the lifestyle of the nomad as uncouth; regionally, it referred to someone whose primary language was Arabic. In this sense, a group could become 'Arab' over time. This process, known as Arabization, was not an anomaly in the region: there was Amharization in Ethiopia and Swahilization on the East African coast. The third meaning of 'Arab' was 'privileged and exclusive'; it was the claim of the riverine political aristocracy who had ruled Sudan since independence, and who equated Arabization with the spread of civilisation and being Arab with descent." Is the definition of an Arab a question of taking your pick from among these different meanings Mamdani offers? The "pejorative reference to the lifestyle of the nomad" is literally and metaphorically a joke in much of the Arab world. Arabs know too well that the historic civilization, which is Arab, came from the Arabian peninsula. It is a culture and civilization they are proud of. Arabization does not result from merely speaking Arabic as a primary language; it involves the acceptance and adoption of Arab culture as a package. Yes, the Arab identity in the Sudan has been characterized by privilege and exclusivity. That is why the marginalized majority of the Sudanese are putting up resistance to its domination.

In the history of the relations between Arabs and Africans, from time immemorial, Arabs have been masters and Africans slaves. Indeed, black in much of the Arab world is equated with slave. Till today in Egypt, the so-called *bawab* (doorman, gate-keeper) is invariably a dark-skinned Nubian from Egypt or the Sudan. We are reminded that, "the *bawab* class is the lowest of the low."12 Amharization in Ethiopia and Swahilization on the East African coast has not gone on unchecked and unquestioned. In our lifetimes, we know that in Ethiopia, Amhara cultural dominance has been one of the factors underlying some of the conflict we have seen in the area. Swahilization remains largely a linguistic affair; it includes in its mould Christians, Moslems, African religionists and a whole variety of African language-speakers. Swahilis in East Africa do not control the state anywhere. They are Africans. Arabization is a different kettle of fish, effectively and eventually, it totally effaces the cultural characteristics of Africans, this is why Africans in the region, who historically were Christians before they became Muslims, today regard themselves as Arabs and are prepared to embark on genocidal wars in the service of Arabism and Arabization.

In Search of Africans

When he comes to the issue of who is an African, Mamdani shifts into post-modernist over-drive and writes that, " 'African', in this context, was a subaltern identity that also had the potential of being either exclusive or inclusive. The two meanings were not only contradictory but came from the experience of two different insurgencies. The inclusive meaning was more political than racial or even cultural (linguistic), in the sense that an 'African' was anyone determined to make a future within Africa. It was pioneered by John Garang, the leader of the Sudan People's Liberation Army (SPLA) in the south, as a way of holding together the New Sudan he hoped to see. In contrast, its exclusive meaning came in two versions, one hard (racial) and the other soft (linguistic) – 'African' as Bantu and 'African' as the identity of anyone who spoke a language indigenous to Africa. The racial meaning came to take a strong hold in both the counter-insurgency and the insurgency in Darfur. The Save Darfur campaign's characterisation of the violence as 'Arab' against 'African' obscured both the fact that the violence was not one-sided and the contest over the meaning of 'Arab' and 'African': a contest that was critical precisely because it was ultimately about who belonged and who did not in the political community called Sudan. The depoliticization, naturalization and, ultimately, demonization of the notion 'Arab', as against 'African', has been the deadliest effect, whether intended or not, of the Save Darfur campaign."

Mamdani must not underestimate the power and relevance of language as an identification reference point. Language is a central feature of most cultures. Arguably, it is the most crucial feature and at the same time, one of the principal distinguishing features of *homo sapiens* as a culture creating animal. It is through language that we relate societally, through language that we transact our social lives.

I personally knew John Garang, for many years. Indeed, I spoke to him on the phone, long-distance, about a month before his very strange death. Nowhere does he define who an African is, in the political terms Mamdani writes about. Garang was always a proud Dinka from Bor. Mamdani's so-called inclusive definition of an African as "anyone determined to make a future within Africa" is most perplexing. When I read this definition to an intern in the Centre for Advanced Studies of African Society (CASAS), Cape Town, Nana Kofi Appiah, his immediate and hilarious response was that this is an invitation for the pillagers of Africa. Does this sort of idea apply to other people in other parts of the world? Does a similar formulation apply to Chinese, Indians, Arabs or Europeans? If I arrived in China or India with a wish to make a future in these places, do I, on the basis of my wishes, become Chinese or Indian? Cecil Rhodes, Verwoerd, Ian Smith were all people who were "determined to make a future within Africa", were they Africans? I dare say they never even wished to be so regarded. Mamdani's understanding of the so-called inclusive definition of an African makes Africaness very cheap. I say, "if everybody is an African, then nobody is an African."

We all know that, by appearance and looks you cannot tell a Sunni from a Shia, Northern Irish Protestant from a Catholic, a Palestinian from an Israeli, a Pakistani from an Indian, or numerous such examples. Black, in Darfur, does not really help us to identify an Arab from an African. The difference is more subtle and decisive. Africans are attached to more eclectic varieties of Islam than Arabs, they are more likely to be cultivators than pastoralists, and they identify themselves as Africans and speak more African languages. They form the overwhelming majority of the population. For an American audience, black as understood in African-American parlance does not help us to understand the nationality dynamics of Darfur. Africans are first and foremost a historical and cultural group. They identify themselves as such. Most are black, but there are blacks who are not African. From South India through Sri Lanka to Melanesia many such groups are to be found. Years ago, I argued elsewhere that; "The racial definition of an African is flawed. It is unscientific and hence untenable. No serious mind today would use the race concept in any way except as an instrument for poetic imagery. What I am saying is that no group of people has been 'pure' from time immemorial. Notions of purity belong to the language of fascists and the rubbish-bin of science. But before my observations are misunderstood let me take the argument into another direction. Most Africans are black, but not all Africans are black, and not all blacks have African cultural and historical roots."[13] Additionally, one must not forget that Arabism in Africa came largely through conquest and cultural domination. Therefore, even today, Arabization and Arabism for Africans represent instruments of thralldom in a tradition, which precedes Western colonialism by a millennium.

Notes

1 Mahmood Mamdani. How Can We Name the Darfur Crisis? Preliminary Thoughts on Darfur. In, *African Voices on Development and Social Justice. Editorials from Pambazuka News, 2004*. Mkuki Na Nyota Publishers. 2005. Pp. 256 – 262. See also, K.K. Prah. Darfur Beyond the Crossroads: Struggles of African Nationalism. In, *African Voices on Development* ….. Ibid. P. 249-256.

2 See, the London Review of Books. Vol.29. No.5. March 2007.

3 Jack Goody. How ethnic is ethnic cleansing? *New Left Review*. 7. January – February, 2001.

4 See, Gamal Nkrumah. Masters at holding on. *Al-Ahram Weekly*. 5-11 April. P.9.

5 Emily Wax. 'We Want to Make a Light Baby'; Arab Militiamen in Sudan Said to Use Rape as Weapon of Ethnic Cleansing. *Washington Post Foreign Service*. Wednesday, June 30, 2004.

6 See, Documenting Atrocities in Darfur. US State Publication 11182. Released by the Bureau of Democracy, Human Rights, and Labor and the Bureau of Intelligence and Research. September 2004.

7 See, Experts Appeal for Action to Resolve Darfur Crisis. http://www.law.virginia.edu/html/news/2007_spr/darfur.htm

8 Ibid

9 Quoted here from, Harakati Shaka Lumumba. Darfur: A Wake-up Call for Africa. (Mimeo), Nairobi, Kenya. 12 November 2006. Appearing in *Tinabantu*. Vol.3. No.1. 2007.

10 Harakati Shaka Lumumba. Ibid.

11 Abel Alier. Southern Sudan. Too Many Agreements Dishonoured. Ithaca Press. Exeter. 1990.

12 See, Amina Abdul Salam. A doorman's lot is not a happy one. *The Egyptian Gazette*. March 29. 2007. P.6.

13 Kwesi Kwaa Prah. Beyond the Color Line: Pan-Africanist Disputations. Africa World Press. Trenton. 1998. P.36

Chapter 8

SLAVERY AND APARTHEID IN MAURITANIA

Garba Diallo

After ousting his former boss on 3 August 2005, the head of the new Junta in Nouakchott took significant steps towards better governance. However important those steps were, the new regime of Colonel Ould Vall failed to address what Mauritanians term as the national Question: the issue of state racism which discriminates against black African citizens in every aspect of their daily life. The other life and death issue that the regime did not take any measures to alleviate was the continued practice of chattel slavery against over one third of the population by the ruling Moorish caste. The move towards democracy while maintaining the status quo, was seen by black Mauritanians as attempt at democracy a la Apartheid in favour of the white Moors.

In this article, I present and analyse the factors behind the coup and the impossibility of its stated mission to introduce real democracy without opening the political space for Mauritanians to freely dialogue in order to replace the old system of Moorish monopoly of power on account of their assumed ethnic superiority over the majority blacks. The article will moreover discuss the origin, mechanism, effects and implications of the Moorish ideology. The article will also discuss the features of racism in Mauritania from which black citizens have been suffering from daily discrimination, massacre, banishment, confiscation of their land and forced arabisation etc.

The military coup

As Baba Galleh Jallow eloquently commented:

> "The current scenario in Mauritania is all too familiar to observers of African politics. Total disenchantment with an African despot who's been in power for decades provides an excuse for a group of semi-illiterate soldiers to seize power. To appease the world, the soldiers declare that they are only out to root out corruption and return the country to civilian rule within a few years. The condemnations continue for some time and then die down, replaced by the sleepy and indifferent silence of the pre-coup days."1

Therefore, the success of the August 3rd 2005 military coup in Mauritania did not come as a surprise to informed observers of the socio-political and economic situation prevailing in the country. What many had not expected was that the coup was carried out by the very insider Colonel Ould Vall. Prior to the coup, Colonel Vall had been the state security chief of the repressive military regime of Colonel Ould Taya, since 1978., making him the most loyal associate of the deposed dictator. They are from the same area with the same supremacist ideology. Abdarahmane Wone, North American representatives *of FLAM,* remarks:

> "I always say that the situation in Mauritania is similar to the situation in (Apartheid) South Africa. If Ely Ould Mohamed Vall is smart enough he will try to be the Mauritanian de Klerk and not the Mauritanian PW Botha. But I'm still very pessimistic because he didn't call for the resolution of this matter."

Thus, the reasons behind coup can be summed up as follows:

1. The insiders decided to turn against their former leader because they wanted to save their own skins. The former ruler had become so corrupt and paranoid that he turned the whole state system into personal fiefdom, making him lose perspectives of what was happening around him and his close cronies. The bloody coup attempt of 8 June 2003 was followed by repeated mutinies and desertion in the lower ranks of the military hierarchy from excluded ethnic groups, particularly in east and south. A successful coup by younger officers outside of the narrow circle of power would have spelled disaster for top ranks of the Taya regime, their families and clans.
2. As a nationalist Pan Arab, Colonel Vall was not happy that Colonel Taya had exchanged his hitherto pan Arab policies for close relation with Israel and the USA.
3. After more than 20 years in power - since 1984- Taya's regime degenerated into one man, one clan, and one family regime. This alienated the other sections of the Moorish community. It threatened to divide them, which could be fatal to the state system based on supremacist minority rule. So, the general consensus within Moorish community was breaking apart because of Taya's greed and personalized system of government. Thus, the new military dictator wanted to restore unity among the Moors vis-à-vis the blacks.

4. The new regime issued decrees to write new constitution, release political prisoners, and organize elections within two years to hand over power to elected civilian government.
5. However, as happened in the previous changes of rulers in the country, the new regime of Ould Vall maintained the status quo. They avoided the core underlying national issues of the country: Coexistence in equality between the African and Moorish sections of society, slavery of Africans and form of government reflecting the cultural, economic and geographical realities and needs of the country.
6. The fate of the tens of thousands of black Mauritanian refugees was not on the priority list of the Vall regime. During hi state visit to Senegal, Colonel Vall avoided discussing the issue of the refugees with his host. Although he was as directly responsible for the banishment of over 100,000 black citizens Vall continued to deny the existence of the refugees. Like his former mentor, Vall maintained that the border was open and all Mauritanians are free to come back.
7. Therefore, what the new regime tried to do was to sustain the system, just by changing the persons on the top while maintaining the Moorish monopoly of power and slavery of black citizens. In an interview with Bill Weinberg on WBAI Radio in New York City, Mamadou Barry and Abdarahmane Wone, North American representatives of the FLAM, commented:

   > "There was a policy of building a system in which blacks would be second class citizens, since our independence in 1960 up to now, all the dictators have worked on building this system. And in 1989 what happened is in order to have fewer blacks in Mauritania and to keep the fertile land in the south, the racist government, helped by Saddam Hussein, decided to deport more than 120,000 people from Mauritania to Senegal and Mali. Those people are still living in refugee camps in those countries. And today we're talking about a change of president, but those people still can not come home".

Mamadou Barry adds that "We are happy to see one of the most racist and dictatorial regimes gone, but there have been so many, it's like a chain. But one gone may be a sign of hope for change"

Artificial entity

More than any other state on the continent, Mauritania appears to be the most artificial and least viable colonial creation. For their colonial agenda, France carved Mauritania out from the fault line between black West Africa and Arabised North Africa. As such the creation of this vast desert enclave was done in total disregard of the historical background, current priorities and future aspirations of the majority of the population. Occupying over one million square kilometres, the estimated three million inhabitants comprise a majority black Africans and minority white Moors (also known as Beydane or Arabo-Berber). Numbering about 35% of the population, free black Africans consist of Fulani, Soninke, Wolof and Bambara. The other black African group is the Haratin (former and current slaves of the white Moors) who make up some 40% of the population. The Haratin were captured, kidnapped, and mostly bred and assimilated to the culture and language of their white Moor masters. The enslavement process has been going on for centuries. As the Fulani, Soninke, Wolof and Bambara have their relatives across the borders in Senegal and Mali; the white Moors share their cultural identity with the various Berbers groups in Mali, Algeria and Morocco.

North South Conflicts in the Sahel

By nature every foreign invasion does ride on certain ideological supremacy of the conqueror. The invaders of North Africa were no exception. The Moors justified their march from the north toward the south by the mission to spread the light of Islam in the Dark Continent. This was based on the assumption that African religions and belief systems were heathen from which the natives needed to be rescued. As they saw Islam as a universal religion with no borders and timeless, there was no end to the continued march to convert and "civilise" the blacks. As Mauritania developed into 100% Muslim and became Islamic Republic in 1960, the subjugation and enslavement of black citizens could not be justified by the need to convert them. The issue became cultural assimilation to Arabise the blacks. This is because as the language of the Koran, Arabic, was assumed to be superior to the African languages of Fulani, Wolof, Soninke and Bamaba, each of which is spoken by millions across West Africa. Since the arbitrary imposition of Arabic as the only office language of the country in 1966, language has been one of the most disputed issues in the ethnic conflict in the country. Although spoken as the mother tongue by less than half of the population, Arabic is given superiority in education, the media, administration and religion. It has been the most effective weapon to favour the Moors and marginalise the blacks. The other factors that encourage the continued march from the north to the south include rapid environmental degradation and the restless lifestyle of the Moorish nomads. Since the prolonged droughts of the 1970s-1980s, the hitherto nomads have been forced to move to the south to seek water, food and pasture. This movement prompted the successive Moor dominated regimes to enact racist land laws to confiscate African farmlands to redistribute them to the Moors from the north. The land law was imposed arbitrarily by the military regime in 1983. The law was applied only on the lands owned by the black farmers in the south.

Thus for centuries, conflicts have been raging along the Sahel belt until the French invaded and occupied the area in the early 20th century. As the British had their north and south policies in the Sudan, the French colonial rule was divided into north- south policy. This policy was biased against the blacks, a bias that culminated in the creation of Mauritania as the land of the Maurs. As soon as France transferred power to the Moors, the latent conflict between the north and south surfaced. France not only exploited existing contradictions between the Africans and Moors, they sharpened and intensified them even further by allying with the light skinned Moors, thereby sowing the seeds of future conflicts.

Franco Berber Alliance

The imperialist Franco-Moorish alliance was meant to help France maintain Algeria as an integral part of its territory and to prevent the creation of any viable West African federation grouping Mali, Senegal and Southern Mauritania. In exchange for the Moorish collaboration, the French created Mauritania as buffer entity, which effectively ended the Moroccan expansionist dream to reach the Senegal River. In order to maintain Mauritania as an Apartheid enclave that would neither be Arab nor African, the French did the following:

1. Turning the Senegal River into a borderline to cut through the black African community into Senegalese on the south bank and Mauritanian on the north. Until the colonial knife cut deep in the heart of the region, the African community had always and still does consider the river their lifeline and cultural glue that keeps them together.
2. The Moors were allowed to keep and develop their language and culture by setting up schools, giving the country their ethnic name (Mauritania) which created the myth that the country is an exclusive land of the moors. Thus, the flag, a capital in their area, the national

anthem and all the state symbols reflected only the Moorish side of the country.

3. The Moors were allowed to maintain their social order including the continued practice of slavery and slave trade of black victims.
4. During colonial times, unlike their black compatriots, the Moors were exempted from paying taxes, serving in the colonial army or sending their kids to the colonial schools.

Thus, the Apartheid infrastructure was in place when Mauritanian gained formal independence in 1960. The first priority of the post independence regime was to gain international recognition while internally it implemented anti African policies. For this purpose, the first head of state, Mokthar Ould Daddah used black Africa to counter Moroccan claim over Mauritania. Apart from Tunisia, all Arab countries supported Morocco's attempt to annex Mauritania.

Inside, he pursued aggressive apartheid policies to turn the country into a monocultural Arab nation. By 1969 the Arab countries were convinced that Ould Daddah was serious in serving Arab interests in that part of Africa. Mauritania was recognised by all Arab countries including Morocco in 1969. This opened the gate for the country to join the Arab League in 1973 and build intimate ties with the Arab world, particularly Libya, Iraq, Algeria and Syria.

The result of this new development was that as Mauritania moved closer to the Arab world, it turned its back on Africa. The regime took various measures to portray the country as a "pure" Arab nation by cultural genocide against African community to the point that it was made illegal to discuss ethnic problems or possess literature in, or teach African languages. As the suppression of African languages intensified, thousands of Arabo-Berbers were sent off to learn Arabic and get indoctrinated into Arab nationalism in various Arab institutions.

Hence the design and application of Arabisation laws that discriminate and marginalise the African citizens in both the public and private sectors. At school African children have to battle with foreign languages, learn history, culture, values and symbols of the invaders rather than their own, and their culture is repeatedly insulted and at the exam, get they excluded and pushed to drop out. Mauritania did not have a university until 1984 and up to now it has only a handful of faculties that cater for about 2000 students. Higher education depends on the state giving scholarships to students to study abroad. For every 100 students that get scholarship, there are normally less than 10 black students. The very few who complete their education would often stay abroad as refugees because they would have no chance of suitable employment should they return home.

As a tribal and Apartheid enclave riddled with nepotism and corruption, black citizens also face cruel discrimination in the labour market, vocational training, in the issuance of export and import licenses as well as opportunities to obtain loans from the banking system. Even opening a shop in the market is nearly impossible for black citizens. The rare black owned enterprises are subjected to constant police harassment and intimidation. In the early 1970s, African shops dominated the main market in the capital but by the late 1980s, the last surviving enterprise was set ablaze.

The fact that Mauritania is 100% Islamic does not stop the racist discrimination from extending even to the sacred realm. With their deep-rooted prejudices against blacks, Arabo-Berbers do not consider black people equal Muslim. Thus, out of some 30 main mosques in the capital there was only one whose imam was black. The minister of culture and Islamic Orientation appoints imams.

Taya's tyranny

With the support of the local Ba'ath and Nasserite nationalists, Colonel Ould Taya seized power on December 12, 1984. His first policy initiatives were aimed at the rehabilitation of relation with France to give him access to loans from the western financial intuitions and repair relations with oil rich Arab states while increasing alliance with Iraq.

Internally, he avoided the key demands of the African community to end racial discrimination, allow equal representation in all national sectors at all levels, end slavery, abrogate the racist land law and introduce democracy. As the new regime sank deeper into the IMF/World Bank trap, the major part of the economy was transferred to private enterprises.

Thanks to the pervasive tribalism, corruption and nepotism, the primary beneficiaries of the liberation were the family and of Taya together with his Smasid tribe and his political supporters. As public services crumbled, the regime exploited the IMF Structural adjustment Programme (SAP) dictate to ethnically cleanse the public sector further. Black people were either fired or forced to prematurely retire. Moorish business people were given loans from the various Islamic and Arab banks to set up private schools, enterprises and drive blacks away from their lands.

The African Liberation Forces of Mauritania (FLAM)

The escalation of racial repression led to the formation of the African Liberation Forces of Mauritania (FLAM) in November 1983[2]. FLAM's key objectives are to end the discrimination, exclusion and persecution of black Mauritanians, to effectively end slavery and introduce real democracy based on a federal system that gives the different ethnic groups autonomy. The movement believes that democracy in Mauritania can only be hoped for when the racial discrimination and slavery have been eliminated.

Although neighbouring Senegal and Mali no longer allow FLAM to operate openly from their territories, the organisation is very active in the black Mauritanian refugee camps just across the Borders in Senegal and Mali. It has strong active representation in France, Belgium, Scandinavia and the US. FLAM also uses its website (FLAM-Net) and its newsletter (Flambeau) to publish, network and disseminates information on the situation in the country and activities of the organisation. FLAM also participates actively in African and international forums to expose the regime's policies and mobilise support for the struggle for equality, justice and democracy.

The regime's response to FLAM call for national dialogue

The regime's reaction to FLAM's call for national dialogue through the publication and distribution of the Manifesto of the oppressed Black Mauritanians was violent. Hundreds of African intellectuals were rounded up, 50 were tried and sentenced to between six months and five-year prison terms with hard labour. They were taken to the desert death detention camp at Walata where they were routinely tortured, insulted, humiliated and starved to death. As part of the racist attitudes and obsession with slavery, the commanding officers of the prison were white Moors and the torturers were black slaves. Although political prisoners, FLAM detainees were put together with common criminals and often referred to as slaves and dirty Jews and their jailers boasted to be representing Hitler.

Another wave of arrest and imprisonments of black intellectuals and officers took place in October 1987. Three officers were sentenced and put to death on December 6, 1987. The event triggered the biggest ethnic purge of the armed forces in the history of the country. Thousands of black service men were purged, banned and confined to their native villages from where they had to report to the police every day.

The banishment of blacks

The war on blacks culminated in the April 1989 massacre of more than one thousand black citizens and West African nationals in Mauritania. The killings triggered a conflict with Senegal and the decision by both countries to repatriate their respective nationals. The regime used the occasion to banish over 100,000 black citizens after having confiscated all their properties and national papers. The deportees included villagers who had never been involved in any political activities, intellectuals, students, civil servants and army officers. As Jane Fleischmann put it:

> Long before "ethnic cleansing" entered popular parlance, its pernicious effects were painfully apparent in Mauritania. Between 1989 and 1991, tens of thousands of black Mauritanians were stripped of their citizenship and forcibly deported, and hundreds more were tortured or killed. An undeclared military occupation of the Senegal River Valley subjected those who remained to harsh repression. The campaign to eliminate black culture in Mauritania, orchestrated by the white Moor rulers, continues today, yet authorities in Nouakchott flatly deny that any of these abuses have ever happened[3].

The ruling Moorish caste is still denying the existence of Mauritanian refugees in Senegal or Mali, though they have just commemorated their 17th anniversary in exile. Like the Tutsi Rwandan refugees in Uganda, the Mauritanian refugees are gathering momentum to return home to take back their land and homes, now occupied by settlers from the north.

Auto Amnesty

In spite of the consistent denial of human violations, the regime passed a blanket amnesty law for all the crimes that were committed by the security and armed forces between 1986 and 1993. The auto amnesty was passed in the run up to the UN Conference on Human Rights in Vienna in June 1993. This was done while the regime still denied any wrongdoing. The associations of the widows and rights groups collected information with the names of all the victims along with those who gave the orders to torture and kill the political detainees in October-November 1990. The waves of arrest and torture to death took place in the shadow of the 1990-91 Gulf War over Kuwait. The local Arab nationalists were convinced that Saddam would win the war. For them it was an opportunity for a final solution to the "black" problem. All the 600 victims who were tortured to death or executed without any form of trial were black while all the commanding officers who ordered the crime were white Moors. Twenty eight of the victims were put to death on the occasion of the "national" day on 28 November while 12 others were "sacrificed" on the anniversary of Taya's seizure of power on 12 December. Some of the officers were forced to dig their own graves, in Nazi style massacre, to be buried alive.

Slavery

In spite of the repeated declarations of abolition, chattel slavery is still alive and well in Mauritania and there is no hope that those whose undeserved privileges depend on the slave system will ever abolish slavery voluntarily. Centuries of dependency on free slave labour has made the white Moors addicted to preying on the victims, that they would not let go on their won free will. On the contrary, the masters employ every means imaginable to breed more slaves. As modern media and communication and human rights groups make it more difficult to buy slaves in the open market; slavers have resorted to subtle ways of acquiring more slaves. The most common way is to mate one male slave with several female slaves to breed slaves to the benefit of the owner of the mothers. The other method is for the white master to mate with his own female slaves for the purpose of breeding new batch of slaves. In Islam the slaver has legal right to use his female slaves as concubines as he will. He does not have to acknowledge the kids as his own blood and flesh. This means that the master ends up using his own children as his slaves that he can sell, give way as gift, bride price, kill, torture, lend off or sexually exploit at his whim.

In addition to employing the slaves to wage racist war on blacks, exploitation of their labour and for sex, the masters do use the slaves in the foreign financed development industry. Already in the 1980s, I noticed that slaves were used to plant trees in Scandinavia-funded environmental projects in Mauritania. Pieter Smit's 2002 report entitled "Slavery on World Bank Projects in Mauritania", confirms the pervasive nature of slavery in Mauritania. Smit writes:

> In its 1994 Mauritania poverty analysis, the World Bank writes that slavery, in spite of being abolished by law, still exists, and that it will take a long time to disappear. The report claims that in the traditional system the formally ex-slaves are still widely treated as slaves, and that they in many cases provide labour to their owner's families without receiving wages. They are also not allowed to own any means of

production. In the World Bank's report the extreme importance of this last fact for poverty reduction strategies and chances is totally missed[4].

Abolition of slavery

Thanks to its obsession with slavery, Mauritanian is the last country on earth to abolish this shameful practice. Slavery was abolished in the country in 1905, 1969 and yet in 1981 again. The 1981 abolition was reconfirmed by the 1991 constitution. Yet slavery lives on as nothing ever has been done by the authorities to eradicate this crime against humanity in practice. The latest high profile abolition, embodied in Ordinance No. 81.234 of November 9, 1981 reads:

- First article: Slavery in all its forms is definitively abolished throughout the territory of the Islamic Republic of Mauritania.
- Second article: In keeping with the Shari'a law, this abolition will imply a payment of compensation to those (slave owners) entitled to such.
- Third article: A national commission, composed of ulama (religious leaders), economists, and administrators will be instituted by decree to study the modalities of the compensation. These modalities will be fixed by decree once the study is completed.
- Fourth article: The ordinance will be published without delay and implemented as law.

Nouakchott, 9 November 1981
The President: Lt. Col. Mohamed Khouna Ould Haidalla.

Slavery continues alive and well

After a fact finding mission to Mauritania in 1982, the London based Anti-Slavery Society estimated that there were at least 100,000 full time slaves and more than 300,000 semi-slaves still held in bondage to the white Moors[5]. Four years latter, a UN mission confirmed the total absence of any concrete measures by the authorities to put an end to slavery[6]. As Roland-Pierre Paringaux writes in his paper entitled "The Desert of the Slaves":

> ... ten years after the 'final' proclamation of abolition, slavery is far from being a thing of the past in the Islamic Republic of Mauritania..[7]

On the 10th anniversary of the famous abolition of 1981, Human Right Watch/Africa published a report entitled, Mauritania slavery Alive and Well, 10 Years after it was last abolished. Human Rights Watch argues:

> Our criticism is not that the Mauritanian government has tried to eradicate slavery and failed, but that it has not tried at all. We are not aware of any significant practical steps taken by successive governments to fulfil the important responsibilities Mauritania undertook when it passed laws and ratified international agreements prohibiting slavery[8].

20 years later, Amnesty International published a report in November 2002 entitled: 'Mauritanian: A future free from slavery', and noted:

> Despite the legal abolition of slavery in Mauritania twenty years ago, the government is yet to take practical steps {to] ensure its abolition in practice. The Mauritanian government must stop violating its own laws and urgently end slavery, which is an abominable attack on human dignity and freedom. Mauritanian laws and international human rights obligations prohibit slavery, but anyone escaping slavery has no legal protection. There is considerable discrimination against former slaves. No government official is willing to take the necessary remedial action to fully eradicate slavery and put an end to impunity for the perpetrators[9].

In the same month of November 2002, the Dutch human rights consultant Pieter Smit reveals in his report that slavery is also rampant on World Bank projects in Mauritania. As he noted:

> Their [the slaves} number might be on the rise because of high birth rates, and because development money and years of good rains have provided slave owners with many new opportunities to exploit slave labour. The process of liberating slaves from their slave status has come almost to a halt. An unresolved conflict exists between modern Mauritanian law, (in which slavery is abolished, but in which also Islamic law is recognised), and Mauritania's version of Islamic law, in which slavery, including all the political and economic exclusion measures to restrict slaves from getting away of slavery, are still firmly in place and widely used by owners of slaves, almost unopposed by any government action. State courts in most cases refuse to take up cases against slavery, and have never yet sentenced any person for keeping slaves... slavery has moved into development, and exploited it successfully. A sizeable section of the well educated political and economic upper class have used development funds, programs and projects to continue with or even expand the application of slave labour, especially in irrigation and livestock. In this way development money from the World Bank and other donors has supported slavery. This has been known at different times by different managers and staff within the World Bank since 1977...[10].

The African Conspiracy of Indifference

Black Mauritanians often wonder why their oppression has not generated the same attention, reaction and support from black Africa. This is more so when successive regimes persecute black citizens in the name of pan Arabism. During the 2001 world conference against racism and xenophobia in Durban, a West African president was lobbying at the NGO forum so that racism and slavery in Mauritania would not be included in the final declaration. Among the reasons the African conspiracy of silence and indifference suggested by African experts are:

- The sensitivity of the Afro-Arab dimension of the conflict makes many Africans prefer not get involved.
- The neighbouring African countries are Islamic and receive petro dollars from oil rich Arab countries in exchange for diplomatic support against Israel.
- The old OAU's non interference doctrine and general lack of concerns and respect for the life and wellbeing of ordinary Africans make the official persecution of black citizens by their government a non issue.
- Due to outward oriented education systems and modern communication media, few African intellectuals and politicians know about the situation in Mauritania. Inter African communication and networking is still weak.

This is why African leaders looked away when Colonel Taya was butchering black citizens, which is the same reason why African leaders did not demand that Colonel Vall put an end to racism, slavery and allow organised return of the banished black citizens.

The resistance

No doubt black Mauritanians do face a long and complex struggle for equal rights, justice and emancipation of the estimated one million slaves who are still held in Moorish bondage. With the near total lack of African and international support for the liberation struggle, black Mauritanians are increasingly relying on their own means of resistance. As both Senegal and Mali refuse FLAM and other freedom fighters bases in their countries, the struggle is taking various forms. People are increasing realising that in order to liberate the country; they have to liberate their minds first. Part of decolonisation of the mind is to revive, use and develop their culture and language. Many people now learn and teach their languages to their families, friends and neighbours. People have also started to use African names instead of foreign and slave names, African styles and outfits instead of the imported foreign items. Some of the slaves and former slaves are becoming aware of their African-ness. With the internet, FLAM and other human rights organisations inform and mobilise people to resist the regime in their own ways. Participation in African and international forums was another means of exposing the regime and mustering supporters. Books, audiovisual materials and newsletters have become available to researchers whose findings shed more light on the dire situation in Mauritania. The works of the Cape Town based Centre for Advanced Studies of African Society is one of the most important in exposing the persecution of Africans in Mauritanian and Sudan. In the African Diaspora a lot of good work is being done on the issue of slavery in the Afro-Arab borderland.

The chances for real democracy in Mauritania

Although the AU made its usual noise and empty warnings against the military take over in Mauritania, ousting Ould Taya was met with joy among the vast majority of Mauritanians and international human rights groups. Most people are against coups, but coups appear to be a convenient way of getting rid of repressive dictators whose tenure is often longer the average life expectancy of the citizens. Initially the regime made some improvement. Among the most significant achievements of the new regime was sending Taya to exile without blood shed, halting the country's slide toward economic collapse, allowing press freedom for the first time in the history of the country, passing laws banning members of the Military Council for Justice and Democracy and its appointed civilian government from standing in the planned year elections, improving relations with neighbouring countries, setting up relatively independent electoral commission to oversee the upcoming elections, real wage increases, appointing new judges who had no record of corruption, sacking some of the big corrupt fishes, more transparency in the new oil sector with improved national share – 20%. Perhaps the most notable, albeit symbolic, achievement was the acknowledgement of the continued existence of slavery for the first time. Furthermore, the new junta granted the SOS-Esclaves and the Mauritanian Association of Human Rights legal status after having been operating outside the law since both were established in 1991.

However, it is noticeable that the junta failed to address the national question of interethnic coexistence, the organised return of the black

Mauritanian refugees, their rights to their land, homes, jobs and compensation for the confiscated belongings by the government. Like the previous regime, the new junta's position was to ensure that the refugees remain in Senegal in the hope that they would be naturalised. According to the Moorish ideology of domination, the return of the refugees would have serious demographic implications for the ruling white Moor caste. There was also no move to recognise the African Liberation Forces of Mauritania, which called for dialogue after the downfall of the Taya regime. The new regime equally failed to take any concrete measures or at least put forward any visions on how it intended to put an end to the enslavement of over one third of the country's citizens. Another important issue that was not on Vall's agenda was the return of Mauritania to the ECOWAS fold. The new regime furthermore failed to address the fate of the 600 African soldiers and civilians who were murdered in government custody in 1990-1991. It equally made no moves to bring those responsible for the racist massacre to justice.

Thus, the plans to hold municipal, legislative and presidential elections by March 2007 will at best only lead to partial liberal democracy a la apartheid as the situation was under the Malaans and Bothas in apartheid South Africa. What Mauritania needs as A. Wone points out is a Mauritanian de Klerk, not Botha. As the Boers failed to sustain apartheid in spite of their military, technological and economic might and backing from the West, less important Mauritania will not be able to sustain the system of apartheid. The new discovery of oil will not prevent the unjust system from crumbling. As Roland-Pierre Paringaux maintained in his article "The Desert of the Slaves" in the Le Monde on 22 October 1990:

> "Held back by the past and surrounded by arrogant certainty, the beidane (white Moors) intend to preserve the Moorish order against the shifting ides. However, without even considering morality, neither time nor numbers are on their side… The verdict of demographic growth – if not that of history- is clear: in Mauritanian, unlike the slaves and the freed slaves, the owners are becoming more of a minority every day"[11].

The Implications of the Situation in Mauritania

The racial persecution of black Mauritanians has congealed the conflict into Arab versus African, north versus south and white versus black. This has pushed the white Moors closer to the Arab world and black Africans closer to Africa. Mauritanian's withdrawal from ECOWAS in

December 1999 in protest of the planned West African monetary union has to be seen in this context. While Mauritania withdrew from the West African body, the military regimes moved closer to the union of the Maghreb Arab.

From environmental point of view, the advancing Moors into the south have interacted with the advancing desertification from the north to the south. As the desert pushes Moorish nomads, they push the blacks in the south. The movements of nomads from the north towards the south is not only limited within Mauritania. The country sends both traders and animals across the border to its black neighbours to the south and southeast. White Mauritanian retail traders have dominated the corner shop trade in Senegal, Gambia and are expanding into Guinea Bissau, Cote d'Ivoire and Niger. Obviously Mauritania has a lot to lose when hostilities threaten regional stability. Mauritania cannot expect to benefit from this vital lifeline without peaceful relations and cooperation with those countries. Environmental protection and combating desertification requires joint efforts. Peaceful relations and fruitful cooperation with black Africa cannot be viable as long as the war on blacks persists.

Notes

1 Mauritania: An All Too Familiar Story August 9, 2005 Posted on allafrica.com.

2 Garba Diallo, Mauritania – The Other Apartheid 1993

3 Janet Fleishman, 1992, Ethnic Cleansing in Mauritanian

4 Pieter Smit, 2002, Slavery on World Bank Projects in Mauritania

5 Mercer, 1982, Slavery in Mauritania Today

6 Human Rights Watch, 1990, Slavery Alive and Well in Mauritania

7 Paringaux, 1990, the Desert of the Slaves

8 See Human Rights Watch, 1990, Slavery Alive and Well in Mauritania

9 Amnesty International, 2002, Mauritanian: A future free from slavery

10 Pieter Smit, 2002, Slavery on World Bank Projects in Mauritania

11 The Desert of the Slaves, Le Monde, 22 October 1990.

Chapter 9

STATES WITHOUT NATIONS: SUDAN AND NIGERIA

Franco Henwood

This article examines the nature of the conflicts in two key borderland states, in Nigeria and Sudan[1]. Sudan appears to be the classic example of an ancient conflict between African and Arab and in Nigeria the division between Christian and Muslim appears to confirm that what we are seeing in these countries is a 'clash of civilisations'[2]. This contribution disputes this. These conflicts are not expressions of two antagonistic cultural and ethnic blocs between pan-Arabism and pan-Africanism. This is too crude and one grand theory cannot account for the complexity of the conflicts we see within the borders of these states. The causes of these conflicts are internal. They do have wider significance in that they reveal the central weakness of most post-independence African states: they are states in name only. These states are vulnerable to tribal and ethnic centrifugal pressures because no national identity exists that could command allegiance across region and tribe. The article then proceeds to discuss the nature of this problem and argues for the creation of genuine national multi-party politics to overcome this division, with suggestions as to how this might be achieved.

Introduction

Sudan is a divided nation. It is divided by religion – between the Muslims of the North and the Christians and animists of the South[3]. It is divided by ethnicity - between Sudanese of African Arabic origins and others. It is divided by tribe and economic activity - between nomadic and sedentary cultures. The county has been at war with itself for 39 out of its 50 years of independence, mainly between North and South. The first civil war lasted from 1956-1972; the second from 1983-2005. At the time of writing (autumn 2006) renewed conflict in the province of Darfur, on-going since 2003, looms.

The present division between north and south stems from the days of British colonial rule. Present day Sudan was governed loosely under Ottoman rule until overthrown by a national religious revolt in the1880s. But the rebels failed to establish coherent administration. The ensuing chaos allowed British forces to invade and conquer the country from Egypt in 1898. The British divided the country into two colonial administrations: one for the Arab/ Islamic North and another for the black African/ Christian/Animist South. In so doing the British created arbitrary borders that rode roughshod over established patterns of ethnic and local allegiances. The British entrenched this division by neglecting administrative and economic development in the south. Hence when the British fused the two halves of the country in 1947, the new union was not on equal terms. The north enjoyed privileges in terms of population and economic development. For the South, independence (in January 1956) meant the substitution of British for Northern domination. Enduring legacies of bitterness existed in the south against the north - perpetuated by memories of raids by northern traders in search for loot, plunder and slaves in the pre-colonial period fuelled fears in the South of marginalisation by more populous North in an independent Sudan. Southern army officers mutinied in 1955, eventually forming Anya-Nya guerrilla movement, ahead of the country's independence in January 1956.

Faced with this division, the north opted for coercion rather than compromise in order to maintain the unity of the country. As we shall see, this remains the preferred policy of choice for successive northern governments right up until the present day. In 1958 General Ibrahim Abboud opted to promote the use of Arabic and sponsor the propagation of Islam in the South as a means to achieve national unity. Resistance on the part of the South led to civil war. A popular uprising forced Abboud out in 1964 but a series of Arab-dominated governments continued to prosecute the war. Fighting continued uninterrupted until 1969 when General Gaafar Numeiri seized power - who proceeded to seek accommodation with the South. A negotiated settlement to the first civil war was successfully concluded in Addis Abada in 1972, with Southerners granted considerable autonomy.

However unresolved issues regarding the precise balance of power between North and South, the discovery of oil deposits in South Sudan in 1978 (and disputes over how to divide the proceeds) gradually destabilised the 1972 agreement. Provocatively, the government continued to pursue a course of Islamisation and deployed Northern troops to the oil-rich town of Bentiu. In 1983 Numeiri abandoned the Addis Abada agreement altogether and declared an Islamic Republic. He revoked the South's constitutional guarantees and declared Arabic the official language and Islamic Shari'a as the sole source of Sudanese law.

Civil war broke out once again. The Sudanese People's Liberation Army (SPLA) led the resistance in the South. In 1986 elections in the North brought Sadiq Al-Mahadi into power, leader of the radical Islamic Umma party. Al-Mahadi intensified efforts to transform Sudan into an Islamic state (Numeiri himself was overthrown in a coup in 1985). By 1989 however the SPLA effectively controlled the South, forcing the government to enter into renewed peace negotiations. This provoked Northern General Omar Bashir to stage a coup, in June 1989, to halt moves towards peace.

General Al-Bashir instituted a dictatorship of unprecedented ruthlessness, tolerating no opposition, whether from Christian or Muslim, Arab or African, Northerner or Southerner. Despite intensifying the war, Al-Bashir failed to defeat the Southern rebels, forcing him to conclude peace in January 2005.

The signing of the Comprehensive Peace Agreement (CPA) the same month incorporated the former rebel group, the SPLA into a Government of National Unity (GNU). The Islamist government however continued to obstruct implementation of the CPA, particularly over oil revenue sharing and the demarcation of the north-south border. Whether the January 2005 peace agreement would be the basis for an enduring settlement between north and south remains to be seen.

This question aside, the point to be made is that the conflict in Sudan is not a battleground between two trans-national ideological forces. The most prominent line of division has been between the Christian/Animist/African South and the Arabic/Islamic North. But repression has not followed this neat schema. Bashir's regime directed repression against Muslim sects such as the Khatmiyya and Ansar movements and detained, tortured and killed hundreds of Muslim Arab Northern dissidents. The regime extended the war to the Muslim populations of the Nuba Mountains, in reprisal for their resistance of land grabs by Northern businessmen. Most recently the regime sponsored a violent campaign against the Muslim residents of Darfur. The sources of these were and are internal: the repeated attempts by the Sudanese government to overcome regional, confessional and ethnic divisions by coercion rather than compromise.

Darfur

By way of illustration of the main argument, it is worth pausing to consider the example of Darfur in greater detail. This conflict provides further illustration to the argument presented above: the weakness of the

Sudanese state and its preferred option of pursuing integration by repression to overcome this weakness. This, I would submit, presents a far stronger and more plausible explanation of the conflict in the country than any version of the clash of civilisations theory.

At first sight this appears to be an Arab/African conflict between Arab nomads and settled African pastoralists. One commentator described the conflict as a 'continuation of the Afro-Arab conflict that commenced 14 centuries ago when the Arabs set foot on African soil.'[4] Ethnic antagonisms between African and Arab do exist and these sharpen the conflict. But the presence of these antagonisms is neither necessary nor sufficient cause of the conflict. Neither are they sufficient explanation. To attribute the origins of the war to ancient hatreds between Arab and African attributes a timeless, ahistorical nature to the conflict, overlooking highly specific local causes. The conflict in Darfur is of recent historical origin. Arab and African in Darfur have not always been at each others' throats for centuries and centuries. There was a peace in Darfur – albeit fragile and uneasy but a peace nonetheless and it broke down only recently. Why?

Darfur's settled communities are indeed generally non-Arab and African groups, such as the Fur, Masaalit, Tama, Tunjur, Bergid, and Berti. The pastoralists are mainly Arab groups such as the northern Rizeigat, Mahariya, Irayqat and Beni Hussein. A system of mutual co-operation allowed the farmers to provide food for the nomads' animals and in turn for the nomads' animals to fertilise the farmers' fields.

Clashes between nomadic and settled communities did occur. But traditional forms of conflict resolution measures contained these somewhat. Deaths resulting from clashes between opposing groups were frequently atoned with payments of diya – blood money.

As a result of population pressures and desertification, this delicate system began to break down. The amount of arable land available for grazing diminished. The competition for scarce resources meant settled communities began to accumulate their own herds and barred nomads from grazing on their fields. Simultaneously, the nomads wanted farmland to settle down on. Clashes became more frequent, greater in intensity, and, on account of easy availability of small arms, resulted in heavier casualties. The government ignored the root causes and responded with a state of emergency in 2001. At first the government directed repression indiscriminately against nomadic and settled groups but this resolved nothing. Attacks by nomadic militias against settled communities continued unabated.

In February 2003 armed groups from the settled population rebelled against the central government – protesting that the government was marginalising the province and failing to protect them from nomadic raids. Fighting under the name of the Sudan Liberation Army (SLA), rebels from settled communities launched a series of raids against government targets. A second armed group – the Justice and Equality Movement (JEM) – arose shortly after, voicing similar demands to the SLA and drawing its support from African settled communities. The government responded by arming the militias of the nomads – the so-called Janjawid – to attack settled communities.

Much media coverage refers to the Janjaweed (armed men on horses) as Arab. But not all Arab groups have joined the Janjaweed. Janjaweed are reported to refer to their black African victims as 'blacks' and 'slaves'. But these racial overtones are as much recent products of the conflict as much if not more than the expression of ancient differences. All participants are Sunni Muslims. There has been much intermarriage between the two groups and many African groups are bi-lingual, speaking both Arabic and an African language. Some African groups have been nomadic and some groups of African origins have become assimilated into Arabic groups. Some Arabic groups in Darfur have refused to join the Janjaweed.

As in the former Yugoslavia, a prolonged period of peace eases differences but war revives them. Since the intensification of the conflict in Darfur, groups such as the Fur, Masaalit and Zaghawa, have begun to identify themselves as "African" and "marginalized," in contrast to earlier self-definitions as Sudanese or Darfurian[5]. They increasingly see the attacks on their communities by the Sudanese government as racially and ethnically motivated ones. Differences in other words are sharpened and deepened by conflict but are not necessarily the sole cause of conflict. The war in Darfur therefore is not an expression of some ancient conflict between Arab and African. It is an expression of the malaise of modern day Sudan: namely the repeated attempts by successive governments of the country to overcome the country's divisions by repression and violence. It is quite mistaken to see the conflict as part of some pan-Arab expansionist project like the Third Reich's lebensraum in Eastern Europe during World War 2[6]. The Sudanese state acts a position of weakness rather than from a position of strength. If we are looking for an explanation of the Sudanese state's behaviour in broader terms, then we will not find it in some pan-Arabist expansionist scheme. Rather we will find it in the weakness of the post-colonial African state, which Sudan shares with the majority of Sub-Saharan post-colonial states, namely its failure to build true nation-states - meaning states that command a national allegiance beyond tribe and ethnicity and are not just organised rackets for a narrow elite. This is a theme that will be expanded in the final section of this paper.

Nigeria

Present day Nigeria incorporates several streams of ethnic traditions. In the North the theocratic Sokoto Caliphate retained its independence right until the beginning of the 20th Century, when the British finally conquered it. This is the historical home of the Hausa-Fulani. The so-called Middle Belt of the Country – where most of the country's 250 plus ethnic groups reside - represents the transitional zone between North and South. The coastal and forest areas west of the Niger are home to the Yoruba and among several groups residing in the East, the Igbo are dominant. These divisions are rough and ready and simplify a variety of complex realities at local level but they suffice as a rule of thumb when describing the approximate ethnic distribution in the country.

It is often assumed that these divisions are somehow timeless. They are not. 'Ethnic identities are not a natural given, despite the substantial impact that such an identity has played in the country's history. Ethnic identities are historical constructions with political value. Their 'truth' is not based on indisputable fact but on subjective conviction, allegiance and mutual identification'[7]

As in Sudan, the immediate origins of these divisions are comparatively recent. Nigeria's borders are less than a century old. They date from the 1914 amalgamation of the Protectorates of Northern and Southern Nigeria. Colonial rule then sealed the future division between North and South. As in Sudan, the British rule treated North and South differently[8]. The British ruled the North indirectly through the Sokoto emirs. The Northern elites shored themselves up by undermining any sign of progress, especially in education. The emirs consolidated their hold on the Middle Belt of the country they had never been able to conquer as an independent emirate. Southern immigrants were housed in separate quarters in northern cites, creating enclaves of separation, exclusion and prejudice.

In the South Christianity and Western education, freely permitted by the British, created modern Western-style elite and stimulated aspirations for independence, as was the pattern elsewhere in the British Empire. The British's decision to preserve pre-modern forms of political organisation laid the foundation for the ethnic and confessional violence we have witnessed in the country in recent times. As in Sudan the two halves of the colony proceeded along separate paths of development. The scene for confrontation was set as soon as the two halves yoked together under the aegis of one state.

Therefore no national party emerged at the time of independence, one that could claim to represent the three main ethnic groups (Hausa/Yoruba/Igbo) and 250 additional ethnic groups, each with their own language and consisting of one third of the population. The North, with three-quarters of Nigeria's land area and about half of its population, enjoyed the strongest position and was determined to maintain that advantage. The key to maintaining domination was control of the federal state. The advent of an independent federal and secular state presented a possible threat to the position of northern elites, privileged under the British. Memories of the privileged position the North enjoyed led to resentments in the South against the North.

Politics was dominated by three major regional and ethnic parties: the Northern People's Congress with its support base drawn mainly from the Hausa-Fulani, the Action Group, based on Yoruba support in the Western region, and the Igbo-dominated National Council of Nigeria and the Cameroons, with its support in the Eastern Region. Control of the federal apparatus meant consolidation of the position of one grouping at the expense of another. For this reason politics became a winner takes all, zero sum game. Each community feared the outcome of an unsuccessful political contest – subordination to opposing communities or even outright annihilation. Politicians on all sides incited ethnic divisions to consolidate their appeal, appealing to the worst instincts of their followers, playing on fear, loathing and suspicion of opposing ethnic groups. Political debate resembled a beer hall brawl. The crunch came with an election victory of the Northern-based Nigerian Democratic Party in elections in the Western Region, a stronghold of anti-Northern opposition. The Northern party's victory was accomplished by blatant vote rigging and fraud. The party's bid for supremacy and the resulting violence provoked an army coup in 1966, terminating the country's first democratic experiment after six years.

The stated intention of the coup leaders was to bring a genuine unity to the conduct of politics. Principally Eastern Igbo officers however led the coup. Northerners, fearing a loss of their pre-eminence, staged a counter-coup. Pogroms and massacres of Easterners living in the North followed. A million refugees fled to the East. Fears of an impending genocide of Easterners pushed the Igbo into outright secession, proclaiming the independent state of Biafra in 1967. The resulting war lasted until January 1970 and claimed between a million to two million lives.

Thirteen years of military rule ended with elections presided over by General Olusegun Obasanjo in 1979. Nigeria was divided into a federation of nineteen states to ease the division of the country into three dominant groups. The election was won by the National Party of Nigeria (NPN), which, although Northern-based, enjoyed genuine three way ethnic and regional support. The discovery of oil in the country however intensified the usual struggle for control of federal state power. With the federal state's command of oil revenue, the stakes were even higher. The resulting slide into anarchy provoked another army take over in 1983.

Before we turn to consider the religious conflicts in the country, we need to expand on the underlying pattern of post-independence politics, expressed by this seemingly endless cycle of crisis upon crisis.

The failure was as much normative as it is institutional – actors were not prepared to play by the rules of the democratic game and recognise the values of compromise and accommodation as setting limits in the pursuit of power. The Westminster Model Nigeria inherited at the time of independence was undermined by the refusal of political actors involved to accept these norms. The restoration of democracy does not appear to have been accompanied by any fundamental shift of attitude on the part of Nigerian politicians. Many, if not most remain sectarian gang leaders rather than truly national politicians.

Second the nature of the Nigerian federation reinforces local sectarian interests. Consisting of a three-tier system of 36 states and 774 Local Government Areas, the system is a recipe for fragmentation and chaos. In 1939 the British carved out three regions with a dominant ethnic group in each- Hausa-Fulani in the north, Yoruba in the west and the Igbo in the Eastern Region. Post-independence governments have extended this practice, laying the foundation for the three-way split in Nigerian politics ever since. Local elites have driven much of this, for the creation of fresh administrative apparatus allows them to consolidate their hold over their own immediate locality and military governments encouraged as a form of administrative divide and rule,

'increasing the number of states to nineteen in 1976, twenty-one in 1987, thirty in 1991 to thirty-six in 1996. The consequences have been over expenditure of state revenue, administrative rivalries and confusion and numerous bureaucratic obstacles for business. Most perniciously, the creation of new states and administrative units is accompanied by a distinction between 'indigenes' and 'non-indigenes' residents, the latter excluded from any entitlements of internal citizenship. Nowhere are these terms properly defined. The issue of internal citizenship remains a disputed issue that fuels local violence all over the country.'

In short, this process of administrative division creates fresh differences in a country already rent by differences.

Third, this administrative divide and rule is lubricated by the federal government's command of oil revenue. Oil has forced up the exchange rate enfeebling Nigeria's agricultural, manufacturing and mining sectors, depriving the country of no other viable means of earning its way. Buildings collapse and airliners fall out of the sky because in so many routine aspects of administration, the federal government is unable to extend its writ beyond Abuja. The principal incentive for the states to enter any dealings with the federal government is through the latter's control of oil revenue. The federal government has little else to command allegiance from the states. State and local politicians are in turn parasitical on the revenue dispensed – using it not on productive investment but buying allegiance through patronage and rent seeking. The country's oil wealth is squandered on buying the allegiance of corrupt and venal local elites.

The corruption that accompanies this has made Nigeria a by-word for corruption with a worldwide notoriety. Few Nigerians see any benefit from the country's oil. Nigerians on every measure of human welfare are worse off now then their parents were at independence.

The religious conflicts in Nigeria

The clashes between Christian and Muslim in recent years must therefore be seen against this backdrop of strong centrifugal and regional identities as outlined above.

In recent years the death toll from repeated outbreaks of inter-denominational violence has been staggering: more than 14,000 deaths and three million displaced since the restoration of democracy in 1999. However it is not the return of democracy alone that is the principal cause. The drift to sectarianism began many years before. Perhaps the most crucial development was the promulgation of the 1979 constitution. The issue of the status of Shari'a law was resolved by permitting Muslim dominated states to implement in certain areas (e.g. sexual and personal conduct) but providing for the Nigerian supreme court to be a secular arbiter (although with three judges versed in Islamic law permitted to sit on the bench).

This attempt to broker a compromise between Muslim and Christian did not ease tensions. Relations between the two were increasingly defined by suspicion of each others' intentions. A series of decisions undertaken by General Babangida in the 1980s inflamed the religious divide by appearing to show partiality to Islamic interests. In 1986 Babangida decided for Nigeria to join the Organisation of Islamic Conference (IOC), without consulting his Christian ministers, the external affairs ministry, the Armed Forces Ruling Council or any other significant power centre in the country.9 In 1989 he banned the importation of *The Satanic Verses* and in the same year allowed for the Islam in Africa Organisation to base itself in Nigeria – with the organisation concluding a conference the same year with a resolution stating that 'we are ready to go to any length to get Shari'a established in this country whether we are alive or dead.'

In the early 1990s these tensions flared into open conflict, with thousands of victims. Massive repression quelled the violence but did nothing to heal the underlying divisions in the country.

At times it has appeared that the country's principal fault line has moved away from the tripartite Yoruba/Hausa/Igbo division to that of a binary division between Christian and Muslim. The reality is otherwise. Despite appearances, as in Sudan, the conflicts are not expressions of a trans-national clash of ethnic and confessional loyalties, but local ones. A riot in Kano in 1982 was sparked by reconstruction work at a church near a mosque. An attempt in the same state by a German evangelist preacher to stage a rally provoked another bout of violence in 1991.

The appeal of Shari'a law in the Muslim, Northern states rests with the disillusionment with the federal government's judicial and administrative apparatuses to secure order and justice. This much can be said of the situation in the South with the rise of protestant revivalism with its stress on personal salvation and withdrawal from public life.

Religious revivals cohere around existing differences, especially between North and South. That much is true. But there is nothing inevitable about this. Recall that the difference between North and South was a contrived one, a product of the nature of colonial rule. Since independence, Nigerian political elites have failed to build a true Nigerian with a national identity that transcends these differences. Indeed as we have seen above, they have actively deepened and entrenched them through the creation of a federal structure that weakens allegiance to the centre but reinforces it in the regions.

Once created, these divisions are difficult to efface. Regional politicians stoke up these divisions to gain legitimacy and consolidate their power base. Politicians without a power base and a mob to mobilise are nobodies. Nigeria's bewildering ethnic and confessional diversity has prevented the emergence of national political parties with cross-regional, ethnic and confessional support. Such parties might have served as possible vehicles for national unity and consolidation. But this failure is not just sociological – too many leaders have had a stake in perpetuating these divisions. As Nigerian novelist Chinua Achebe wrote in 1983:

> "There is basically nothing wrong with the Nigerian character. There is nothing wrong with the Nigerian land or climate or air or anything else. The Nigerian problem is the unwillingness or inability of its leaders to rise to the responsibility, to the challenge of personal example which are the hallmarks of personal leadership".

The Problem and Possible Solution Stated

In both conflicts, the appeals of Pan-Africanism and Pan-Arabism are weak. These ideologies appeal to a supposed ethnic solidarity that transcends national boundaries. The fact is that such appeals have gone largely unheeded. Local solidarities continue to trump trans-national ones. To attribute these conflicts to a 'clash of civilisations' between two cultural and religious blocs is unfounded. These ideologies simply do not generate sufficient emotive appeal. There is a degree of validity in referring to the vast zone stretching from Western to the Horn of Africa as the borderlands. There is indeed a zone of transition between the two halves of Africa. But to attribute this boundary of difference in itself as a source of conflict is not in itself sufficient explanation for the conflicts we see in the borderlands. Africa is a continent rent divisions; that in the borderlands is just one of a myriad of divisions. In sourcing the roots of today's conflicts, there is no reason to ascribe this division with any greater significance than any other.

It might also be added that the clash of civilisations theory – or versions thereof – are over deterministic and let too many participants off the hook. If such conflicts are the expression of ancient hatreds, then no one is really responsible for the violence and atrocity that mars the borderlands. They are not merely the expression of some genetically determined reflex.

However the conflicts do have wider significance. The dynamics of the two conflicts outlined above are repeated elsewhere in sub-Saharan Africa. These conflicts reveal the central weakness of the post-independence African state: many of them are creations in name only. They are hollow states, states without nations: Nigeria without Nigerians; Sudan without Sudanese. Primary allegiances are owed to race, ethnicity or tribe. The state in these circumstances is not seen as a tool to be employed to create a nation and civic identity, but as a weapon to be deployed in the struggle for ethnic self-preservation or domination. The conflicts we have examined in the borderlands are best understood in these terms. To find a solution, one needs to understand the problem. To look for an explanation in terms of a clash between pan-Arabism and pan-Africanism is to misunderstand the problem entirely. The remainder of this chapter discusses more broadly how this problem might be overcome.

African states owe their nature to the colonial past first and foremost. But that is not a complete explanation for the persistence of these divisions. It is true for example that the division between Hutu and Tutsi in Rwanda was an artificial one. But the responsibility for the genocide in 1994 was not Belgium's but that of the Hutu power elite. They chose genocide as a policy option and before genocide they chose to entrench the inherited divide between Hutu and Tutsi that made the genocide possible. The post-genocide government in Rwanda is attempting to build a genuine Rwandan nationalism that effaces the distinction between Hutu and Tutsi. Again that is a conscious policy choice - albeit pursued at considerable cost to respect for basic human rights. Regrettably, the Rwandan government restricts press freedom based on the claim that it would serve to revive and incite ethnic antagonisms. This is not a valid conclusion to draw: the operation of Radio Mille Collines during the genocide was not an expression of the proper operation of a freedom of expression. Nonetheless, a policy that aims to transcend ethnic division is to be welcomed in principle, if not in all aspects of its implementation, because it shows that these divisions can be overcome. The crucial determinant however is leadership. African leaders will either opt to build truly national polities or they will continue to try to legitimate themselves with tribal and sectarian appeals.

Given however these realities, what is the best way to proceed? I would submit that in the longer term the priority must be to build working multi-party democracies to overcome these divisions. The justifications for this will be set out below but first it is necessary to deal with objections.

Julius Nyerere, former president of Tanzania, concluded that only a single mass party could overcome tribal differences and build a nation. Nyerere argued that multi-party politics provided a recipe for ethnic chaos as the political parties could become vehicles for inter-ethnic conflict. His observation was valid: this is precisely what happened in so many post-independence states. However he failed to appreciate that a one-party state was no less susceptible to ethnic capture. The dismal record of one party rule in Africa in deepening rather than overcoming ethnic divisions since independence confirms this.

It is not the existence of a multi-party system that is the cause of inter-ethnic competition and chaos. The problem is with the formation of parties along ethnic lines rather than parties with cross-ethnic appeal. Ethnic parties vie for supremacy by appealing to group solidarity in opposition to other groups, defined as threats that must be combated against rather than compromised with. National parties appeal to an identity that transcends sectarian allegiances[10]. The Labour Party of the United Kingdom's slogan 'New Labour, New Britain' is a platitude. But it would not make sense if there were no understanding of a shared national interest that transcends regional, ethnic and class divisions of the United Kingdom that the slogan appeals to. The understanding of this shared interest may vary depending on if you live on a run down local authority housing estate in Glasgow or the commuter belt of Surrey. But the point is that there is a shared recognition that a higher national interest exists and needs to be protected against intrusion, against any sectional interest, even against your own interests. The continued existence of the welfare state and the National Health Service is defended on precisely this shared understanding. Even though vast swathes of the population could afford to opt out of the service, any party that advocated its abolition would commit electoral suicide.

The key is that whatever the ideological orientation of the party concerned, its appeal must not rest on sectarian allegiances alone. It must have a national appeal. The need to frame the appeal to reconcile or balance a variety of interests inhibits narrow, sectarian appeals. In doing so, compromise and conciliation is necessary to accommodate the interests of a variety of groups. Of course, if no sense of allegiance to higher interests outside the tribe or group exists, such an appeal is impossible. Once this identity exists, then stable multi-party politics are possible. How is this to be achieved?

There are enormous obstacles in the path of constructing such an identity. What is needed is to find a way to weaken the basis of ethnic and sectarian allegiances that form the power basis of Africa's strongmen. In effect, so many Africans are not citizens of their nominal country. They are subjects of their local strongman – whether a sectarian politician, warlord or dictator. Nonetheless, creating a national democratic identity of independent democratic citizens to break the power of the strongman is a vital prerequisite in constructing a national identity that transcends national divisions.

This contribution will conclude with three suggestions as to how this might be accomplished.

First of all, respect of the human right of freedom of expression and media freedom especially - press, television and radio. This is not to claim other human rights are marginal or irrelevant. It is to say that the hold of the strongman on his subjects depends on his ability to deny them alternative sources of information to judge his words and deeds. Sectarian appeals and incitements to violence thrive on distortions and falsehoods. A free, critical media is the antidote. Media freedom is a key tool to hold the strongmen to account. While it is possible for media outlets themselves to be tools of sectarian interests, allowing the foundation of alternative outlets to challenge sectarian appeals best counteracts this. The answer is not a crackdown on a free media.

The second priority is ending impunity. The strongman's hold on his subjects depends not just on the favours he can confer but also on fear. The strongman's subjects may offer their allegiance willingly, especially in the absence of any suitable alternative: a gangster's protection racket is preferable to anarchy. But the bottom line is the subject's knowledge that the strong man confers not just favours but that he also holds the power of life or death - and there is no escaping him. As was said of Charles Taylor during the Liberian civil war - 'He killed my ma, he killed my pa but I'll vote for him' (And remarks like these were uttered by his victims!). Therefore that Nigeria surrendered Charles Taylor to the war crimes tribunal in Sierra Leone represents a welcome step. It serves as a salutary warning to others of his kind and provides some encouragement for the strongmen's victims elsewhere.

Third is the creation of property rights. The strongman does not just hold political power. He frequently commands wealth and economic power His followers frequently do not have the means to subsist independently of the strongman. A simple measure would be to grant Africans legal recognition of the land or informal shacks they own.

Without title deeds they cannot raise collateral and get access to credit. Farmers cannot obtain the tools they need and entrepreneurs do not have the means to expand. And not only that, the absence of formal property rights allows the strong to steal from the weak. In Africa, the unexploited value of informal urban shacks and informally owned fields is estimated at almost a trillion US dollars, three times the annual GDP of all of sub-Sahara Africa. The potential here is vast: if the power of the strongman is to be broken decisively, then his subjects need the means to earn a living independent of him[11].

If one needs practical illustration of this, then one needs to look no further than the practice of forced demolitions. Over three million Africans have been forcibly evicted since 2000 . The mass eviction of informal urban dwellers in Zimbabwe in May 2005 was the most egregious example. African governments justify these evictions on grounds of development or urban regeneration and therefore for the greater good. Such reasoning is irrational. As mentioned above, the so called shanty towns and shacks are in fact potential productive assets. The demolitions represent asset wrecking on a colossal scale. The motives of the demolishers are principally political: Zimbabwean urban dwellers tended to be supporters of the political opposition. In the Dar Assalaam camp in Sudan, more than 12,000 people were forcibly evicted in August 2006. The majority of the evictees had been previously displaced through conflict in Sudan and settled in camps in or around the capital Khartoum. On other occasions they are the expression of rapacious and callous elites seeking to clear real estate and an opportunity for corrupt and venal law state agents to indulge themselves in a spot of loot. In any case, the problem boils down to lack of enforceable property rights. The poor have no security of tenure and therefore cannot invest and accumulate and have no means of redress once their assets have been robbed from them.

Taken together these suggestions amount to some tall orders indeed. Their successful implementation would require normative shifts as well as policy shifts. No doubt many objections practical and principled can be mustered against them. But they are offered to stimulate debate and they are based on one undeniable truth: that the continuing failure to build true national as opposed to ethnic states in Africa has had and continues to have unacceptable catastrophic human consequences.

Notes

1 The inclusion of Nigeria may surprise some readers.

2 The phrase popularised by American political scientist Samuel Huntington in his 1996 book of the same name.

3 The estimates being 70 per cent Muslim, 25 per cent animist and 5 per cent Christian respectively.

4 Peter Adwok Nyaba, 'Arab Racism in Sudan: Its Historical Source and Modern Manifestation', Cited in Kwesi Kwaa Prah, 'Towards a Strategic Geo-Political Vision of Afro-Arab Relations', *African Renaissance* Sep/Oct 2006, 131 This is in a sense a version of the clash of civilizations theory.

5 Human Rights Watch, Darfur in Flames: Atrocities in Western Sudan, Human Rights Watch, London and New York, April 2004 http://hrw.org/reports/2004/sudan0404/3.htm#_Toc68525371

6 See Chinweizu. „Why Black Africa Should Resist Arab Domination of AU" or The „Arab quest for Lebensraum in Africa and the challenge to Pan Africanism", Paper presented at the Global Pan African Reparations and Repatriation Conference (GPARRC) on 25 July, 2006, at the University of Ghana, Legon, Accra.

7 Elizabeth Isichei, A History of Nigeria (London, Lagos 1983) cited in International Crisis Group, Nigeria: Want in the Midst of Plenty, African Report No.113 19 July 2006 p.2

8 As in Sudan and elsewhere in the British Empire (notably India) the British often treated Islamic pre-colonial elites preferentially. The British considered Islam as a monotheistic, prophetic religion as a 'higher' religion than African polytheistic, animist forms of religious expression (although not quite as 'high' as Protestant Christianity, of course)

9 See Toylin Falola, Violence in Nigeria. The Crisis of Religious Politics and Secular Ideologies (Rochester, 1998)

10 Why multi-party politics rather than a single party? A single party does not have to compete for a national vote to retain power. A single party has no disincentive to arrogate greater powers to it.

11 See the argument of Peruvian economist Hernando de Soto, *The Mystery of Capital. Why Capitalism Triumphs in the West and Fails Everywhere Else*, New York, 2000. De Soto estimates that the value of 'dead capital' in developing countries - that is, property that cannot be capitalised because of a lack of title deed - is forty times the value of aid received throughout the world since 1945. See also Robert Guest, *The Shackled Continent: Africa's Past, Present and Future*, London, 2004 pp. 15-16 for a discussion of De Soto's ideas as they apply to Africa.

Chapter 10

SOUTH AFRICA AND THE NEW AFRICA: CHASING AFRICAN RAINBOWS

Monique Theron and Gerrie Swart

Introduction

Africa, Africanness and the African have always been subjected to brutal stereotypes – the 'dark continent', conflict-ridden, underdeveloped and beyond hope. For decades Africa has been trapped in its own middle ages, unable to overcome not only the internal politics of identity, but also the struggle to reconstruct its perceived identity outside the continent. Small successes are always overshadowed by the general despair that the continent finds itself in. Nowhere on the continent has this politics of identity been more prominent than in South Africa, during the pre- and post-apartheid eras. Identity, in the form of race, was at the core of the apartheid state's existence. With its relatively peaceful transition to democracy, it had the opportunity to reconstruct its identity, internally and externally, although this was not an easy task and is still a work in progress. According to Bekker (2001:2) at present there appears to be no current elegant theory on the construction and elaboration of ethnic identities, which may be applied across countries, cultures and continents. Another argument held forth is that ethnic identities are constructed and manipulated, not "given". Though they may often be considered and even experienced as ascribed, this does not detract from their constructed nature. For some scholars, identity refers to "people's source of meaning and experience" and to "the process of construction of meaning on the basis of (culture)". South Africa has taken on the mammoth task of identity construction. Despite pressing demands to pay attention to the domestic issues of nation-building and redistributing the benefits of the new political system to all its citizens, it nevertheless took on the complex task of championing not only its own interests, but also giving a new vision to the whole continent.

Somewhere over the Rainbow: Transcending race and colour

The concept of the "Rainbow Nation" is not just a nation-building tool for the new South African nation, but also an ideology that South Africa is exporting to the rest of Africa to pursue the reconstitution of the African identity at large. The concept, which was coined by Desmond Tutu, widely used by Nelson Mandela, and now an everyday part of the South African political vocabulary, is not just a people-centered identity and nation-building tool, but also a state-constructed tool with a larger political agenda. South Africa's "miracle" transition created the hope for the rest of the continent that it is possible to overcome and reconstruct institutionalized identities and stereotypes, be it political or economical.

Discussing South Africa and its identity politics is not as simple as merely discussing the politics of black and white. Underlying the "colour" politics of South Africa's identity issues, is a much more intense debate about identity. South Africa's African identity is not constructed around the conquering of the black African over the white oppressor. It does not revolve around race, culture, nationality or territory, but rather an identity of solidarity, reconciliation and renewal. For the new South Africa, 'Africanness' and being African is synonymous with the rainbow. The rainbow is not just a symbol of a new South Africa that embraces all its peoples, but more importantly a symbol of renewal and what it means to be a "new" African. It regards values as more important attributes to identity than constructs of creed.

At the heart of South Africa's post-1994 foreign policy lies the belief that South Africa's future is inextricably linked to that of the rest of the continent. In order for South Africa to be able to achieve its goals, not only for itself, but also for Africa as a whole, it has to identify itself as a part of the continent in every sense possible. Post-1994 it needed to re-assert its 'Africanness'. Even though South Africa is not under a minority white rule anymore, it still has many "western" or "more-developed" attributes than its African counterparts, such as its economic strength and moral authority. In order for South Africa to do business with the continent (politically and economically) it needs to be able to accommodate all actors and stakeholders in the continent, regardless of their ideologies or beliefs. South Africa, as a "new kid on the block" has an ambitious reform or renaissance agenda for the continent and has to convince Africa's old-school "big men" that its plans are feasible. Therefore, the rainbow concept is not just an all-inclusive metaphor for nation building within South Africa, but most importantly a metaphor for the new African nation – a nation in which there is a place for each and every one on the continent. It places emphasis not only on who we are, but on what we are working for. It is a move away from "who is truly African" to "what is Africa" as a force to be reckoned with in the global order. It is a reconstruction of Africa's social and economic stereotypes and a move away from race and creed. After all, the new South Africa's existence is based on its fervent non-racialism and it is now using this value to transform what it means to be an African.

The South African Government: Promoting multiple South African identities and consolidating African unity

The African National Congress (ANC), significantly the *African* National Congress and not the *South African* National Congress, proved that the stereotype oppressed African can escape from the cage of inferiority that the "West" has entrapped it in for such a long time. It is the final victory over colonialism in Africa. And along with this victory came the even bigger ambition of conquering neo-colonialism and proving to the world that the time of the New Africa and the New African has arrived. South Africa under the leadership of Thabo Mbeki has announced this renaissance in Africa's identity.

South Africa's then-Deputy President, Thabo Mbeki eloquently addressed the issue of identity and citizenship when he addressed South Africa's Parliament on the occasion of the adoption of a critical piece of legislation- The Republic of South Africa Constitution Bill in 1996:

During his landmark address to Parliament, Deputy President Mbeki encapsulated the essence of his perspective on identity and citizenship:

> "I am an African....
>
> I owe my being to the hills and the valleys, the mountains and the glades, the rivers, the deserts, the trees, the flowers, the seas and the ever-changing seasons that define the face of our native land".... A human presence among all these, a feature on the face of our native land thus defined, I know that none dare challenge me when I say - I am an African!" (Mbeki 1996).

During his speech the Deputy President interestingly expanded upon his African identity to include other multiple identities, which also form part of his African identity and therefore exist alongside one another:

> "I owe my being to the Khoi and the San.... I am formed of the migrants who left Europe to find a new home on our native land..... In my veins

> courses the blood of the Malay slaves who came from the East. Their proud dignity informs my bearing, their culture a part of my essence...... I am the grandchild of the warrior men and women that Hintsa and Sekhukhune led, the patriots that Cetshwayo and Mphephu took to battle, the soldiers Moshoeshoe and Ngungunyane taught never to dishonour the cause of freedom. .... I am the grandchild who lays fresh flowers on the Boer graves at St Helena and the Bahamas..... I come of those who were transported from India and China... Being part of all these people, and in the knowledge that none dare contest that assertion, I shall claim that - I am an African." (Mbeki 1996).

This vivid portrayal of identity in Thabo Mbeki's speech contextualizes the very nature of the South African identity that has emerged and the great diversity of cultures that have assumed their rightful place as members and citizens of a united South Africa that returned to the fold of nations, following the 1994 elections. Interestingly this also formed the central theme of the historic Presidential Inauguration of Nelson Mandela, South Africa's first democratically elected Head of State. The central theme of the celebrations was entitled "Many cultures, One Nation", which ultimately gave birth to the rainbow nation, a term coined by Anglican Archbishop Desmond Tutu. The term was intended to encapsulate the unity of multi-culturalism and the coming-together of people of many different races. The phrase was elaborated upon by President Nelson Mandela in his first month in office, when he proclaimed:

> "Each of us is as intimately attached to the soil of this beautiful country as are the famous jacaranda trees of Pretoria and the mimosa trees of the bushveld- a rainbow nation at peace with itself and the world." (Mandela 1994).

From these extracts it is clear that the leaders of the new South Africa have embarked on reconstructing not only the South African identity, but the African identity. Shifting the focus to the fact that being African is about being connected to the continent's soil, being dedicated to certain values such as freedom and human rights and being determined to work for the upliftment of the continent's people. Being "African" is therefore no longer a question of race, culture, religion, language or any of these social constructs, but rather an ideology or belief.

The problem is that the rainbow identity is a top-down, instead of a bottom-up project. It is a state-driven project, instead of people-driven. This can clearly be seen with the 21st century pan-African projects (mostly driven by South Africa). These projects include the African Union, the New Partnership for Africa's Development, the Pan-African Parliament and the like. To what extent individual South Africans perceive themselves to be part of this rainbow nation is debatable. With new political rights a given, for many South Africans the missing pot of gold at the end of this rainbow, makes it difficult for all South Africans to embrace their rainbow identity. Yet, the South African Government continues to use this rainbow construct to pursue its broader foreign policy and other interests in Africa and the world. This is perhaps the rainbow's greatest pitfall – the fact that it is a political and economic tool that chases the pot of gold, instead of finding a place for all peoples of the continent in this rainbow. There is considerable skepticism emerging from other African nations about South Africa's intentions. There is also a reluctance to accept this new African identity as constructed by South Africa. Some African leaders still perceive South Africa as a puppet of the West and this new African identity just as an infiltration of Western ideas. Instead of promoting "African solutions to African problems", it often appears that South Africa is propagating "South African solutions for African problems".

Along with South Africa's re-entry into international relations and trade after 1994, came a new generation of South African business men, who want to find their place in the capitalist world system. The generation of old-school African liberation leaders (or "traditional" Africans) is making way for the younger generation of change-hungry neo-liberal Africans. This change involves a move away from "us against them" or "Africa against the colonizers". It calls for new partnerships within and outside Africa. It is a realization that co-existence is not only possible, but a necessity in a globalised world.

South Africa: 'The Politics of Branding and Exporting Identity'

South Africa has adopted a symbolic approach towards entrenching a uniquely South African identity on various fronts. Perhaps the most visible symbol of projecting this newfound identity is the country's new coat of arms - deemed to be the highest visual symbol of the state. Encapsulated within the motto of the coat of arms was yet another definitive reflection of South Africa's attempt towards fostering a greater sense of oneness amongst its people. !ke e: /xarra //ke, written in the language of the /Xam people, literally means Diverse People Unite. It calls for the nation to unite in a common sense of belonging and national pride. Just as South Africa is exporting its products and its "miracle formulas" for conflict resolution and development to the rest of the continent, it is also attempting to export its new ideology and values. Despite difference amongst South Africa and some African leaders, South Africa and especially Thabo Mbeki, has consistently advocated African solidarity and consensus, regardless of differences.

Many Africans, One Africa

In South Africa, being "African" is not a mutually exclusive concept; it is not a matter of Africans co-existing with "non-Africans" (whichever way this is defined), but rather a matter of people on the African continent co-existing with the legacies of the past, the challenges of the present and a vision for the future. As the proverb states - the soul would have no rainbow, if the eyes had no tears.

South Africa has come a long way in trying to eradicate the politics of race. In the context of this book, it would be wrong to remain in the paradigm of the South African past, namely by discussing 'Africanness' in terms of race. The Rainbow Nation concept creates a sphere for all South Africans to define and identify themselves in whichever way they prefer, whether this identity is based on culture, religion, race, ethnicity or gender. The question that should be investigated is therefore not who is "African" within the South African nation, but rather what makes South Africa part of the African continent. In the apartheid years South Africa was perceived as a European outpost in Africa and even today some still perceive South Africa as a country in Africa, but not of Africa. Perhaps to an extent this is still the case in the sense that South Africa can not truly identify with the problems of other African nations. But what this chapter is arguing is that even though South Africa cannot now claim to have been truly "African" all along, it is now taking the lead in constructing Africa's new identity and revolutionizing what it means to be African. And at the same time, South Africa is integrating itself into the continent, a continent in which it used to be the outcast.

I am, because we are: redefining African identity

The concept of *'ubuntu'* perhaps best describes the South African approach to reinterpreting identity and providing for a more constructive debate on the construction of African identity. Louw (1998) suggests that the concept of ubuntu, the Zulu maxim *umuntu ngumuntu ngabantu* ("a person is a person through (other) persons", defines the individual in terms of their several relationships with others. *Ubuntu* has been viewed as one of the founding principles of a new South Africa and is intimately connected to the ideals of the African Renaissance. In the political sphere the concept of *ubuntu* is used to emphasize the need for unity or consensus in decision-making, as well as the need for a suitably humanitarian ethic to inform those decisions. Perhaps the concept of *ubuntu* could serve as a common lens through which the construction of African identity could be approached.

In the Shona language, which a majority of people speak in Zimbabwe after English, ubuntu is unhu. The concept of ubuntu is viewed the same in Zimbabwe as in other African cultures, and the Zulu saying is also common in Shona: *munhu munhu nekuda kweyanhu. Stanlake J.W.T* Samkange (1980), highlights one of the defining maxims *of Hunhuism or Ubuntuism* which shape this philosophy: This maxim asserts that: "To be human is to affirm one's humanity by recognizing the humanity of others and, on that basis, establish respectful human relations with them'.

The meaning of the concept becomes much clearer when its social value is highlighted. Group solidarity, conformity, compassion, respect, human dignity, humanistic orientation and collective unity have, among others been defined as key social values of *ubuntu.* Because of the expansive nature of the concept, its social value will always depend on the approach and the purpose for which it is depended on (Mokgoro 1998). Thus its value has also been viewed as a basis for a morality of co-operation, compassion, communalism and concern for the interests of the collective respect for the dignity of personhood, all the time emphasising the virtues of that dignity in social relationships and practices.

A second important overlap between *ubuntu* and a decolonising assessment of the other according to Louw (n.d.) in a paper entitled "Ubuntu and the Challenges of Multiculturalism in post-apartheid South Africa" pertains to the extremely important role which agreement or consensus plays within this assessment. Without a common scale, that is, without an agreement or consensus on criteria, the beliefs and practices of the other simply cannot be judged without violating them. *Ubuntu* underscores the importance of agreement or consensus. African traditional culture, it seems, has an almost infinite capacity for the pursuit of consensus and reconciliation (Teffo, 1994a:4, cited in Louw n.d.). Democracy, the African way, does not simply boil down to majority rule. Traditional African democracy operates in the form of a (sometimes extremely lengthy) discussion or *indaba* (Shutte, 1998a:17-18; Du Toit, 2000:25-26). Although there may be a hierarchy of importance among the speakers, every person gets an equal chance to speak up until some kind of an agreement, consensus or group cohesion is reached. This important aim is expressed by words like *simunye* ("we are one", i.e. "unity is strength") and slogans like "an injury to one is an injury to all".

However, the desire to agree, which - within the context of *ubuntu* - is supposed to safeguard the rights and opinions of individuals and minorities, is often exploited to enforce group solidarity. Because of its extreme emphasis on community, *ubuntu* democracy might be abused to legitimize what Themba Sono calls the "constrictive nature" or "tyrannical custom" of a derailed African culture, especially its "totalitarian communalism" which "...frowns upon elevating one beyond the community" (1994:xiii, xv). The role of the group in African consciousness, says Sono, could be

> "...overwhelming, totalistic, even totalitarian. Group psychology, though parochially and narrowly based..., nonetheless pretends universality. This mentality, this psychology is stronger on belief than on reason; on sameness than on difference. Discursive rationality is overwhelmed by emotional identity, by the obsession to identify with and by the longing to conform to. To agree is more important than to disagree; conformity is cherished more than innovation. Tradition is venerated, continuity revered, change feared and difference shunned. Heresies [i.e. the innovative creations of intellectual African individuals, or refusal to participate in communalism] are not tolerated in such communities" (1994:7; cited in Louw,n.d).

Shifting Paradigms: Moving Beyond Defining African Identity, moving towards Being African

For South Africa, being African means being part of the rainbow, believing in renewal, embracing diversity and being part of a continent that is transforming itself for a better future. Being African (or a "New African") is about working towards creating a new image and space for Africa in the world. South Africa is redefining what it means to be African (the South African way!). It is a state of mind and being, rather than a construct of race or creed. It is about breaking away from stereotypes and being able to accommodate everyone and everything, and therefore, being able to do business with anyone. And despite embracing diversity, it focuses on that which all people on this continent have in common, namely creating a better future for all who inhabits it. South Africa has shifted the debate about what is African from being identity-based to being issue-based.

The Sri Lankan-born Canadian, Vithu Jeyaloganathan perhaps best encapsulates the debate on identity and citizenship that forms the core of this and a discussion that is likely to continue well beyond the confines of this book when he stated that *"The identity of one changes with how one perceives reality"*. Indeed many perceptions of African identity will continue to shape the continent, but should not dictate or overshadow the importance of striving towards a unified Africa.

References

Bekker, S.2001. Identity and Ethnicity in *Shifting African Identities, Volume II in the series Identity? Theory, Politics, History* edited by Simon Bekker, Martine Dodds and Meshack M. Khosa. Pretoria: HSRC Press

Du Toit, Cornel W. 2000. Roots of violence: Is a South African common good possible?, pp.15-41 in C.W. du Toit (Ed.). *Violence, truth and prophetic silence*. UNISA, Pretoria: Research Institute for Theology and Religion, cited in Louw (n.d.) Ubuntu and the Challenges of Multiculturalism in post-apartheid South Africa, http://www.phys.uu.nl/~unitwin/ubuntu.html, Date Accessed: 30 July 2007

Louw, D.J. 1998. *Ubuntu: An African assessment of the religious other*, Twentieth World Congress on Philosophy

Louw,D.J. n.d. Ubuntu and the Challenges of Multiculturalism in post-apartheid South Africa, http://www.phys.uu.nl/~unitwin/ubuntu .html, Date Accessed: 30 July 2007

Mandela, N.R.1994. *Statement of the President of the African National Congress, Nelson Rolihlahla Mandela on the occasion of his inauguration as President of the Republic of South Africa*, Pretoria, Union Buildings, 10 May 1994

Mbeki, T.1996. Statement of Deputy President TM Mbeki on Behalf of the African National Congress on the Occasion of the Adoption by the Constitutional Assembly of the Republic of South Africa Constitutional Bill 1996, Cape Town: 8 May 1996

Mokgoro, J.Y.1998. *Ubuntu and the Law in South Africa, paper presented by Justice J.Y. Mokgoro, Judge of the Constitutional Court of the Republic of South Africa*

Samkange, S. & Samkange, T.M. (1980) *Hunhuism or Ubuntuism: A Zimbabwe indigenous political philosophy*. Salisbury [Harare]: Graham Publishing.

Shutte, Augustine. 1998. *Ubuntu: An ethic for a new South Africa.* Cape Town (unpublished cited in Louw (n.d.) Ubuntu and the Challenges of Multiculturalism in post-apartheid South Africa, http://www.phys.uu.nl/~unitwin/ubuntu.html, Date Accessed: 30 July 2007

Sono, Themba. 1994. *Dilemmas of African intellectuals in South Africa.* Pretoria: UNISA cited in Louw (n.d.) Ubuntu and the Challenges of Multiculturalism in post-apartheid South Africa, http://www.phys.uu.nl/~unitwin/ubuntu.html, Date Accessed: 30 July 2007

Teffo, Lesiba J. 1994. *The concept of Ubuntu as a cohesive moral value.* Pretoria: Ubuntu School of Philosophy cited in Louw (n.d.) Ubuntu and the Challenges of Multiculturalism in post-apartheid South Africa, http://www.phys.uu.nl/~unitwin/ubuntu.html, Date Accessed: 30 July 2007

Chapter 11

IDENTITY POLITICS: TOGO FROM 1963-1993

Marcel Kitissou

> "The people of the earth are at war to decide whose interpretation of the past is going to shape the future of mankind. The ethos that will eventually conquer the minds of people will be the one that succeeds in creating a framework of historical understanding for which a believable and inspiring future of mankind may be constructed".
>
> J. T. Fraser. *Time: the familiar stranger*. The University of Massachusetts Press, Amherst, 1987, p. 352.

Introduction

"As the Prime Minister of England, Lord Salisbury, expressed in his famous speech in the Albert Hall on May 4, 1898, 'One can roughly divide the nations of the world into the living and the dying.'" It was an image that came frighteningly close to reality. The weak nations become increasingly weaker and the strong stronger, Salisbury went on. It was in the nature of things that "living nations will fraudulently encroach on the territory of the dying", wrote Sven Lindqvist in *Exterminate all the brutes* (New Press, 1996, p. 140). The situation is not much different today, 110 years after the speech of Lord Salisbury. The living nations are still fraudulently encroaching on the territory of the dying ones. And within nations themselves, the pattern is repeated thousands of times. Togo is not an exception, more so in the decades following its independence in 1960.

This chapter discusses the doing and undoing of the process of nation building in Togo, the dialectical relationship between the living and the dying; the resilience of the dying and the pain inherent in the act of living. The line between the two is not always clearly defined. A tragic sense of life as the Spanish philosopher, Miguel de Unamuno, would put it. Above all, overshadowing the efforts at nation building is identity politics. Who is citizen? And who is African? The case of political conflict in Togo between 1963 and 1993, following the1963 military coup d'etat, is symbolic of political development in Africa more generally speaking.

Togo as a symbol

Maybe because of its small size in terms of geography (56,000 km2), and of population (5.4 million in 2005, when President Eyadéma died), Togo has been a political laboratory. The Germans, during their occupation from 1884 to 1919, used to call it "unsere musterne kolonie", our pilot colony. The "Loi Deferre" of colonial decentralization was first tested in Togo from 1956 to 1958 with Nicolas Grunitzky as Prime Minister. And in 1963, the first experience in destabilizing a political regime in the post-colonial sub-Saharan Africa took place in Togo.

African leaders understood the menace. They first refused to recognize the regime. The same year, in May 1963, the Organization of African Unity (OAU) was created in Addis-Ababa (Ethiopia). As a major concession from OAU founding members, and with support from some francophone countries, Togo was admitted at the conference with the status of Observer, not as a founding member.

Thereafter, military coups d'etat began to fall onto Africa as a rain of crickets, completely changing the initial agenda of those who led the independence movements on the continent. The era of identity politics and of instability began, along with unfulfilled promises of independence.

Coup d'etat and its aftermath

Early in the morning of January 13, 1963, I was a teenager playing soccer with friends on the streets of Lomé, the capital city of Togo. The sky was very cloudy that day. Things looked strange. I then noticed that the traffic was very sparse. I was wondering if it was because it was too early in the morning to play on streets. Suddenly, trucks full of heavily armed soldiers began to pass by. Some slowed down and the officers, one after another, would shout: "Kids go home, quickly, this is no time to play on streets. Things are not good!"

What was happening? Tension was so high between the Togo of Sylvanus Olympio and the Ghana of Kwame N'Krumah that we began to speculate among us: maybe Togo and Ghana were at war. So, we went home. Once there, adults told us that foreign radio stations announced that there was a coup d'etat in Togo and that President Sylvanus Olympio was assassinated. Foreign radios knew what was happening better than the local population! None of us believed that Olympio could die because of the magical aura around him. After all, he put an end to French colonization, not an ordinary task. So, we believed that he was clothed with the veil of immortality and that his end could be nothing less than an apotheosis. We went as far as to think that those who assassinated him shared the same belief. That was why, our reasoning continued, his body was said to have been mutilated so as to prevent him from resurrecting. And that was also why people were shocked to the point of political paralysis. There was no significant public demonstration against the coup in spite of the great popularity that the President seemed to have enjoyed. Then, another mystery spread throughout the city like wild fire. The dead body disappeared. A few of us ventured to the scene. We saw the soldier who, presumably, shot him. And bullet impacts on walls of the private house of the defunct President were evidence of the violence of the assault.

A few months later, I was visiting a friend from my school soccer team. There was a man in his neighborhood, obviously well off, as evidenced by the size of his house, his shining car, and his dress style. Furthermore, there was a mystery surrounding him well beyond the display of his personal wealth and social status. I asked my friend: who is that man? My friend responded, both annoyed and surprised by my ignorance: "You don't know him? He is the man!" - "Which man?" I asked. "The man who stole the body!" "Which body?" "Sylvanus Olympio!" replied my friend. And so the secret was revealed. The man had a Brazilian (Portuguese) last name as did Olympio. He was said to have gone to the scene of the murder, removed the body (some said he stole it), put it in the trunk of his car and, despite road blocks and closed borders, successfully managed to reach Agoué.

Agoué was a village on the other side of the border, in Dahomey. It was the place of birth of the first Togolese President, Sylvanus Olympio. By accident of colonization and decolonization, the village happened to be in the neighboring country, and not in the country that Olympio led to independence, the newly created Republic of Togo. So, the body of the defunct President was out of reach of the new Togolese authorities. However, by the same token, he lost *de facto* and *post mortem* Togolese nationality and was presented as a foreigner, returned to his place of origin, Dahomey at the time of independence, and currently known as the Republic of Bénin. Other Togolese partisans and supporters converged to Agoué to have Olympio properly buried in his native village. How did the "man" accomplish that feat, I still don't know. That was never explained to me. And I was too scared to talk to him directly.

However, my weltanschauung was shaken. I was born in the colonial era, under a foreign power. I was convinced that independence was a good thing not because I understood its meaning and benefits but because I lived among people who fought for it, and sacrificed their blood and lives for it. Their champion died for no apparent reason other than his resistance to incorporate in the new national armed forces former colonial soldiers. During their active duty in the French colonial army, they were used to repress African movements for independence. With the death of Olympio, the belief in a transcendental force guiding the collective destiny also died out. Rumors had it that the coup was orchestrated by a foreign power, France, to restore its influence over a country ruled by an independent-minded President. Not only was Olympio a fallen god but also the new propaganda machine tended to demote him from his Togolese nationality. Furthermore, his African identity was questioned. As the propaganda went, not only was he not from Togo but from Dahomey (current Bénin) where his body was buried, but it was also publicized that his father was a Brazilian. The name was an evidence, but the reality was not so evident.

"Brazilians" (Olympio's father was one of them) came to the Gulf of Guinea in the 19th century, before Togo became a German colony. The presence of Afro-Brazilians in the Gulf of Guinea has a long history that predates the colonization of Togo. In particular, the slave revolt of January 1835 in Bahia (Brazil) spread the fear of another Haiti in the region. For reasons related to social and political stability, Brazilian authorities encouraged freed African slaves to return to Africa. While Afro-Brazilians practiced Africanism in Brazil, Brazilian-Africans were attached to Brazilianism in Africa. That distinctive status allowed them to free themselves from the constraints of African traditions and traditional authorities and, later on, afforded them a privileged treatment under colonial powers. As part of the local intelligentsia, they were able to articulate the grievances of the colonized and participated in the leadership of the movement that led the country to independence.

Notwithstanding the propaganda of the military junta, Sylvanus Olympio was associated with the southern part of the country and was perceived as such. The military coup leaders were from the north. And I was already wondering at that time, how the former French administrative territory would ever become a unified nation-state with a bloody coup d'état taking place three years after formal independence and dividing the country.

Meaning of the coup

Coup d'etat was, in 1963, neither a familiar concept nor an anticipated event in the aftermath of the wave of independence in sub-Saharan Africa. It caught everyone by surprise. The regime of Sylvanus Olympio had already weakened itself by establishing a one-party system, thus dismantling and demobilizing the dynamic groups which, ultimately, helped him to lead the country to its independence. These groups and their activism could have been a deterrent to potential coup makers. However, after January 13, 1963 the "Comité Insurrectionnel", the military junta, did not directly assume political power. Instead, it set up a temporary government headed by a civilian and former Prime Minister (1956-1958), Nicolas Grurnitzky. Grunitzky's mother was a Togolese native but his father was of Polish origin. And the "yovovi" (the white) would not hold for a long time his weak power.

The soldier who reportedly shot the President was promoted to the rank of sergeant. In a four-year period, he became Lieutenant Colonel. He implemented the second successful coup in the history of Togo on January 13, 1967 and, subsequently, became known as General Etienne Eyadéma. He held power for almost four decades, until his death in February 2005.

General Eyadéma made January 13th a national holiday, the "Day of National Liberation", in commemoration of his second coup d'Etat. By so doing, he minimised the celebration of the Independence Day of the country, April 27, 1960. Also, while part of the population officially celebrated January 13 as "La Fete de Libération Nationale", another part, unofficially, celebrated it as the Memorial Day of Sylvanus Olympio. All political activities were suspended from 1967 to 1969 when another one-party system was established. In between, the country was ruled by presidential decrees and ordinances. There was not much change in practice afterward when the regime became a one party-state ("parti-Etat") as opposed to nation-state. The party was placed above the government. Party affiliation being compulsory for all citizens, political loyalty became more important than professional competence. To be a good mathematician, one had first to be a good party militant. Security was so tight that one could say, without exaggeration, that the country was ruled like a military principality. It was a satrapy where the French influence replaced the German one that prevailed under Olympio; an absolute one-man rule, where political institutions, economic policies, military and law enforcement activities revolved around the strong-man;

and a minority regime were the military and civilian urban elite concentrated in the capital city of Lomé ruled over the rest of the country. The political atmosphere thus created reminds one of the allegory written by the Greek poet, Hesiod, in *Work And Days,* around 8th century B.C. The story was describing the power relationship between the hawk and the nightingale:

This is what the hawk said when he caught a nightingale with spangled neck in his claws and carried her high among the clouds. She spitted on the claw hooks, was wailing pitifully but the hawk, in his masterful manner, gave her an answer: 'what is the matter with you? Why scream? Your master has you. You shall go wherever I take you, for all your singing. If I like, I can let you go. If I like, I can eat you for dinner. He is a fool who tries to match his strength with the stronger. He will lose the battle, and with the shame will he be hurt also!' So spoke the hawk, the bird who flies so fast on his long wings.

In that logic, farmers were exempted from paying taxes. The general population became what was locally termed an "applaudimeter", called to applaud wherever the "Timonier National" (the National Helmsman) appeared and whenever his name was mentioned in public events. The youth, in large part, was on duty to sing and dance at public events and for visiting foreign dignitaries.

In 1991, however, events took place that General Gassingbé (no longer Etienne) Eyadéma qualified as a civilian coup d'état. There was a "Conférence Nationale Soverraine". Representatives of civilian associations from all walks and from all over the country held a national conference in the capital city, Lomé. The conference declared that it was the expression of the will of the people, and appointed itself the incarnation of the national sovereignty. It dissolved the existing constitution. It replaced the parliament with a "Haut Conseil de la République". It proclaimed a temporary constitution and appointed an interim Prime Minister in charge of organizing new presidential elections within a 12-month period. By virtue of this constitutional arrangement, the sitting President was made *de facto* (and *de jure,* if one accepts the sovereign character of the "Conférence") transitional. The one-party system, with the principle of party-state, collapsed. Many political parties emerged. And the son of the slain President, Sylvanus Olympio, became one of the key figures of the opposition: Gilchrist Olympio. "Brazilianism" was no longer an issue. But the north-south division became sharper.

During the "Conference Nationale Souveraine", General Eyadema was harshly criticized, openly accused of "kleptocracy" (but never tried) and of gross violations of human rights (with no means to prosecute him). The opposition went as far as to deny him the direct responsibility of the assassination of 1963. It was alleged that the coup was orchestrated by France and the man who actually shot the President was a non-African, his French Military Advisor. The opposition claimed that he shot the President when he was running to take refuge in the US embassy adjacent to his private house.

It took three years rather than 12 months to organize elections, which General Eyadema managed to win through a combination of intimidation and maneuvers. The military sabotaged electoral materials, created or supported militias to disrupt civilian life, and sent opposition leaders into exile. During the electoral campaign, Gilchrist Olympio fell victim of an assassination attempt in 1992. He received more than a dozen bullets while campaigning in the northern part of the country. He too, like the body of his father thirty years earlier, was carried through bushes by his driver into Benin where he received urgent care before being evacuated to London for treatment. He survived and has remained a key player in Togolese politics. Following this event, in 1993, half a million Togolese fled to neighboring countries in a matter of weeks due to a sudden escalation of military repression and raids in neighborhoods sympathetic to the opposition. Elections were held, but were boycotted by the opposition and thus had predictable results.

However, beyond personalities lie realities. And those realities were not particular to Togo. Togo was, in a sense, a mirror of the general political evolution of Africa particularly in 1963-1993 time period. Characters and events that took place in Togo were highly symbolic of the political life on the continent.

Symbolic capital

The concept of symbolic capital is both similar and different from the idea of role model. Role modeling is practically teaching by example. Symbolic capital parallels financial capital. You have a certain amount of money and you invest it to diversify your assets. With symbolic capital, you build a success in a certain area (culture, education, business, sports) and you use it or allow it to be used in order to achieve a more general social status.

There is a critical question: the encounter of history and personality. Does personality create history or does personality translate history?

Maybe a little bit of both. A brief study of the respective lives of Sylvanus Olympio and Gnassingbé Eyadéma will illustrate this dilemma.

Sylvanus Olympio, as aforementioned, had a Brazilian background. His father belonged to the reverse Afro-Brazilian Diaspora to the west coast of Africa. He was part of the long tradition of pre-colonial modern intelligentsia in West Africa. He studied political economy in London and became the representative of the British company U..A.C. (United African Company) in West Africa. He was the first African to be appointed to that position in the colonial era. His social status was not at the mercy of France. He could oppose France's colonial policies without risk of losing his job. He spoke English better than German, and German better than French.

After World War II, France wanted to reform the colonial administration and created an "AssembléeTerritoriale." According to a surviving eyewitness I interviewed in 1992, the elite of the territory was invited to a meeting to basically endorse this idea. Olympio was the one who truly dared to voice his opposition. For him, a territorial assembly had no meaning if its function was to approve the decisions made in Paris; the local legislative power would have no meaning without local executive entity. Many people rallied supported this idea and, subsequently, launched a political movement, which would spearhead the struggle for independence. The French then encouraged the emergence of an opposition party which advocated autonomy but cooperation with France. My own father, Mathias Kitissou, was a founding member of Olympio's C.U.T. (Committee for the Unity of Togo) for independence and reunification with British Togo. However, Mathias Kitissou grew up as a roommate and schoolmate of Nicholas Grunitzky, leader of the other party. Torn between his friendship with the "Polish-African" and his support for the political ideas of the "Brazilian-African", my father gave up his political activism altogether. Many others certainly found themselves in a similar situation.

In 1956, Grunitzky became Prime Minister when the Autonomous Territory of Togo was established. In 1958, while Olympio was held in prison, he was elected Prime Minister. Deeming, however, that the country was not ready for immediate independence, he asked for a two-year waiting period and the independence was declared only on April 27, 1960. Between his election and the declaration of the independence (1958-1960), he was Prime Minister. Togo remained an autonomous territory under France until then. He held the title of President only after the official declaration of independence on April 27, 1960.

The biography of Etienne Eyadema is much less complicated. Native of the inland, the northern part of the country, he dropped out of elementary school and joined the French colonial army. His first appearance on the political scene was in 1963 when he was said to have shot President Sylvanus Olympio. However, Eyadema represented more than an individual. In spite of France's "mission civilisatrice" in Africa, this mission was not universally applied. Development and education were based on the need of the colonial power. It was a typical pattern of colonial economy. Also ports, as outlets for export of tropical products, tended to develop more. Hence, the south offered more job opportunities and the elite were concentrated in the south. The territorial disparity thus created gave southerners a sense of superiority.

The north was comparatively less developed. And because of lack of job opportunities, the "nordistes" tended to serve in the army and police forces. By virtue of circumstances, repression of political opponents mainly from the south, was done by military forces recruited mainly from the north. The colonial army, though, was regional and was sent as needed to different administrative territories of France's empire. However, it was well known that in coastal countries, the police were from the inland, and in land-locked countries the police came from the least developed areas. One should keep in mind that migrations were east-west vs. north-south. Therefore, when one traveled south-north one was likely to cross different ethnic groups more than in the east-west direction.

Internally, differences began to build up, based on invidious ethnic comparison, education and professional achievements and activities. Continent wide, on the one hand solidarity emerged among political leaders and, on the other hand, a sense of fraternity was created among African colonial military. The colonial armed forces were a real melting-pot of various African ethnic groups. And between the two groups there was a gap. Sylvanus Olympio, skeptical of their loyalty to the country, denied the request for integrating demobilized colonial soldiers into the armed forces of the newly independent country. However, the symbolic meaning of that denial was three-fold: it was excluding the northern (military) elite from the national pie; it made the northern elite lose their symbolic capital within their own communities, and it was creating a precedent on the continent as far as France's regional influence and own symbolic capital were concerned.

Interface of internal and external factors

First of all, there is a distinction between independence and freedom. With the wave of independence of African countries in the 1960s, France undertook to dissolve its colonial armies. While some men had the option of integrating into the French army, most of them had to return to their native countries with pensions but no other credentials than those of colonial war veterans. France, then, was pushing the newly independent francophone governments to form their national armies with the debris of its colonial forces. Francophone governments, in general, complied. However, Sylvanus Olympio, believing that freedom came with independence, refused. These were his four main reasons for doing so:

First, Togo had no resources for sustaining an external war and had no intention of attacking anyone. Therefore it didn't need an army.

Second, what was needed was rather a small but well-trained police force for the stability and internal security of a new state.

Third, the demobilized colonial soldiers were illegally recruited in the first place. Togo was not a French colony. France had trusteeship of the territory first from the League of Nations after Germany was defeated in World War I; then, from the United Nations after World War II. The international status of the former German colony did not allow France to recruit soldiers from the territory. Either those soldiers were not from Togo or, if they were, they were illegally recruited. Actually, to get recruited into the French colonial army, candidates used to cross the border and apply in Dahomey, the current Republic of Bénin, which was a French colony.

Fourth, not only were they illegally recruited but also their request to be integrated into the new national army was deemed illegitimate. As Olympio put it, "we were being massacred by those men when we were fighting for our independence. How can we place the security of our independence once acquired in the hands of the same men?"

It is also important to understand the logic of Eyadéma and his companions. Eyadéma and his men found themselves in an ambiguous situation. For France, they were soldiers from Togo; for Togo, they were soldiers for France and potential troublemakers at home. For Togo, they were retired soldiers with pensions from France; for France, they were in transition to their national armies. Hence, technically, the coup of 1963 was not a military coup. It only became a military coup after the "Comité Insurrectionnel" assumed political power. Besides, as Eyadéma himself explained later, the atmosphere of suspicion surrounding him and his companions was so thick that he couldn't sleep. He was afraid that someday, "they" would throw weapons over his walls, then knock on his door and say, "We found weapons in your house, you are preparing a coup." He had to do something about that; it was a matter of survival.

Politicization of Ethnicity

The mutilation of the dead body of Sylvanus Olympio, aforementioned, was highly symbolic. With the emergence of former colonial military officers on the political scene in Africa, it signaled an abrupt return of colonial methods of government. Notorious were other former colonial officers who, when heads of state, committed gross violations of human rights: Idi Amin Dada of Uganda, Jean-Bédel Bokassa who crowned himself Emperor of Central Africa, and Mobutu Sesse Seko who changed the name of Congo into Zaire during his dictatorship.

The Cold war era had no room for morality. Those regimes played the West against the East and managed to survive by successfully negotiating the backing of one block or the other. Then, they were practically free to run internal affairs as they wished.

However, as far as internal affairs were concerned, the 1963 coup d'etat in Togo and its aftermath raised ethnic issues to the highest level. As in colonial times, ethnicity returned as a method of government. For example, the use of traditional chiefs both as representatives of ethnic groups and channels through which government orders were carried out, and the reinforcement of customary laws both politicized and legalized the existence of ethnic groups. On another level, the colonial power had educated intellectuals in the south and recruited the forces of repression (police and army) from the north. The new regime practiced an "affirmative action" policy that favored the north in order to restore balance. However, that policy angered many in the south and increased the social divide. At the start of efforts at nation building, the killing of a southern president by a northern military created five interlocking conflicts: a) north vs. south, b) military vs. civilian, c) francophile (pro-France) vs. francophobe (pro-Germany), d) modern elite vs. traditional elite, e) "metis" vs. "natives", in addition to a complete reorientation of Togolese foreign policy in compliance with France's wishes.

The intellectual tradition, the location of central administration and business activities gave individuals from the south many more options. The lack of those options and the general relative poverty in the north gave little social mobility opportunities to northerners. The ambitious youth of the north had only one true option, the army, which happened to be, in the case of Togo, a forbidden fruit due to the post World War I and post World War II status of the territory. Being treated after independence which was to benefit all citizens, at best as pariahs and at worst as traitors looked like double punishment for the northern military elite. The politicians of the south, having borne strong resentment against the army due to past anti-colonial struggle, failed to show an understanding of the national inequalities and to envision policies that were inclusive and conducive to national unity. A political program of that sort, if it existed, was poorly managed by Olympio and his team.

Then, when Eyadema took power in 1967, he could not expect support but from the north. This limitation was aggravated by his original sin: he reportedly killed the former President. Therefore, as his first step into the halls of power, he suspended the constitution, political parties and political activities, and practiced a method of government in which the association of traditional chiefs played a prominent role. Thus, ethnicity was highly politicized. When the one-party system was created in 1969 an apogee of identity politics was reached.

Ethnicization of politics

The initial move of President Eyadéma was to appoint "technocrats" (vs."politicians") in his cabinet. "Technocrats" often mean officials with no political base and personal influence. Then, they were made to serve as the government spokespersons in their respective ethnic groups. The one-party system, started in 1969, was meant to reinforce this method of government and transform the cabinet into a kind of a forum for interethnic dialog. However, the "dialog" promoted by the regime was conducted with military ethics and discipline. As chief of the national village and the commander-in-chief of the armed forces, the General wanted from every citizen both the loyalty of a clan man vis-à-vis the chief and, at the same time, the obedience of a soldier. Instead of a nation-state, there was a hybrid entity combining ethnic-state and party-state. Any deviation was therefore perceived and harshly punished as a betrayal. The place that that type of solidarity could be best ensured and enforced was the ethnic group of the President himself. Therefore important political and administrative positions were given to members of his ethnic group, with more than 60% of the armed forces recruited from his region while two thirds of the population lived in the southern part of the country. Any political opposition, particularly when repressed by the army, tended to take the form of an ethnic conflict.

The Living and the Dying

A distinction emerged on the continent: a distinction between, as Ali Mazrui put it in a conversation, between coup-prone and coup-proof countries. Togo was among the coup-prone states.

It can be assumed, however, that the distinction, in general, lies in the degree of integration of the intellectual class and the military elite, and "natives" and "foreigners", when perceived differences between regions are not too sharp and when social and ethnic groups don't perceive political power as a zero sum game or the only means available for them to survive and to protect their interests. Having failed to achieve that integration, Togo lived in a constant fear of coup since the days of independence. The result was an obsessive security system and an excessive atmosphere of repression. The Eyadema regime lasted for almost four decades thanks to a constant use of mirror tactics (accusing the enemy of one's own intention) which amounted to a situation of permanent coup d'etat.

The pesonalization of the political conflict, for four decades, between the Olympio and Eyadéma's families made the political conflict intractable and created what one could call an atmosphere of political vendetta. Negotiations between the government and the opposition never reached full conclusion. Gilchrist Olympio once requested a face-to-face meeting with Gnassingbé Eyadema. The latter refused and the former returned to exile in Ghana.

Interlocking Conflicts

Most of the time, political and social conflicts are interlocking conflicts. Many who enter the game on each side of the dividing line do so with their own agenda. There are layers of issues but negotiations focus only on the most conspicuous ones. However, like the Hydra of Lema, which constantly grew its lost heads back, once an issue is resolved another one emerges. Violence only makes conflicts more and more complicated and a coup d'etat tends to create the conditions for another coup d'etat, hence a permanent state of alert and repression. In the case of Togo, in the period of 1963 to 1993, it seems that issues were accumulated without resolution and that what kept the appearance of peace was the strength and discipline of the army combined with the weakness of the opposition.

The repercussions of the assassination of Sylvanus Olympio went well beyond the borders of Togo. Instead of restoring balance between the regions of the country and creating a sense of national justice, the blood spilled on January 13, 1963 sharpened the division between north-south, civilian-military, intellectuals-soldiers, and metis-natives. The first heads of state to visit independent Togo were Emperor Haile Selassie of Ethiopia and President Henrich Lubke of West Germany. One of the first Presidents to receive a visit from Sylvanus Olympio was John F. Kennedy. Besides communism, the situation most feared by France in the first decades of independence, was to see its influence overshadowed by American presence. France, then, started to play the role of a regional power in Africa. In the particular case of Togo, the return of the influence of the former colonial power, former West Germany, was an additional component in France's policy vis-à-vis Togo.

Conclusion

In many ways the 1990s in Togo, when the struggle for democratic reforms started, looked like the 1960s when internal tensions were high. In the early 1990s, April 27 was revived by many and celebrated as Independence Day. January 13 was considered the most important national holiday by some and a day of mourning by others.

There were, however, some differences between the 1960s and the 1990s. In 1963 the struggle was about independence. In the 1990s, the movement was about freedom. In the early 1960s, the government was supported by the US and Germany and the opposition by France. In the 1990s, the government was supported by France and the opposition by the US and Germany. Subsequently, the US suspended its economic assistance in 1993 and Germany used its weight to have the European Union suspend its cooperation with Togo. In the 1960s, as in the 1990s, policy differences between France and Germany were noticeable.

Would Togolese internal conflict be panafricanized again within the new African Union or regionalized within the Economic Community of West African States? That is less than sure. These organizations are now more focused on economic development and peace building, trying to create space so that parties can negotiate and find a solution to their domestic problems.

In the absence of the resolution of conflict such as during the reign of Gnassingbé Eyadéma (1967-2005), authoritarian imagination, in the form of ideology and propaganda, was used to support an imaginary authority that did not really take roots in the country. The strong-man appeared strong but political institutions were weak. Administrative failure led to political failure. In a country where parents could not talk to their children about the founding fathers of the "nation", or when the first President was deemed non-African, in a country where the school teacher could not pronounce the name of a former president without fear of being arrested, there could not be nation building. And in a situation where the difference in the interpretation of collective experience was so sharp and the vision of a common future so controversial, the failure of the state was a predictable outcome.

"It is not knowledge we lack. What is missing is the courage to understand what we know and draw conclusions", wrote Sven Lindqvist in his book, *Exterminate All the Brutes.*

PART 3

CAN AFRICA-NATION BE CONSTRUCTED?

Chapter 12

THE GOLDEN AGE OF ARAB-AFRICAN RELATIONS

Gamal Nkrumah

Introduction

I recall the common vision Egypt's Gamal Abdul-Nasser shared with African leaders of the 1950s and 1960s. In this article, I outline the main features of contemporary Arab-African relations since the end of the Cold War, the rise of militant Islam as a thorn in the flesh of Pax -Americana, and the politics of oil.

Leaders And Trendsetters of Arab African Solidarity

On 28 September 1970, Gamal Abdel-Nasser died, but his anti-colonialist legacy lived on in the minds of many Africans. The socialist, anti-imperialist Egypt he constructed was systematically dismantled by his successor Anwar Sadat. Nasser's Africa policy was quickly discarded. And, Africa featured less prominently on the Egyptian political agenda.

As the most populous, politically and culturally influential Arab state, the change of direction had a profound impact on other Arab countries. It was only with the Libyan leader Muammar Gaddafi's zealous embrace of pan-Africanism in the late 1990s, that the foundation stones of Arab-African relations carefully built by Nasser, were partially reassembled.

The historical reference point and golden age of Arab-African relations shall always be the late 1950s and early 1960s. Even though the first official Arab-African summit was convened in Cairo in 1977, the foundation stones of African-Arab relations were laid down a decade or two earlier. Sadat presided over the 1977 African-Arab summit, but the African leaders most prominent at the summit were, to put it bluntly, neo-colonial stooges - Mobutu Sese Sekou of Zaire, Jaafar Numeiri of Sudan and Sadat himself. No longer was there a common anti-colonial bond to bind the Arab and African struggles for national liberation and emancipation from Western hegemony, poverty, underdevelopment and social injustice. Rather, Africa was ruled by men determined to make the most of a subservient, neo-colonial relationship with Western powers.

Indeed, whenever Arab-African ties come into question, one cannot help remembering the days when colonialism was the threat closer to home, and one Arab leader was always at hand to lend support to those Africans who wished to throw off its yoke. That was the time of solidarity, of a common Arab-African dream, of nations taking their first steps to freedom. That was Nasser's time.

The solidarity between Arab and non-Arab Africans is not an historical accident. It is rooted in a common vision, drawn from a common cause. It all started in the late 1950s and early 1960s, when Africa's leaders-to-be were still freedom fighters, and Nasser was their closest ally.

For Nasser and his fellow African leaders, African liberation was an historic duty. They lived and died for the cause of national liberation. Few Arab leaders of Nasser's stature were involved as intimately as he was in the struggle to liberate Africa from colonial rule. It was this dedication to the cause of African liberation that endeared him to like-minded African leaders. What they had in common was a radical agenda of social change, a task they knew would not be easy, and a mission that remains, to this day, incomplete.

It is difficult for me to write about the icon that Nasser was without mentioning something of the man. His role in rescuing my family from possible perdition in the aftermath of the bloody 24 February 1966 coup that overthrew my father, Kwame Nkrumah, has been documented elsewhere. Nasser's personal involvement with the fortunes of his fellow African leaders and their families was based on a political outlook characteristic of the time. Personally, I had an unusual opportunity to watch Nasser's Pan-African contribution at close quarters and observed the close friendship he had with those who spearheaded the anti-colonial struggle in Africa.

"With feelings of great bitterness and shock, we, in the United Arab Republic, have heard of the sad events to which the people of Ghana were exposed ... I agree with you that the forces of colonialism are always trying to undermine the independence of African states, and to draw them again into spheres of influence in order to continue exploiting their resources and shape their fates. What has happened in Ghana is actually part of this imperialist plan. To face colonialism in the African continent requires of us all continuous efforts and a sustained struggle to liberate it from old colonialism and neo-colonialism. The setback that has occurred in Ghana must act as a driving force for all of us to continue the struggle for the consolidation of the independence of African peoples and their liberation from imperialist forces." Nasser wrote this in a letter to Kwame Nkrumah less than 48 hours after the coup, which toppled the latter's government.

Nasser's commiseration letter to Ghana's first president was typical of the friendship Nasser had with African leaders of his time such as Guinea's President Ahmed Sekou Toure and Congolese Premier Patrice Lumumba. As comrades, to use the parlance of the period, they developed a sense of personal solidarity within the larger context of African liberation. "I thank you for your kind felicitations on the Ramadan Bairam and send my best wishes to you and your family," stated a letter from Nasser to Nkrumah dated 25 January 1967.

Nasser's African connection was in no way restricted to the Nkrumah family.

Indeed, he took a special interest in the resettlement of Lumumba's family after the Congolese leader was brutally assassinated at the hands of the henchmen of Mobutu Sese Seku, the late Zairean military strongman. Lumumba's widow and children fled to the safety of the Egyptian embassy in Kinshasa and they were spirited away to Cairo in a harrowing rescue mission. Nasser's gallant gesture further enhanced his stature in the entire African continent. Nasser's Egypt became the Lumumbas' adopted home.

Curiously enough, Mobutu Sese Seku later emerged as a staunch proponent of the establishment of a League of Black African Nations as a counterbalance for the Arab League. Membership of Mobutu's League was to be strictly limited to African states south of the Sahara, to the express exclusion of Arab African states.

Egypt's July Revolution was an inspiration to people who lived under colonial rule across the world, especially for Arabs and Africans. For the first time in three millennia, Egypt was ruled by an Egyptian, one who was just as proud of his African heritage as he was of his Arab identity. Nasser embarked on a radical policy of land reform and redistribution. He confiscated 2,430 square kilometres of farmland from the tiny land-owning elite and gave them to dispossessed peasant families. Nasser's socialist-inspired policies prompted him to nationalise banks and major industries. But the turning point, perhaps, was his nationalisation of the Suez Canal in 1956. This was the act that brought him instant admiration across the Third World, and the wrath of former colonial powers, particularly Britain and France. Soon after the evacuation of British troops from the Suez Canal zone in June 1956, Britain, France and Israel attacked Egypt in what became known in Egypt as the Tripartite Aggression.

Now, more than 30 years after Nasser's death, is any of the above still relevant? I believe so. There have been growing calls in Africa for reparations over the medieval Arab slave trade. There is open hostility to a perceived "Arab agenda" in the African continent. The unresolved Sudanese crises - in the south and in the west - has mistakenly been portrayed in the international media as a conflict between Arab Muslims on one hand and African animists and Christians on the other. This conflict was made to look as if it was an unavoidable consequence of a fault line separating Arab and non-Arab Africa.

The Israeli and far right lobbies in the United States and the West have been fanning anti-Arab and anti-Muslim resentment among African Americans and the predominantly Christian and non-Muslim parts of Africa. Africa may have its own grievances with the Arab world. But these grievances are not medieval, and certainly not atavistic. When oil prices surged spectacularly in the wake of the 1973 war, African countries hoped for Arab economic aid and financial assistance, and were sorely disappointed. Arab countries, even with their newly acquired wealth, were developing countries, after all. They didn't have the technological and administrative means of promoting economic development in Africa. The frustration was understandable. But the insidious plots, when they happened, were hatched in other lands.

African leaders like Nasser and Nkrumah were aware that the world was watching their political, social, and economic endeavours. It was the success, not the failure, of Nkrumah's policies that triggered the CIA-inspired coup of 24 February 1966. Nkrumah, like the core leftist African leaders of his generation, looked to Nasser's Egypt as a bulwark against colonialism and imperialism. Socialist leaders in Africa watched closely the agrarian reform and the ambitious industrialisation drive of Nasser's Egypt.

Just as Egypt had built the High Dam in Aswan; Ghana, too, embarked on the construction of a dam to harness the country's vast water resources and its largest river, the Volta. Nkrumah's Ghana needed electricity for its ambitious industrialisation programmes. The inauguration of the Volta Dam in January 1966 brought Ghana close to economic independence. Nasser and Nkrumah had a similar outlook. Both espoused a philosophy of national liberation infused with a strong dose of socialism. While Nasser propagated what was known as Arab socialism, Nkrumah opted for what he termed scientific socialism.

Nasser was the first Egyptian leader to put Egypt firmly within its African context. Successive Egyptian and other North African regimes followed that trend. For Nasser, Egypt's identity drew upon three circles: the Arab, the Islamic and the African. Nasser saw no contradiction in Egypt belonging to the Organisation of African Unity, the Arab League, and the Organisation of Islamic Conference. Prior to Nasser, Egypt's rulers were mostly Mediterranean, if not outright European, in their outlook. Nasser deliberately shifted the focus with his introduction of the Arab, African and Islamic "circles." Nasser's stress on those three circles brought him into close contact with the leaders of the African liberation struggle.

Nkrumah, too, had a similar vision for the African world. In his Consciencism: Philosophy and Ideology for Decolonisation, Nkrumah says that the African personality draws upon three major elements: the African, the Western Christian and the Arab Islamic. Nasser's The Philosophy of the Revolution, echoes the same sentiment.

On a personal level, however, the two men were quite different. Nasser was one of the first ordinary Egyptians to ever graduate from the prestigious Military Academy, Previously, admittance to the Military Academy was strictly limited to members of the country's predominantly Turco-Caucasian elite. Nasser took part in the disastrous 1948 war against Israel. Upon his return from the battlefront, he joined the Free Officers, the secret group that was later to topple the monarchy.

Nkrumah, meanwhile, only learnt how to use a gun when he was well into his fifties. He was educated in the West, first in the United States (where he attended the University of Lincoln, Pennsylvania, then reserved for African Americans) and then in London. As a young man, he was very active in student politics in both the US and Britain and was heavily influenced by the African American experience. Pan-African leaders like W.E.B. Du Bois and Marcus Josiah Garvey were Nkrumah's mentors. He drew much inspiration from their writings and was particularly influenced by Garvey's political activism, his Universal Negro Improvement Association (UNIA), and its paper The Negro World.

Because of Egypt's geographical location at the crossroads of Africa and Asia and because the country was, and still is, the cultural heart of the Arab world, Nasser was inevitably drawn into the vortex of Arab politics. The 1958 unification of Egypt and Syria in the United Arab Republic, UAR, was the first successful attempt at Arab unity. Egypt and Syria were soon joined by Yemen. Still, the UAR unceremoniously broke up in 1961, and with it floundered the dream of Arab unity.

In Africa, several attempts were made at unification. One was the Ghana, Guinea, Mali Union in the early sixties. Another was the short-lived union between Nkrumah's Ghana and Lumumba's Congo, signed a few months before Lumumba's assassination. The parallels were many. The Arabs and Africans were exchanging notes. "In Accra, Kozonguizi and I contacted the special representative of President Gamal Abdel Nasser of Egypt, who came to attend the Positive Action Conference. He gave us a very sympathetic hearing. Egypt's first practical help came from President Nasser's special representative who gave £100 sterling to each of us. With part of the money I was given, I bought an Olivetti portable typewriter, which I used for many years during the struggle and which I still have," wrote Namibian President Sam Nujoma in his autobiography Where Others Wavered.

"At the beginning of March 1961, I attended the third All-African People's Conference in Cairo ... I requested President Nasser to offer the opportunity of military training to SWAPO members. Nasser assured me of such opportunities if I could get a group of SWAPO members from South West Africa. He urged all African independent countries to render the necessary assistance to the national liberation movements, including military training, in order to free their countries from colonial occupation and foreign domination. He also urged the independent African states not to allow the imperialist powers to maintain and promote neo-colonialism and disunity among the African countries," Nujoma said in his tribute to the late Egyptian president. This was how the July Revolution inspired African leaders throughout the 1950s.

"When in 1963, the first group [of Namibian freedom fighters] went for military training in Cairo, this was possible because President Gamal Abd el-Nasser of Egypt had offered me training and tickets. Nasser was a dedicated supporter of African liberation," Nujoma added. Small wonder that when Nasser passed away on 28 September 1970, many Africans felt the loss.

"The world has lost a great man and all those who fight for freedom and human dignity have lost a brother in the struggle. The people of Namibia join you in mourning President Nasser's tragic death," Nujoma, still a political exile and freedom fighter, lamented. Nujoma attended Nasser's funeral in Cairo. "Nasser had inspired us in Namibia as far back as 1956 when he fought against the British, French, and Israelis after he had taken the Suez Canal. When we read about the fighting, in the newspapers in then South West Africa, we were firmly on the Egyptian side," Nujoma said.

There were, of course, some controversial decisions made during the Cold War era such as the military assistance Nasser's Egypt provided to the federal government in Nigeria in its fight to subdue the breakaway Biafra during the Nigerian civil war of 1967-70. But Nasser's decision has to be seen in the context of African nation's struggle for sovereignty, unity and territorial integrity. Africa was balkanised in the immediate aftermath of the 1883-84 Berlin Conference. Most African countries were economically non-viable states at independence. African countries were characterised by a host of crippling constraints - small markets, poor standards of living and debilitating socio-economic woes.

Arab countries, too, suffered from much the same problems. Leaders like Nasser, Nkrumah, Lumumba and Algeria's Ahmed Ben Bella instinctively understood that the entire continent north and south of the Sahara suffered from similar ills. Why now, 32 years after Nasser's death, is tackling this issue of any consequence? The Zionist and Christian fundamentalist lobbies in the Western world, and in the United States in particular, have fanned the flames of religious hatred and spread a most virulent anti-Arab and anti-Muslim sentiment among the African Diaspora in the Americas and among Africans south of the Sahara, especially in predominantly Christian and non-Muslim parts of the continent.

Pax-Americana: A Decisive Factor in Contemporary African-Arab Relations

The Cold War might be a distant memory in most African countries, but its after-effects linger on in certain places - the Horn of Africa and southern Africa. Most African leaders, however, now look to Washington for political guidance and economic salvation.

Pax Americana rules supreme in Africa. The Arab ruling elites, too, are firmly in the grip of American economic, political and especially military might. The political map of Africa has seen radical shifts and realignments in recent years. The new democracies of Africa have inched ever closer to Washington. In the Arab world the situation is a little more complex, but by and large all Arab states - including Libya - can now be considered as economic partners of the US. Still, as the tense and untenable situation in Iraq and Saudi Arabia demonstrate, pockets of resistance to US hegemony survive - and it is not just the militant Islamists who are defiantly anti-US.

Contemporary Arab-African relations cannot be properly viewed outside the context of the turmoil in Iraq, Palestine and the oil-rich

Arabian Gulf. These Arab countries and regions are not geographically located in Africa, but the Arab countries of North Africa, including Egypt, have been profoundly impacted by what is happening in Iraq, Palestine and Saudi Arabia. Ironically, and in the wake of the 11 September attacks on New York and Washington, the subsequent invasion and occupation of first Afghanistan and then Iraq, the states of North Africa, in particular, have emerged as the most staunchly pro-American on the African continent. They have long battled against their own militant Islamists, long before Washington became aware of the Islamist threat.

It is difficult to trace the changing and contradictory perceptions of Africans in the Arab world. One fact holds true today: The US has strengthened its political grip on both African and Arab countries since the demise of the former Soviet Union and the end of the Cold War. The US is no longer propping up dictators such as Mobutu Sese Sekou of Zaire (now the Democratic Republic of Congo) and paramilitary protégés such as Jonas Savimbi the late leader of the National Union for the Total Liberation of Angola better known by its Portuguese acronym UNITA. But, Washington turns a blind eye to human rights abuses and undemocratic practices in Arab and African countries closely aligned to the US.

The political map of Africa has seen radical shifts and realignments in recent years. Indeed, the ruling Movement for the Liberation of Angola (MPLA), formerly a close political and military ally of the former Soviet Union and Cuba, has inched ever closer to Washington and can now be considered a key economic partner of the US in Africa.

Contemporary Arab-African relations cannot be seen outside the context of the after-effects of 11 September 2002, and even before that with the bombing of the American embassies in Nairobi, Kenya, and Dar es-Salam, Tanzania. The point, I wish to stress, is that contemporary Arab-African relations cannot be properly understood without the magnifying glass of US foreign policy and especially the US-led international war on terrorism. African- Arab relation are also influenced by three other important developments. First, US interest in developing the oil reserves of Africa as a counterbalance to dependence on Middle Eastern oil. Second, Libya's about face vis-à-vis the US and other Western powers. Third, the Sudanese political crisis and attendant civil wars and humanitarian catastrophe.

With the commercial exploitation of vast reserves of oil in West and Central Africa, the continent stands poised to be a sharply better place.

Oil production is poised to increase considerably among old-timers like Angola and Nigeria. And newcomers like Chad and Sudan are literally converting swords into ploughshares heralding a big change in oil markets. The relative proximity of West African oil to the US is of critical importance. West Africa is expected to emerge as a major supplier of crude oil to the US - supplying as much as 25 per cent of America's oil needs by 2015, thereby greatly reducing the superpower's dependence on Middle Eastern oil. These factors must be taken into account when assessing contemporary African-Arab relations.

Sudan - the binding factor in African Arab relations

The situation in Sudan is being fiercely debated in many Pan-African circles as well as in many international forums. Egypt and the rest of the Arab world want a united, territorially integral Sudan.

The international community is most concerned about the humanitarian catastrophe in southern and western Sudan. Human rights violations, talk of ethnic cleansing, and the scorched earth policy adopted by the Sudanese government and allied Arabised militias are sources of concern. "This is the most vicious hostile campaign this government has ever faced,' warned Sudanese Foreign Minister Mostafa Othman Ismail recently.

The Sudanese government, however, doesn't have a leg to stand on. Privately, African governments condemn the Sudanese government policies. Publicly, however, they don't. The United Nations Human Rights Commission in Geneva, Switzerland, recently expressed concern about the overall situation in Sudan's war-torn province of Darfur. But it stopped short of condemning the Sudanese government. Many Arab and African countries were responsible for letting the Sudanese authorities get away with mass murder.

The Sudanese government and the country's main armed opposition group, the southern-based Sudan People's Liberation Army (SPLA) have been holding peace talks in Naivasha, 80 kms northwest of the Kenyan capital Nairobi. The Sudanese peace talks are taking place under the auspices of the Inter-Governmental Authority for Development (IGAD), a regional organisation which groups seven East African countries, including Sudan. The real propelling force behind the Sudanese peace process, however, is the US.

Sudan, or rather the Sudanese crisis, brings into sharp focus the key importance of US foreign policy as a determining factor in contemporary Arab-African relations. The political fate of Sudan hangs on the balance.

If Sudan breaks up into two states - an Arab Muslim north and a southern non-Arab, non-Muslim south - then that will negatively impact African-Arab relations. The very existence of Sudan as a country has been living proof of intertwining fortunes of Arabs and Africans. A united Sudan will confirm that Africans and Arabs can live in one continent peaceably. If Arabs and Africans cannot live amicably together in Sudan, then neither can they do so on the continent at large.

But Sudan's unity will entail the democratisation of Sudan's political and socio-economic institutions. The southern Sudanese will never accept living in a Sudan that is dominated by an Arab, militant Islamist elite as it has done since independence from Britain in 1956. For Arabs and Non-Arabs to live together peacefully in Sudan, the principles of democracy and respect for human rights must be enshrined in the Sudanese constitution.

The lessons one can draw from the Sudanese crisis must not be underestimated or played down. A peaceful, democratic and prosperous Sudan is key to cementing Arab-African relations. Sudan must be at peace with itself for Arab-African ties to be strengthened.

Back to the past

But, the lessons of the past must not be forgotten, either. It is at turbulent times like these that one is tempted to draw back on the lessons of Nasser's experience. The Egyptian Revolution erupted in July 1952. After a brief stint in office by Mohamed Naguib, Nasser, the chief architect of the Revolution, assumed the reins of power. For the first time in three millennia, Egypt was ruled by an Egyptian. Not since the days of the Pharaohs was Egypt ruled by an Egyptian.

Nasser personified the Arab dream of national self-determination and emancipation from colonial servitude, poverty, illiteracy and backwardness. Nkrumah, too, embodied Africa's aspirations of freedom and social justice.

Both Africa and the Arab world have been undergoing series of changes since the death both Nasser in 1970 and Nkrumah two years later. Sadly, four decades after the establishment of the OAU, Africans have on the whole left the control of their destiny to others, and especially to the former European colonial masters and the US. Africa's role, as the New Partnership for African Development (NEPAD) makes clear, is that of a timid co-pilot at best. NEPAD - the current blueprint for African economic survival - is as strongly supported by Arab countries like Algeria and Egypt as by the non-Arab Senegal, Nigeria and South Africa.

"In spite of all good intentions, in spite of our plans, the naked fact, alas, is that Africa is still an impoverished continent, immobilised by the lack of political cohesion, harassed by imperialism and ransacked by neo-colonialism," warned Nkrumah.

Chapter 13

PAN AFRICA OR AFRICAN UNION? *

Bankie Forster Bankie

In the Foreword to the French language book dedicated to Tarek Aziz, the former Iraqi diplomat, edited by Beatrice Bouvet and Patrick Denaud,(2000), there is a quotation from Henry Kissinger as follows:

> Whereas the intellectual analyses the functioning of the international order, politicians create that order … and there exists a great difference between the perspective of the analyst and that of the politician.

Background

In international relations 'no position is permanent' and only self-interest remains as a continuous guiding principle in diplomatic exchange. From a bipolar world, we are now in the unipolar phase, before proceeding to a multi-polar world some years hence. So too the pursuit of foreign policy must be under constant review taking consonance of the shifting nature of domestic and foreign interests.

The text finds its origins in the paper 'Pan Africanism or Continentalism'? (see Bankie, 1995), which was originally presented on March 13, 1991 at the Institute for African Alternatives in London, England. The introductory note of that text stated:

> 'The linkage of Africa with its Diaspora is merely one of the important elements in the advancement of the Pan African Project. This linkage is only one of the keys to Pan Africanism – another is the issue who is an African – yet another is the question of Pan Africanism or Continentalism?'

The OAU which emerged as a compromise from the earlier Pan Africanist struggles, based its project for unity on unequal Afro-Arab relations, which did not reflect the lived experiences of the Afro-Arab interchange, which was less than cordial at the point of contact in the Sahel. The marginalization of Africans in the area was, after all, not a new phenomenon and had been centuries in the making. One of the foremost exponents of the OAU approach to unity had married an Arab to symbolize his aspirations for continental union, by a co-habitation. So it was that the Organisation of African Unity (OAU) had failed to act on one and a half million lost lives in the Sudan since 1983 and four million displaced, or when thousands were massacred or displaced in Mauritania, and reports filtered through of genocide in other parts of the 'Borderlands', and of the harassment of African communities. The 'Borderlands' is that area of Africa running from Mauritania on the Atlantic Ocean, eastwards through the Sahel, to Sudan on the Red Sea.

With hindsight one increasingly asks how the leaders of the 1950s and 1960s believed that they could short- circuit centuries of history and move to immediate union with a people who had pursued a policy of expansion over centuries, and who by the mid-twentieth century had created their own pan-movement for Arab solidarity, led by the Nasserite revolution, which captured the imagination of the Arab world and spawned the Arab nationalist Baath parties of Syria, Iraq and the Libyan Arab Jamahiriya. The policies pursued by the Baath party and the Jamahiriya were but a continuation of the age-old policy of Arab expansion into Africa, with the Iraqi Baath party training the elite military structures of the Mauritanian army, the Republican Guard; with Iraq supplying mustard gas to Khartoum to be used in south Sudan and with Libya seeking to annex Tibesti in Chad, creating chaos and anarchy in west Africa (e.g. Liberia, Ivory Coast, etc), whilst seeking to extend its influence in the Central African Republic, Zimbabwe and elsewhere.

Apparently the Founding Fathers of the OAU, or at least some of them, did not know the real nature of Afro-Arab interaction in the Sahel, and were ignorant of the grassroots conflictual relations which exploded into violence in Nouakchott, Mauritania for the first time in 1966 (Diallo, 1993). As the movement, which was largely driven by Libya gained momentum towards the revision of the OAU structures; some observers monitored closely the formulation of the Charter of the emerging African Union (AU). This was not easy, given that the elaboration took place, at least in the early stages, away from public scrutiny and knowledge. From the 'Report of the meeting of legal experts and parliamentarians on the establishment of the African Union and the Pan African Parliament' dated 17-20 April 2000, Addis Ababa, Ethiopia Ref Cab/Leg/23.15/6/Vol IV,[4] paragraph 48, under the rubric 'Consideration Protocol relating to the Pan African Parliament' at the section referring to Article 4 'Objectives', it is stated:

> 'On the issue of composition it was proposed that the prospective members should represent not only the people of Africa and those who

have naturalized, but peoples of African descent as well. However, other delegations were of the view that only African peoples should be represented in the Parliament ....'

At paragraph 55 appearing under the same rubric as paragraph 48 (i.e. Consideration Protocol relating to the Pan African Parliament) in the section referring to Articles 2 and 3 'Establishment and relationship with the OAU', it is reported ...

'After effecting certain amendments to paragraph 1 and 2 of Article 3, the reference to members of Parliament representing all people of 'African descent' was deleted.'

It is no secret that Arabia in the OAU never saw a place for the African Diaspora in its deliberations, whereas Africans in general embrace their 'kith and kin' taken out of Africa through slavery. Mohamed Fayek, Director-General, Dar Al-Mustaqbal Al-Arabi, Cairo, Egypt in his contribution to the Amman Seminar on Afro-Arab relations points out that prior to the Nasserite Revolution of July 23, 1952 Egypt had no organic relationship with the rest of Africa and there existed no linkage movements. He goes on to state that (cited in *Newsletter of the African Association of Political Science*, 2001):

'... The African movement itself, which was initiated by black Americans in reaction to discrimination against them, adopted the theme of the black man's dignity and freedom and his returning to his roots – while the black Americans had neither knowledge nor concrete links with the African continent, other than the colour of their skin. Hence the birth of what is called 'Africanism' based on their African descent – but only with black Africa in mind. African unity was to them as much a way of reviving the ancient African empires of Ghana, Songhai, Mali and others, as it was the unity of black Africa. With this, Africanism, before reaching the African continent itself, took a separate path from Arab Africa. Egypt, therefore, as well as the rest of North Africa, had no connection with this particular African movement.

The Borderlands and the Sudan

It is submitted that the resolution of the problems in Afro-Arab relations, specifically as reflected in the Borderlands will only take place when the African people in general are sufficiently informed and active to bring about change. As these issues are addressed, it will result in the re-orientation of African international relations. It will affect how

Africans see the world, how African unity is constructed and how the rest of the world sees Africa. This strategic shift in intra-African relations represents the first major departure from the interpretations and 'set of problems' left to us by those who formed the OAU in the 1960s, which precepts have remained unchallenged in conventional circles from the formation of the OAU to its re-incarnation as the AU today.

The establishment of the Afro-Arab 'dialogue', if need be, will require, as its principal interlocutors, from the African side, the people of the Borderlands who have co-existed with the Arabs. Not the coastal peoples of West Africa, or the central, east and southern Africans, who have in general chosen to ignore the problems in the Borderlands. It is with the people of the Borderlands that the Arabs north of the Sahel - the Moroccans, Egyptians, Libyans, Tunisians, Algerians (whose government, less we forget, needs to resolve its differences with the Berbers in their midst) *et al* that the dialogue may take place. Some Africans are saying that the issue of reparations for Arab-led slavery should not be addressed in this period, when the Middle East is being regime changed. Here again such tactical questions need to be answered by those living in the areas affected (see Professor Tier's position on this, 2002). We need to remember that Nigeria, Senegal and Uganda have at different times renounced rights to reparations for slavery.

The Arab world in general, as represented by the Arab League, as well as the Palestine Liberation Organisation (PLO), has supported the Sudan government in its war in the south against African nationalism. In the Sudan, as in the Borderlands in general, Africans have had to contend with Arab expansionism. In these circumstances they had to choose whether to Arabise and Islamise or to take the option of African nationalism. Those who chose the latter option, some of whom opted for Christianity, have until recently been fighting the central government in Khartoum. The major opposition is formed by the Sudan Peoples Liberation Movement (SPLM), although other groups in Sudan are also at war with the central government in Khartoum. Kwesi Kwaa Prah (2000) has explained the reasons why the Sudanese conflict has failed to find definitive settlement. It is the oldest war in Africa, having started in its current phase in 1955. Essentially the war in the Sudan represents a clash of African and Arab nationalism, contending for economic, cultural, political and social stakes within the colonial-bequeathed borders of the Sudan. Prah states that the dominant feature in the Sudan situation is the national question. The discovery of large quantities of oil in the Sudan adds further fuel to an inflammatory situation.

Although Sudan on independence rushed to join the Arab League, only 39 per cent of its people consider themselves Arabs. Sudan is, in effect, a minority ruled state. The majority of its people are Africans, who are mainly concentrated in the south, where the cultural features are less Arabised and the people are partially Christian. The north is predominantly Islamic and Arabic, including blacks who opt for Pan-Arabism.

The issues the Borderlands raise date back thousands of years and it is suggested that the area provides a sharper, historically based, holistic definition of African nationalism than that hitherto offered by the black consciousness movements in the Americas and Southern Africa. In the Sudan, as in the Borderlands in general, there exists a minority group of Arabized black people who do not consider themselves Africans and who participate in the oppression and enslavement of the majority African population. Clearly what is at stake is not a matter of colour, but a question of culture. The Borderlands teach us that the African nationality is primarily cultural, not race based. For the African unity movement , one of the implications of this is the need to 'wipe the slate clean' and a need to 'return to the drawing board'. Too much emphasis was placed on geopolitics, economics and race at the cost of culture. Indeed culture is the missing link in development planning (Prah, 2002).

We need to recall at this point how Africa, from the Mediterranean Sea southwards, had been originally populated by black people. The doctoral thesis of Cheik Anta Diop in 1960 established the cultural origins of the Egyptian civilization as being African. This was affirmed in Cairo at the UNESCO- sponsored Symposium (January 28 to February 3, 1974) on the Peopling of Ancient Egypt and the Deciphering of the Meroitic Script, attended by Diop and Theophile Obenga (see Diop, 1992).

The author saw at the National Museum in Khartoum in December 2002 irrefutable evidence that the earliest civilizations in the present day Sudan were African cultures. We know that with the passage of time other Indo-European peoples entered North Africa through the Nile Delta pushing southwards the Africans they met, so that today the Borderlands define the point to which Africans have been pushed southwards, generally to arid, infertile areas. In the Borderlands, due to the Arabisation of its people, some of those leading the fight southwards are black people culturally Arabised, who have been denationalized and thus reject their African national identity.

References

AAPS (2001): "Report of the Meeting of Legal Experts and Parliamentarians on the Establishment of the African Union and the PanAfrican Parliament" in, *Newsletter of the African Association of Political Science.* Vol.6, No.1 January-April, Harare, AAPS) Pp.15-16.

Bankie, B.F. (1995): "PanAfricanism or Continentalism?" African Opinion Series No. 4. Cape Town; Harps Publications.

Bouvet, B & Denaud, P. (2000): *Tarek Aziz: Le Diplomate De Saddam Hussein,* Paris; L'Harmattan P.13.

Diallo, G. (1993): *Mauritania – The Other Apartheid?* Uppsala; Nordiska Afrikainstitutet P.9.

Diop, C.A. (1992): "Origin of the Ancient Egyptians" in Sertima, I.V., Ed *Great African Thinkers* (Rutgers, New Jersey: Transaction Books) Pp. 35-63.

Fayek, M. (1984) "The July 23 Revolution and Africa" in Khair El-Din Haseeb Ed, *The Arabs and Africa* (London: Croom Helm) Pp 90-91

Prah, K.K. (2000) "Constitutionalism, the National Question and the Sudanese Civil War" in Nnoli, O. (Ed., 2000): *Government and Politics in Africa – A Reader.* (Harare: AAPS Books) Pp. 392-410.

Prah, K.K. (2002) "Culture, The Missing Link in Development Planning in Africa" in Karikari, K., Ed, *Where has Aid taken Africa? Re-thinking Development.* (Accra: Media Foundation for West Africa) Pp. 107-126.

Professor Tier, A. Dean of the Faculty of Law, University of Khartoum, specialist in Human Rights law, December 12, 2002, in Khartoum endorsed the legitimacy of reparations for Arab-led Slavery.

---

* (Published originally in the May/June 2005 edition of *African Renaissance*)

Chapter 14

REGIONAL ECONOMIC COMMUNITIES AND PAN-AFRICANISM

Issaka K. Souaré & Dossou David Zounmenou

State structures that post-colonial African states inherited were very weak. Likewise, the resources available to meet demands of socio-economic development were greatly limited. But ever since what many regard as the first Pan-African Congress held in London in 1900, the realisation in African thinking has been the conditioning of the continent's uplifting and the well-being of its peoples to genuine and greater integration and unity. In a recent categorisation of pan-Africanism according to historical periods, South African scholar Christopher Landsberg identifies five waves of pan-Africanism. The author puts the establishment of regional and sub-regional organisations or communities in the fourth wave, starting in the mid-1970s. This followed the formal establishment of the Organisation of African Unity (OAU) in 1963, the year that the author argues is the starting stage of the third wave and the culminating and crowning point of earlier waves of pan-Africanism.

Benedikt Franke, however, offers a different analysis with regard to the place of Regional Economic Communities (RECs) in the timeline of the different waves of pan-Africanism. His analysis seems more nuanced with one part of it converging with that of Landsberg. This is perhaps owing to the fact that his study focuses on regionalisms and does not deal with the wider pan-African movement. He identifies two waves of regionalisation in Africa, with the first one preceding the establishment of the OAU. He notes that the competition seen these days between the RECs also characterised their counterparts/predecessors then. This places the formation of the first RECs in Africa in the second wave of pan-Africanism going by Landsberg's categorisation. Their two analyses then converge when Franke notes the significance of the formation of the OAU or the high hopes its establishment raised with black peoples the world over. It was hoped that the new organisation would embody pan-Africanism and put an end to political divisions that had split the continent in preceding years into almost feuding blocs. Another wish was for it to become the supreme political authority with the power to coordinate Africa's many cooperative and regional activities and groupings.

But a cursory look at the state of regionalism in Africa today shows that these high hopes have not materialised. Instead, Africa has seen more and more regional organisations springing up despite significant efforts by the secretariats of the OAU and now the African Union (AU) to minimise these divisions. This state of affairs begs the question: what are the places, roles and effects of the existing RECs on the notion of pan-Africanism and what explains this state of affairs? It is with this thorny issue that this chapter deals.

We divide the chapter into three main sections. The first section briefly looks at the notion of pan-Africanism, the pan-African movement and their linkage with regional groupings in Africa. The second section will look at the state of regionalism on the continent and the factors contributing to this. The third section will look more closely at some of the factors explaining the current state of affairs. Here we identify three main factors: a) multiple allegiances and the prevalence of external dependence; b) the lure of nationalism and personal power policies; and c) lack of commitment, political will and self-esteem. At a time when some are calling for a government of African Union, dealing with these issues is necessary for the promotion of an effective integration in Africa. This will allow us, in the concluding section, to advance some general recommendations with the aim of making the RECs the true pillars and building blocks of pan-Africanism of which the AU, we hope, is or should be the incarnation.

From Pan-Racialism to Pan-Africanism

'Pan-Africanism' is at once a political movement, a social-cultural phenomenon and an ideology containing a set of political ideas and ideals, norms, and values that seek to bring about the unity of African peoples (Landsberg, 2004:117). This definition or description of the phenomenon seems broad and all-encompassing, but it would seem that Landsberg eyes a specific aspect of it, that which reduces it to the continent of Africa. The author makes it clear that his study 'deals with pan-Africanism as politics.' With regard to this 'political pan-Africanism,' he submits that this is 'embedded in an emancipatory project to rid the continent and its people of racism, colonialism, and foreign subjugation' (ibid). According to Abdul-Raheem (1996:13), 'the essence of Pan-Africanism demanded a willingness to surrender petty nationalism for the greater unity of *Africa*' (italic is ours). As it will be clear below, these two definitions or descriptions represent only one form or stage of the concept of 'Pan-Africanism'.

Dealing specifically with its political component, as Landsberg, Chen Chimutengwende's description of the notion is more in line with the broad meaning found in Landsberg's first definition but is more explicit than it. Chimutengwende (2006:109-118) contends that 'Pan-Africanism served as the dynamic and driving force for the black liberation struggle for independence and civil rights.' The term 'black' clearly encompasses all that is African – that is Africans living on the continent of Africa and their descendants that have permanently settled abroad, regardless of how, when and why they came to settle where they are. The phrase 'struggle for independence' is an explicit reference to Africa, while 'struggle for civil rights' refers to Africans in the Diaspora and their fight for equal rights.

The point we are trying to make here is that the broad picture of the concept given above by Chimutengwende includes two phases and/or faces of the subject matter. One is Pan-Racialism and the other is Pan-Africanism. These are two faces and in this order they represent two periodical phases of the movement. The broad definition is what we find in the 'One Africa' call by the pioneers of the movement, such as William Edward Burkhardt DuBois (1867-1963), Henry Sylvester Williams, George Padmore, Peter Millard, Ras Makonnen, Marcus Garvey and CLR. James. The common denominator between these pioneers is that they were all what Ali Mazrui calls 'Africans of blood but not of soil' – meaning they belonged to the African or black race but were not born and bread in Africa. This is why Patricia Romero calls them 'New World Blacks' – Africans of the continent being 'Old World Blacks'.

To Romero (1976:321-336), the pan-African movement can be divided into two historical periods, one marked by the 'One Africa' approach and dominated by Africans of the Diaspora, and the other being led by Africans of the soil and narrowly defined and limited to the continent. According to the author, Ghana's regain of independence in 1957 as the first black African nation to do so marked the end of the transition from Pan-Racialism to Pan-Africanism. Both faces and phases are however called 'Pan-Africanism', which is for more than convenience. For it is clear that whether led by Afro-Americans or West Indians or by Africans of the continent, the main thrust of the movement was centred on Africa, hence Garvey's 'Back-To-Africa' movement.

Indeed, a number of these New World black activists went to live in various African countries once those regained their independence. For example, DuBois moved to Ghana where he died in 1963; Padmore worked in Nkrumah's government; and Makonnen moved to live with his friend and former employee (in Manchester), Jomo Kenyatta in Nairobi (Romero, 1976:327-329).

What does this brief conceptual overview of the phenomenon of 'Pan-Africanism' tell us about the state of African regional groupings today? This is where lies the significance of the analyses of Landsberg and Franke.

As noted above, Landsberg (2004:119) identifies five waves of pan-Africanism. He makes 1880 the starting point of the first wave. According to him, this wave consisted of the struggle against or resistance to European expansionism and colonial occupation between this year and 1945. The second wave was that of decolonisation between the end of World War Two (or the Second European Civil War, as he calls it) and 1962, when most African countries regained their independence. The period between the formation of the OAU in 1963 and 1975 constitutes the third wave, that of African unity. As mentioned earlier, the author places the fourth wave in the period between 1975 and 1989 and identifies it with the establishment of regional groupings in Africa. He contends that this constituted some sort of devolution of pan-Africanism from the OAU to these regional groupings. But this argument is somehow questionable as seen in Franke's analysis above, and we will say more about this below.

Since the end of the Cold War, the author thinks we are in the fifth wave, the wave of the African renaissance. This involves a series of initiatives, such as the Millennium Africa Recovery Plan (MAP), inspired by South African President Thabo Mbeki; the Omega Plan for Africa, a brainchild of Senegalese President Abdoulaye Wade; and the New Partnership for Africa's Development (NEPAD), a compromised amalgamation of the two previous initiatives.

Of all these waves, it is the fourth one that interests us in this chapter, and this is where we bring in Franke. According to this author, Africa experienced the establishment of a whole range of regional schemes for political and economic cooperation during the colonial period. This was more noticeable in French colonies as a reflection of Paris' bent of centralised administration. The links between these 'cooperative' organisations were therefore vertical between them and metropoles rather than horizontal among the colonies. Reference is made here to the

Afrique occidentale française (or French West Africa – AOF), *Afrique équatoriale française* (French Equatorial Africa – AEF), and the Central African Federation (Franke, 2007). Although these were colonial creations for the sole administrative convenience of the metropoles, they came to cement some kind of unity amongst Africans. So much so that the preservation or the breakdown of AOF became a major debating issue between independence leaders such as Sékou Touré of Guinea, Senghor of Senegal, Houphouët-Boigny of Côte d'Ivoire, Ouezzin Koulibaly of what later became Burkina Faso, and Hamani Diori of Niger.

There were other cooperative movements created by African intellectuals and students, mainly in the metorpoles. These tended to be true African organisations or movements. One such movement was the *negritude* movement led by the Senegalese scholar, Alioune Diop, and the great Martinique poet, writer and later politician, Aimé Césaire (June 1913-April 2008), in Paris. One could argue that the negritude movement was the Francophone complement of the Anglophone-dominated pan-African movement, one based in France and the other in England and the US. Although the negritude movement was chiefly cultural, the main thinking of its militants assembled around the publication series *Présence Africaine,* set up in 1947, was that the flowering of black culture was impossible in a situation of political dependence, and that black people needed to be united by solidarity in the struggle for their emancipation (Asante & Chanaiwa, 1999:24-743).

What Franke's article shows is that the fissure observed above in the interpretation of pan-Africanism between the broader Pan-Racial concept and the narrower Pan-African one exhibited itself in the interpretation of the continentalist pan-Africanism itself or how to achieve its emancipating goal. The colonial Anglophone, Arabophone, Francophone and Lusophone demarcations further widened this crack. It led to the creation of various organisations with members of each of them claiming that theirs serves better the pan-African cause than those of others. We are still in the second wave according to Landsberg's chronology, the period from 1945 to the formation of the OAU, during which many African countries regained their independence. As these countries realised the need for cooperation, but given some of the aforementioned factors, Africa saw a proliferation of intergovernmental organisations, federations, unions and economic communities.

Leaders such as Kwame Nkrumah of Ghana and Sékou Touré of Guinea warned against regional federations, lest regional loyalties give rise to power politics and undermine African unity. But there were other leaders who were opposed to such a far-reaching political union. They perhaps did not believe in the notion of neo-colonialism or did not see the threat of it warranting such drastic steps as the derogation of sovereignty to a supranational political authority (Asante & Chanaiwa, 1999:726).

As a result, Africa saw the establishment of such regional groupings such as the Pan-African Freedom Movement of Eastern, Central and Southern Africa (1958), the *Conseil de l'Entente* (1959), the Union of African States (1960), the African States of the Casablanca Charter (1961), the African and Malagasy Union (1961), and the 1962 Organisation of Inter-African and Malagasy States (Franke, 2007; Uda, 2003:140). In the words of Asante and Chanaiwa (1999:726), by the time the OAU was founded, the 33 or so independent African states or their leaders that signed its Charter were greatly divided. They were 'divided horizontally into pro-East and pro-West blocs, and vertically into revolutionaries, progressives, reactionaries, capitalists, socialists, traditionalists and middle-of-the-roaders.'

Of particular importance was their division into two main blocs within the continent. On the one hand were Ghana, Guinea, Egypt, Mali, Morocco, Libya and the Algerian government-in-exile that formed the Casablanca Group and advocated for a greater unity, if not a United States of Africa outright. On the other hand were the remaining former French colonies plus Nigeria, Ethiopia, Liberia and Sierra Leone that formed the Monrovia Group. The leaders of this latter group were more conservative, were keen on maintaining good relations with former colonial powers (most former French colonies in this group had already entered into bilateral defence agreements with France), or feared the real or perceived personal ambitions of some of their counterparts in the other group (Asante & Chanaiwa, 1999:726). For these reasons, the founding of the OAU in May 1963 as a result of a compromise between the two groups and including all independent African states was very significant.

The primary objective of the OAU was to strengthen relations among the newly independent African states, coordinate their development efforts, and assist those other African territories not yet independent to rid themselves of the yoke of European colonialism. As Khadiagala and Lyons (1997) indicate, continental identity, supranationalism and integration in various forms proceeded from the desire to unite disparate geographic units, to pool resources in concerted actions and to increase the leverage of the continent as a whole in world affairs (see also Legum, 1979; Maloka, 2006).

It would seem however that the statist and gradualist approach of the Monrovia Group prevailed over the unionist approach of the Casablanca Group in the new organisation. And perhaps this is what explains what Romero (1976:330) finds strange that on the tenth anniversary of DuBois' death, and on the same anniversary of the founding of the OAU, 'no tribute from that body was forthcoming to the "Father of Pan-Africanism".' But what is of more interest to us here is the observation of Woronoff (1975:68-70) that the OAU Charter did not contain any specific provision clarifying the continental hierarchy of institutions and organisations, nor did it determine the actual relationship between the OAU and the sub-regional organisations and groupings that existed before its founding or that came to be formed later on. In fact, the OAU gave itself (or was given) no supervisory power over these organisations. Nor were the regional organisations required to consult with it or even inform it of their decisions (see also Franke, 2007). We submit that it is largely this problem and other factors that explain what we now turn to below.

The State of Regionalism in Africa

Before proceeding to the subject matter, a brief conceptualisation of the phenomenon of regionalism or regional integration is needed. A definitive and universal theorisation of the phenomenon is almost unattainable, and in any case not envisioned in this chapter owing to the different drives that lead different regions or groups of states to come closer and integrate their economies. Suffice to note here that Daniel Bach, one of the most prominent African scholars on this subject, has defined 'regionalism' as the implementation of a programme and the definition of a strategy, associating it with 'institutional building'. He defines 'regionalisation' as 'processes that may or may not be related to the emergence of institutional structures and patterns of transaction' (Bach 2004: 70). Bourenane (1997:50) defines it as 'a voluntary pooling of resources for a common purpose by two or more sets of partners belonging to different states'.

The process of regional integration starts with the creation of a *free trade area,* when members eliminate all or most trade restrictions against each other's goods. This is followed by the creation of a *customs union,* then a *common market,* which transcends the customs union to free movement of the factors of production (i.e. workers, goods, services and capital). From common market one moves to *economic union,* which is the highest form of economic integration, incorporating the previous stages of integration and extending to the harmonisation of monetary and fiscal policy amongst the member states. The highest form of all integration processes is *political union,* which transcends economic integration to supranational decision-making between the member states (Gilpin 2001:343). It would seem that efforts at African unity aim at one of the two latter stages of regional integration. But does the current state of regional groupings in Africa offer any indication that one or the other of these two stages might be achieved on the continent anytime soon? If not, what explains this?

Let us now take a closer look at the state of regionalism on the continent in the hope that this might help us answer these questions. In geo-political terms, Africa is divided into five natural regions: West, East, North, South and Centre. However, as we finalised this chapter in mid-2008, there were fourteen regional groupings on the continent; that is seven full-fledged RECs and seven smaller intergovernmental organisations (IGOs) with regional dimensions. In West Africa, alongside the Economic Community of West African States (ECOWAS), encompassing all the 15 countries of the sub-region, there is the *Union économique et monétaire oust-africaine* (West African Economic and Monetary Union —UEMOA), consisting of eight ECOWAS member states—all French-speaking with strong links to Paris. Albeit not very active due to political factors, there is a third grouping in the region: the Mano River Union, consisting of three ECOWAS member states (Guinea, Liberia and Sierra Leone – with Côte d'Ivoire striving to join it).

In East Africa, there is the Inter-Governmental Authority on Development (IGAD), whose seven member states come from the Horn of Africa and the northern part of East Africa. There is also the Economic Community of Great Lakes Countries (known by its acronym of CEPGL), consisting of three members of the Economic Community of Central African States (ECCAS), which consists of eleven members across Central Africa. Still in East Africa, there is the *Communauté économique et monétaire des Etats d'Afrique centrale* (Central African Economic and Monetary Union —CEMAC), the identical equivalent of UEMOA in West Africa, comprising six French-speaking ECCAS countries. The East Africa Community (EAC) is made up of COMESA members Kenya and Uganda and SADC member Tanzania – which does not make it in reality a purely East African grouping.

In Southern Africa, there is the Southern African Development Community (SADC), whose fourteen members consist of all of the countries in Southern Africa. But there is also in the region two other economic communities: the Southern African Customs Union (SACU), consisting of five members of SADC, and the Indian Ocean Commission (IOC), made up of four members of COMESA and Réunion. COMESA stands for the Common Market for Eastern and Southern Africa and its name shows its far-reaching span. The 20 countries that make up its membership include all East African countries except Tanzania and seven countries of Southern Africa.

In North Africa, there is the Arab Maghreb Union (UMA), consisting of the six North African countries (minus Egypt) with close links with the Arab League. But it has been stagnant since 1995 because of political discords between its member states, particularly between Algeria and Morocco over the question of Western Sahara. There is also in the region the Tripoli-based Community of Sahel-Saharan States (CEN-SAD), whose 18 member states transcend four geographical regions, feeding its ranks from almost all the five regions of the continent, with countries such as Libya (N. Africa), Mali (W. Africa), Chad (C. Africa) and Swaziland (S. Africa) very active in it.

This is the state of regional integration in Africa as it stood at the time we completed this chapter. Most of these RECs have very sophisticated treaties and protocols guiding their work, which are quite similar, if not identical, to those of other groupings on the continent. Most of them have well-functioning secretariats and they conduct frequent meetings at the summit, ministerial and technical levels (ECA 2004:30). While this shows how determined Africans seem to be to integrate their economies, it is clearly not an indication that the greater continental unity can be achieved unless these various groupings are rationalised. It is perhaps out of the recognition of this fact that the Constitutive Act of the African Union set for itself as one of the objectives the task of 'coordinating and harmonising the policies between the existing and future Regional Economic Communities for the gradual attainment of the objectives of the Union.'

In fact, given that some of these RECs transcend geographic regions, there is a tendency for some countries to have multiple memberships in the RECs. As shown by the Economic Commission for Africa's comprehensive report about regional integration in Africa, of the 54 (53 AU members + Morocco) African countries, 26 are members of two RECs and 20 are members of three. One country (the Democratic Republic of Congo) belongs to four RECs. Only five countries (Algeria & Mauritania (UMA only), Malawi & Mozambique (SADC only) and ECCAS member

Sao Tomé & Principe) maintain membership in just one Regional Economic Community (ECA 2004:40; Souaré, 2006:17-24).

Evidently, this state of affairs does not augur well for the expected harmonisation of these regional groupings in view of forming an all-African common market (Oyejide, 2003; Souaré, 2006:17-24). But before suggesting any remedy to this issue, we must first diagnose the problem, and here again we bring Franke on board. According to Franke (2007), the root causes of these problems as well as the key to overarching issue of competing regionalisms in Africa can be found in five mutually reinforcing determinants. The author lists these determinants as: a) the political-ideological rifts permeating the continent; b) the prevalence of external dependence and influence; c) the lure of nationalism; d) institutional weaknesses resulting from the absence of political will and regional identities; and e) personal power politics.

Abass Bundu, a former Executive Secretary of the ECOWAS, makes a similar diagnosis with regard to this specific regional organisation, one of the most active and effective regional groupings on the continent. He identifies seven main issues. These are: a) the absence of an integration and development culture in the individual West African countries; b) the priority accorded to nation-building in the years following independence rather than collective regional development initiatives; c) differences in ideology and approach; d) the fear of Nigeria's domination; e) the burden of certain institutional and economic structures inherited from colonialism; f) the economic crises that plagued the region from the early 1980s; and g) political instability (Bundu 1997:29).

These two diagnoses show that it is almost the same problems facing regional groupings on the continent, either taken together or individually. We are, however, of the view that some of the points raised by both Franke and Bundu are more like symptoms or results of others rather than independent factors in their own right. We thus limit our diagnosis to three main and interlinked factors. The three main issues that caught our attention are the following: a) multiple allegiances and the prevalence of external dependence; b) the lure of nationalism and personal power policies; and c) lack of commitment, political will and self-esteem. The latter two factors being easy to apprehend than the first one, we shall now take a closer look at the factor of multiple allegiances and only mention the other two in passing.

Multiple allegiances and the prevalence of external dependence

The overlapping membership seen above in the composition of the various regional groupings is an evidence of multiple allegiances of African states. This is at the continental level. It is also worth noting that in addition to this, the continent is divided into various groupings in which the different African states are assembled with mainly their former colonial 'masters'. We are referring here to the British Commonwealth of Nations, the group of French-speaking nations or *l'Organisation Internatinale de la Francophonie* (OIF), the *Jamiatu Adduwal Al-arabiyah* or the Arab League, and the *Comunidade dos Paises de Lingua Portuguesa* or the Community of Portuguese Language Countries (CPLP).

Founded in the 19th century as a forum for states 'owing allegiance to the [British] Crown,' according to the Balfour Report of 1926, 18 of the 53 governments and territories that make up the Commonwealth today are from Africa. That is after the withdrawal of Zimbabwe in 2003. The permanent secretariat of the Organisation is, not surprisingly, in London, the former colonial capital. Africa also provides more than half of the 49 member states and governments of *la Francophonie*. As much as 27 countries are from Africa, and the permanent secretariat, as in the case of the Commonwealth, is in Paris, the imperial metropolis. The main objective of the organisation is the advancement of the French language.

The same can be said about the other two organisations with variant degrees. For example, of its 22 member states, about half (10 members) of the Arab League are African. African countries constitute even a majority in the CPLP, for five of the eight countries of which the organisation consists today are African. As in the case of the aforementioned array of RECs on the continent, each of these organisations have over the years created organs that are somehow supranational in nature, with periodic meetings at the highest political level of member states. All are now engaged in political processes from election monitoring to political co-operation at international venues such as the UN.

Albeit Angola and Mozambique rejected it, the CPLP have even had the courage to propose the adoption of common citizenship between its eight member states. A similar proposal about free movement of people – although bound to fail – has been made within *la Francophonie*. Gulf states would not allow this vis-à-vis the African members of the Arab League, but many distinctive arrangements are in place between the member states, including in visa processing (Souaré, 2005:75-82). In addition to these multilateral blocs, African states are also divided between 'special bilateral partners.'

The point we are trying to make here is that all these contribute to creating distinctive identities and allegiances of the different African states in these different organisations. One is therefore justified to ask the question: where is their African identity? Clearly, with one's hopes and all his aspirations focused on one entity, the devotion and significance that one attaches to this entity cannot be equated to what one may have in the case where you have more entities.

It would seem that the mentality of external dependence, lack of political will and lack of self-esteem (as Africans) that many African leaders have account for much of this state of affairs. Many African leaders appear to accord more importance to how they are viewed in London, Paris and Washington than at home. Many feel more reassured by their membership in these various organisations, especially foreign-based ones, than to work towards strengthening a single or a minimum number of Africa-wide organisations.

This is especially true of those RECs that have close ties with so-called special bilateral partners outside Africa, particularly the two exclusively francophone economic communities (UEMOA in West Africa and CEMAC in Central Africa), which have 'a special' relationship with France. Only recently have these two institutions accepted the membership of other countries outside the "francophone" bloc, with "lusophone" Guinea-Bissau and Equatorial Guinea respectively joining UEMOA and CEMAC. In fact, both communities, especially the West African Economic and Monetary Union were created, if not at the instance of France, then at least by its strong backing in order to undermine ECOWAS, then seen as a Nigerian initiative to fulfil its hegemonic aspirations in West Africa (Adedeji, 2004).

Given the declared long-term objective of the eventual fusion of all the RECs into the African Economic Community – by the OAU in Lagos in 1991 – and then the African Union (in the fullest sense of the word), these multiple and overlapping memberships make this process more complicated. The situation becomes even more complicated when foreign linguistic affiliations play a divisive role among African countries and weaken the process of consensus-building necessary for common decision-making. Africans are now divided between Francophones, Anglophones, Lusophones and, to an extent, Arabophones.

It should moreover be noted that with multiple allegiances come multiple responsibilities. As the AU Commissioner for Economic Affairs rightly said in 2005, 'the RECs are under-funded, the member states are not able to make their contribution to the AU or their respective RECs on time because they have so many commitments. If a country has to belong to just one REC, then that would lessen the financial burden on it' (AUC News, Dec, 2005). The problem of overlapping membership and the rivalry it generates are well illustrated by the relationship between ECOWAS and CEAO/UEMOA in West Africa and between COMESA and SADC in Eastern and Southern Africa (CDD, 2002). Clearly, the whole project of African unity could be in danger if these divided allegiances were to continue to evolve at the pace they now seem to have.

Conclusion

The concept and vision of 'pan-Africanism' emerged at a time when most African states were still under the yoke of European colonialism or subjugation. In fact, the struggle to regain their sovereignty is what gave rise to the pan-African movement. Until African states began to redeem their independence in the second half of the last century, the pan-African movement or ideal was an all-encompassing one, advocating a 'One Africa' approach and a single 'African identity' for African peoples both in Mother Africa and in the Diaspora. The newly-independent states of Africa made their way into a world society that was already both economically and politically structured, with rules of the game long defined and rubber stamped. These structures and rules were of course in favour of those that established and made them.

The urgent need of the newly independent states for social and economic development led most of the new African leaders to realise the interconnectedness of politics and economics. Yet, the micro-states that these leaders had inherited from colonialism meant that many African states were too small to be economically viable and thus be in a position to transform their political independence into economic independence (Asante 2004:51). Although African countries had been greatly divided in their strategies for handling this situation, they eventually came to the conclusion that there was no better way than coming together. This led to the formation of the OAU as a result of that realisation.

The new organisation, however, failed to overshadow regionalised entities that preceded it and did not attempt or manage to prevent the establishment of new ones or assume a coordinating role between them. As a consequence of this and a multitude of other mutually reinforcing factors, the drive for unity in Africa seems to have been reduced to what Franke (2007) describes as 'regionalism without common values' or 'asymmetrical regionalisation.' This trend, instead of unifying the continent, is dividing it into various regionalised and internationalised blocs. This calls for proper rationalisation of regional groupings on the continent and a rethink of the various allegiances that African states have. With all its noble aims, this should clearly take precedence over the idea of a United States of Africa or Union Government. For you cannot build a house over wobbly foundations and expect it to be sustainable.

To that effect, there are two schools of thought. One submits that since the RECs are considered the Building Blocks of the proposed Common African Market or the AU they should be rationalised along the five regions of the AU, which suggests two things. One is for the current 14 RECs and IGOs to be reduced to five. This requires dismantling those RECs whose membership transcends their natural geographic regions or asking those members that are not from the region where the REC is rooted to kindly withdraw from such RECs and maintain their membership in the REC that is representative of their geographic region. The second school of thought contends that the existing RECs and IGOs should be maintained, and calls for efforts to be made to review their mandates and modes of operation so as to avoid duplication of projects and activities.

It is clear though that none of these two suggestions is an easy policy choice but reducing the number of RECs seems a better way to achieve the still-elusive pan-African dream of unity than the second option. A cause of optimism, however, is that the AU seems to be leaning towards the direction of this option. This can be seen for example in the fact that the proposed African Standby Force (ASF) has five regional brigades (for more about this force, see Cilliers, 2008; Fanke 2007). This should be applied to the RECs and the latter should fully cooperate if they are truly committed to African unity. African citizens and civil society groups have a role to play here in terms of putting pressure on their leaders to heed such appeals.

References

Abdul-Raheem, Tajudeen (1996), 'Introduction: Reclaiming Africa for Africans – Pan

Africanism: 1900-1994,' in Tajudeen Abdul-Raheem (ed.), *Pan-Africanism: Politics, Economy and Social Change in the Twenty-First Century* (London: Pluto Press).

Adedeji, Adebayo (2004), 'ECOWAS: A Retrospective Journey,' in Adekeye Adebajo & Ismail Rachid (eds.), *West Africa's Security Challenges: Building Peace in a Trouble Region* (Boulder and London: Lynne Rienner Publishers).

African Union (2005), *The Newsletter of the African Union Commission* (December).

Asante, S. K. B (2004), 'The Travails of Integration,' in Adekeye Adebajo & Ismail Rachid (eds.), *West Africa's Security Challenges: Building Peace in a Troubled. Region* (Boulder and London: Lynne Rienner Publishers).

Asante, S. K. B and David Chanaiwa (1999), 'Pan-Africanism and regional integration,' in Ali A. Mazrui and C. Wondji (eds.), *General History of Africa: VIII Africa since 1935* (Oxford, Berkeley and Paris: James Currey, University Press of California and UNESCO).

Bach, Daniel C. (2004), 'The Dilemmas of Regionalization' in Adekeye Adebajo & Ismail Rachid (eds.), *West Africa's Security Challenges: Building Peace in a Troubled Region* (Boulder and London: Lynne Rienner Publishers).

Borenane, Naceur (1997), 'Theoretical and Strategic Approaches,' in Réal Lavergne (ed.), *Regional Integration and Cooperation in West Africa: A Multidimensional Perspective* (Trenton and Asmara: Africa World Press).

Bundu, Abass (1997), 'ECOWAS and the Future of Regional Integration in West Africa,' in Réal Lavergne (ed.), *Regional Integration and Cooperation in West Africa: A Multi Dimensional Perspective.* Trenton and Asmara: Africa World Press.

Chimutengwende, Chen (2006), 'Pan-Africanism and the Second Liberation for a United New Africa,' *African Renaissance,* 3 (1):109-118.

Cilliers, Jakkie (March 2008), 'The African Standby Force: An update on progress,' *Paper* no. 160 (Pretoria: Institute for Security Studies), available at: www.issafrica.org

Economic Commission for Africa (2004), *Assessing Regional Integration in Africa* (Addis Ababa: ECA Publications).

Franke, Benedikt, F. (2007), 'Competing regionalisms in Africa and the Continent's Emerging Security Architecture,' *African Studies Quarterly,* 9 (3): online at: http://web.africa.ufl.edu/asq/v9/v9i3a2.htm

Gilpin, Robert (2001), *Global Political Economy: Understanding the International Economic Order* (Princeton: Princeton University Press).

Hey, Jeanne, A. K. (1995), 'Foreign Policy of Dependent States,' in Laura Neack, Jeanne A. K. Hey and Patrick J. Haney (eds.), *Foreign Policy Analysis: Continuity and Change in Its Second Generation* (Englewood Cliffs: Prentice Hall).

Khadiagala, Gilbert, M. and Lyons Terrence (1997), *African Foreign Policies: Power and Process* (London and Boulder: Lynne Rienner Publishers).

Landsberg, Christopher (2004), The Fifth Wave of Pan-Africanism,' in Adekeye Adebajo & Ismail Rachid (eds.), *West Africa's Security Challenges: Building Peace in a Troubled Region* (Boulder and London: Lynne Rienner Publishers).

Lavergne, Real, *Regional Integration and Cooperation in West Africa: A Multi Dimensional Perspective* (Trenton and Asmara: Africa World Press).

Legum, Collin I. William Zartman, Lynn K. Mytelka and Steven Langdon (1979), *Africa in the 1980s: A Continent in Crisis* (New York, McGraw-Hill).

Oyejide, Ademola, T. (2000), 'Policies for Regional Integration in Africa,' *The African Development Bank, Economic Research Paper,*

Romero, Patricia, W. (June 1976), 'W.E.B. DuBois, Pan-Africanists, and Africa 1963-1973,' *Journal of Black Studies,* 6 (4) :321-336.

Souaré, Issaka, K. (2005), 'African Membership of the Arab League, Commonwealth, la Francophonie, and the CPLP : Implications of Divided Allegiance for Regional Integration in Africa', *African Renaissance,* 2 (1) :75-82.

_____(2006), 'African Union and Regional Economic Communities in Africa : Minimizing Allegiances and Rationalizing Partnership', *African Renaissance,* 3(1) :17-24.

UDA, Ede, J.V. 2003. 'La Politique Etrangère des Etats africains: Ruptures et continuités d'une diplomatie contestée,' *Revue Juridique et Politique des Etats Francophones,* no. 2 (April-June) :140-156.

Woronoff, Jon (1975), 'The OAU and Sub-Saharan Regional Bodies,' in Yassin El-Ayouty (ed.), *The OAU after Ten Years – Comparative Perspectives* (New York : Praeger).

Chapter 15

ARAB-AFRICAN RELATIONS: FROM LIBERATION TO GLOBALISATION *

Helmi Sharawy

Is it legitimate today to subdivide the African Continent according to the "races" it contains? Can this, moreover, be simply done with an historic content for race, or an idealistic concept of identities? Or are we going to talk about the Arabism of Egypt, Libya or Morocco as if it were an identity gained with the advent of the "Arab Race", implying that these were "lands with no people" - a sort of No Man's Land? Or fragile spaces that could not confront the invading Empire? Or will Arabism equate Bantuism or Negroism at one time, and Haussa and Swahili cultures at other times? If we continue in this vein, we shall end up with Arabism confronting Africanism with no scientific definitions, and thus quit the domain of social sciences, and enter the realm of easy ideologies, in an epoch of the great phantom ideologies.

There is no scope here for a comprehensive study, nor does the author assume an apologetic attitude towards the stances of geography or history, while the catastrophic imperialist globalisation, and its product in the continent and the Arab world leaves no place for escape into past models. However, the scientific mode of thinking may help us comprehend the social, cultural and historic reactions, governed by the laws of "dialectics" and contradictions in the epochs of the great migrations, and empires, until all were encompassed within the logic of the polarising world capitalist system. Thus, the Arabs and Africans entered the colonial era as products of the world capitalist system. In the colonial era, identities did not develop, for they developed and crystallised only in the era of national liberation, as we shall see later.

The phase of demographic intermingling, and interaction, or acculturation, through the advent of the historic empires (which were far more respectful of the peoples than the present day imperialist Empire), saw the Roman Empire, followed by the Arab Islamic Empire. In this latter, the Arab "race" played a limited role, for a short period of time only, but its Islamic Arab culture was disseminated mainly by various elements (from the East, West, or even south of Europe), which prompted the Peoples in the north of the continent, and other parts as well, to adopt this political and social culture.

For historic reasons, Egypt and Morocco became the centres for dissemination, anthropologically as well as politically, and the same factors stood behind its acceptance, or otherwise, at the borders of the Sahara, and limited parts of East Africa, and Andalusia in Europe, and Persia in Asia, etc. The intensity of the force of the local reaction, and the specific historical and geographical circumstances decided the fact that Egypt identified itself as "Arab", Morocco to a lesser degree, while Spain and Iran refused the Arab identity. In Africa, rose the Empires of Mali and the Songhai, as well as the City States in Kilwa, lamu and Mombassa.

The spread of Arab Islamic Empire

The spread of the Islamic Empire "in African Sahara " did not lead to the disappearance or distortion of societies or languages as happened under colonial rule later on. Ajayi, and Davidson, and ogot, and others, speak a lot about this phase of interaction, and the emergence of the empires of the Hausa, the Fulani, the Manding, and the Amhara or Abysinnians, who could not, in their turn, annihilate the Yoruba, or the Mussas, or the Somalis. No one belonging to the Cape Town school or any other, can deny the product of all these empires in two fields: the existence of various forms of class or social exploitation, or enslavement; and the absence of the concept of Africanism in those conditions. The same is true of the absence of "Arabism" in the domain of Islamic culture. The dominant feature was the resistance offered by these peoples along the centuries, in various traditional forms, to colonialism: as demonstrated for instance by the peoples of Egypt, the Fula and the Zulus in their isolated local cultural units. Such empires and kingdoms of the pre-colonial era could have developed into modern states had it not been for the colonial intervention. All these countries lived through the beginnings or the embryo of the modern state at the same era as the European states, but were distorted or interrupted by capitalist colonial invasion. These countries did not suffer the same defeat during the period of the Arab-African interaction. Hence new conditions for the development of new identities emerged, but gave rise to deformed identities in Mamluki Egypt, and Morocco under the Bays, and isolated elsewhere in the continent. We should note here that Egypt and Morocco suffered under "Islamic" Ottoman occupation prior to the capitalist expansion in the rest of the continent, and this Ottoman citizenship predominated up to the environs of Mali and Zimbabwe, with no intimation of Arabism. Similarly, the "Jihad" meant for a long time, the management of the interaction in Morocco and West Africa, still on an Islamic basis.

It will be necessary to point out the fact that Egyptian historians do not generally speak about one Egypt, but rather about Pharaonic, Coptic, Mamluk, or Ottoman Egypt, then modern state Egypt, and Arab Egypt since the Nasser era. Thus, stress is not laid upon any one identity, but rather, on the dynamism of the identity, or its development according to the laws of dialectics. However, some stabilising elements may prove their importance in influencing future developments, even if not consciously concerned with the identity. Here, we note the deep presence of the Arabic language and its traditions in the African North, while Islamic Sciences, and Islamic Ulamas played the deepest role in the rest of the Continent, to the extent of writing some of their contributions in Aajami (African languages in Arabic characters), rather than in Arabic. Such a close loyalty to Islam, and not Arabism, lay behind the different degrees of interaction between the various regions of the Continent. It is therefore astonishing to see some African scholars follow their colonial predecessors in denying the existence of a certain Islamic African Identity (or even Arab as in the case of the Hausa or Fulani), which need not be in full agreement with the models of the identities born of the ideologies in vogue.

Phases of modern identity building

Following this scientific dialectical methodology, we can proceed to the study of one of the main phases of modern identity building - and I insist on speaking of phases and not stable conditions - which shows new characteristics in conformity with the new dialectics imposed by the colonial and imperial epochs.

To be brief, we shall proceed directly to the phase of Pan Africanism and Pan Arabism, which were concurrent with all similar pan movements whether Islamic, Turanic, Slavic, or even Arian (German or Nazi). We shall first examine the traditions inherited by our Arab and African region prior to the emergence of these pan movements, i.e. inherited from the period of the colonial invasion, after the hegemony of the world capitalist system. During that period, lasting two to three centuries, the colonial ideology, the "negation from history" was imposed (see A. Cabral and W. Rodney). The big social entities were negated, as well as the principal linguistic entities at the hands of colonial anthropologists (see K. Prah). Another instance of this "negation", which had almost become a self-choice after being imposed, was the ideology of tribalism (see Archie Mafeje).

The emergence of Pan Arabism or Africanism was more of a political phenomenon than a socio-political development. We have therefore to question the popular content of these pan movements, and their spontaneous consistence with the socio-political movement, and the role of the new consciousness in reforming that movement. Now that building consciousness has become an endeavour in itself, we have to ascertain the role of its actors, and the masses that adhere to it, in order to make sure that this new Africanism or Arabism is the same as the pan movement of before. Since any "policy" has its own social, political and cultural base, it is imperative to define these elements very clearly when studying Africanism and the pan movement. The same holds in the case of Arabs, Arabity and pseudo Arabism. Such a study will show that the new Africanism is much more recent than Pan Africanism, and similarly, Pseudo Arabism is more recent than Pan Arabism.

The Pan African movement was conceived in the Diaspora, and the "other" in its view was not colonialism in particular, but the oppressor, which gave rise to various tendencies within the movement that were not directly related to liberation from colonialism. Such tendencies appeared with Garvey, or Blyden, or the leaders of the Negritude or francophone movements, who did not take a clear anti-colonial attitude except after the development of the National Liberation Movements after the Second World War. Although Du Bois and R. James were clearly anti-colonial, unfortunately they were not the most vocal within the movement, and this condition still persists till today. This may partly explain its weak influence among the peoples of the Continent. We may even contend that weak anti-colonial stand at the inception of the African Movement led to its weak relation with the Arab Movement, which was openly anti-colonial from the start.

On the other hand, the Pan Arab Movement was conceived around the beginning of the 20th century, like its Pan African counterpart. It started in similar conditions on the initiative of certain groups of politicised Christian intellectuals opposed to the tyranny of the Ottoman coloniser. While the African movement started in the Diaspora, this one was partly alienated at the start, for three reasons: first, it was mostly Levantine in origin, second, it was mainly Christian in a predominantly Moslem world, third, it did not gain the whole hearted support of Cairo and its intellectuals at its start, nor did it get the full support of the Maghreb which was on the throes of its "Islamic" insurgence against the

French who gave their efforts for subjugation an anti-Moslem character from the start. Thus, the Pan Arab Movement in its turn did not gain much popularity except after World War II. A thorough analysis of both Movements shows that National Liberation retained the commanding position of the rise and deterioration of both Movements, and their inter-relations as well.

In brief, we may conclude that the political turmoil attached to both Movements was the driving force for their charismatic leaderships after independence, and which put the independence of the Congo at the heart of the Arab Liberation Movement (before that of Aden, and during the Algerian Revolution). It also kept the fight against Apartheid at the heart of both Movements, and led to the creation in Casablanca, in 1961, of a group combining three countries of the "Arab" North, and three countries from Sub Saharan Africa. This group, created its common Post and Customs units, as well as ministerial committees of all sorts, soon to be followed by the creation of the Organisation of African Unity (OAU), in 1963. In this latter, Egypt and Algeria played prominent roles, and especially outstanding, was the role played by the "Coordinating Committee for the Liberation of the Colonies". At that time in the sixties, the Author was a researcher in the team of the bureau detailed by Gamal Abdel Nasser for African Affairs, and was responsible for the various offices belonging to 22 African Liberation Movements, and a member of the expatriate committee that was responsible for the presence and well being of some 20,000 students from all parts of Africa (north and south), who were getting free education like all Egyptian students in all grades of education.

Of course, we had to face certain every day problems from some unruly youths, and a certain cultural tradition of aversion against "black" youth. There was as well some exaggerated talk about the Black Giant, and others about the "civilising" role of Islam and Arabism in Africa, and the insistence of the Islamic Movements on the importance of dissemination of Islam and the Arabic language. Some African governments complained that it was not of much use to have their youth receive religious education in Al-Azhar and not in regular schools and universities, and Abdel Nasser responded by creating special sections to teach in English and French in the Universities for African students.

We lived all through such problems of interaction. However, the discourse against Arabs, and the historic legacy of slave trade, came only from openly reactionary sources as we used to say, and it was no coincidence that such talk came from some of the leaders of the

Negritude Movement, and capitals like Abidjan, Dakar and Nairobi well known for their "Entente" with Imperialist Powers. This was no surprise since revision of history is an ideological process as much as a cultural one. But I would stress that the tune of the common National Liberation was the more prominent, and was much more credible for African unity than the racist accusations, or the negative versions of the historic relations between the Arabs and Africa. This confused attitude to the assessment of social history should receive more attention in future.

From Liberation to Solidarity

"From Liberation to Solidarity, and from Solidarity to Cooperation": This was the trend of Arab African relations down to the nineties of last century when the interaction came almost to a standstill. By the end of the sixties, the symbols of National Liberation had almost all been toppled, by coups d'etat, or by the imperialist Zionist aggression in Egypt's case. The leading "political Voice" grew weaker at the beginning of the seventies, although the armed struggle was still rising in Africa and Palestine as an indication of the continuing unrest of our peoples. The Arab-Israeli war of 1973 was an attempt at breath taking, but it had ambivalent effects. It showed the depth of the African-Arab solidarity (with Egypt, Syria and Palestine) on one hand, but caused some losses to the development plans of the newly liberated nations of Africa due to the rise in petrol prices, on the other hand. At the same time, the Imperialist Powers started their counter attacks against the third world, by imposing the newly conceived policies of so called economic reform, and structural adjustment, which meant the wave of privatisations, the reduction of the commitment of the State, and the resulting deterioration of public services. To better achieve these goals, the mechanisms of third World solidarity such as the Non Aligned Movement, and the UNCTAD were reduced to ghosts of the past.

However, we must note that during the 1970s, the revolutionary fervour was still apparent in Africa, where we saw Algeria assume the role of Nasser at the head of the Group of 77, to build a new Economic Order; and in the centre of the Continent, the armed struggle achieved good results in Guinea Bissau Angola and Mozambique; and rose to new heights against Apartheid in South Africa. Arab and African Liberation Struggle got world recognition when Arafat and Sam Nujoma were received at the United Nations, as the General Assembly recognised "the right of the struggle against colonialism by all means", (meaning the armed struggle). Severing political relations with Israel was another sign of the continued solidarity between peoples whose main concern was still National Liberation. On the Arab side, we saw Libya try to continue the role of Egypt in helping the African Liberation Movements, and the Sudan signing the historic reconciliation agreement with the South in Addis Ababa in 1972, and Morocco recognising Mauritania. This led to Arab solidarity with African nations in their plight due to the rise of oil prices, when the Arab Summit in Algiers created a special fund to compensate the African States for any difficulties caused by the rising oil prices.

Still, we must admit that the discourse of "common liberation" was being replaced by that of "solidarity" in an economic crisis that looked very much like helping the poor relatives by their more affluent relatives. It was a shift from the discourse of "Revolution", to that of "Riches". The issue was no more one of cooperation, but one of give and take. This let the door wide open to compromise solutions with racist regimes, as in the case of the Camp David agreement between Egypt and Israel (1979), and the Komati agreement between Mozambique and South Africa (1984). This all led to the demise of the solidarity trend itself as time went by.

Yet the relations between the two groups continued to develop even against the trend pursued by the World Order to contain any independent blocks, which culminated in the destruction of the Socialist Block itself - the main antagonist to the Imperialist Capitalist Block. We shall not elaborate on the continued institutional forms of Arab-African cooperation, which prove the will of the two sides to keep interacting even under these unfavourable conditions. This will is structural as well as functional, and is bound to stay alive unless the globalisation mechanisms manage to stifle all such trends for cooperation between the oppressed, and not only between Arabs and Africans. Thus, after an Arab-African Summit in Cairo, attended by 62 countries, in March 1977, a development Bank, a Fund for technical assistance, and permanent cooperation committees, were created between the two sides. It was also agreed to create a joint Arab-African Cultural Institute, and a permanent Trade Exhibition. All this demonstrated the deep wish for a common historical presence within Third World Structures, yet it also indicated the nature of the regimes that stood behind that entire endeavour. Those regimes were an integral part of the World Capitalist System, and not merely on its periphery, as proved by the investment of the integral amount of the Oil Capital in American and European financial institutions, and in US Government Bonds. They also comply fully with the policies of the International Financial Institutions (World Bank and

International Monetary Fund) of privatisation, reducing the role of the State, and the exclusion of the masses in the Arab and African Worlds, from any real participation in the production process. All this ended by reducing the above framework into an empty structure, with no effectiveness whatsoever starting from the 1980s.

The spirit of liberation loses its heat

When the spirit of liberation loses its heat, and the feelings of solidarity lie low, and the cooperation institutions deteriorate, between groups of people already imbued with mutual mistrust, it becomes very difficult to mobilise them for united action. This becomes even harder as the governing regimes get more involved with the militarised imperialist leaderships which dare, these days, resort to direct colonisation (in Iraq) to which they had not dared resort for almost a century. In this new atmosphere of globalisation, rife with the ideas of conflict of civilisations, where Islam had assumed the role of Ultimate Evil in place of communism, the Arab-African relations are imbued with new hallucinations about the close connection between Islam and Arabism, as a follow up of the old doubts about the connection between Arabism and Islam in the first place.

There are enough residual problems to keep such doubts lively, as well as certain elements that might entrain a country or other in this anti-cooperation direction. There is also an intentional confusion in the presentation of certain issues. This situation may be better understood, when we remember the global framework in which Arab-African relations take place. The Arab World is subjected to open oppression from the early nineties (in Iraq and Palestine), as an exercise in the military projects of the USA since it assumed the role of the single military Pole. In such a framework, it is easy to make the connection between Islamic Fundamentalism and Terrorism, then over and above, came the terrorist attacks against the US embassies in Nairobi and Dar Es-Salam, and the conflicts between Christians and Moslems in Nigeria, and the application of Shari'a Laws in some Nigerian States. Of course, the American media in spreading such accusations, intentionally ignore that it was the US that was the first to cooperate with the Islamic Fundamentalists in the Arab World to confront the forces of the Left, and recruited and trained the terrorists of Osama Bin Laden to fight the Soviet Union in Afghanistan. We shall not elaborate on this issue here, but it is closely connected to the American, and European position in Somalia and Mauritania (on the borderlines between Arabs and Africans). Similarly, the whole issue of South Sudan is now presented in the light of the "Arab Sin", in the framework of Moslem- Christian conflict. Instead of studying it as social historical problems as it is not the Arabs who are in Nigeria or Somalia, or were in Rwanda some- or all- the times as for as "Cape Town School" would like to assert.

More problems may afflict Arab-African relations with the rise of the role of Israel in the World Arena in contrast with the situation in the seventies. Israel is now playing a prominent role in the Arab region, on behalf of the United States, and enjoys a position of strength in the World Financial Lobby. A special position is reserved for Israel in the measures adopted by the European Union for the Mediterranean Participation Project. It also plays a leading role in the world market for diamonds, and hence meddles in the illicit diamond trade that fuels the ethnic conflicts in Central and Western Africa. It is even trying to meddle in the recent trend for renegotiating the partition of the Nile Waters.

Although all these problems have a global dimension, the constant efforts of the Zionist movement to increase its influence, on the one hand, and the Nationalist, and Fundamentalist reaction on the other hand, urge the Arab side to look forward to some kind of breathing space from the Africans, in order to keep their relations on course as they used to be. It remains to be seen to what extent the protagonists of the Pan-African Movement, and the African Union will respond to this requirement in order to preserve this important block of the Third World. Is it possible to rise above the narrow limits of the local or regional considerations, and let this power realise its due position in the WTO and OPEC? Could these two groups realise that the future of the World Order is **not** necessarily American, especially in the light of the difficulties the US encounters in the Middle East, and the greater role played by an enlarged European Union, and a renewed role for the United Nations? I believe that within such a framework, Arab- African Relations may experience better conditions in spite of the unfavourable situation caused by the hegemonistic mechanisms of American globalisation. Arab and African Intellectuals will have to overcome some issues in the field of ideology and methodology such as:

- History cannot be arrested and transformed to non-historic "still" facts or phenomena, and that the dialectics of the relations between peoples have resulted in the rereading of such phenomena.
- Analysis according to "Race" or "Colour", or even "Tradition" or "Region", is not appropriate in the era of globalisation. Therefore, Arab

or African identities could not be read as "closed units" in on open theatre of the anti – globalisation movement.

- The ideological mechanisms, and the media trumped up by the globalisation circles create the issues that keep us, consciously or unconsciously' at each other's throats.
- Serious debates should be undertaken by intellectuals on both sides to go over the whole agenda and resolve any issues that need to be cleared.

References

Ajayi, J.F.A (1967): A thousand years in West African History (Ibadan, I.U.P).

Cabral, A, (1980): Unity and Struggle (Oxford, Heinemann).

Ki- Zerbo, J (1980): A General History of Africa (Unesco, Vol 1)

Mafeje, A. (1970): "The Ideology of Tribalism" in Journal of Modern African Studies Vol 9-2.

Ogot, B.A (ed., 1985): Kenya in the 19th century (Nairobi, Bookwise).

Prah, K. (1995): African Languages for the Mass Education of Africans (Bonn 1995).

Rodney, W. (1970) A History of Upper Guinea Coast 1545-1800 (Oxford, Clarendon Press).

---

* Originally published in *African Renaissance*, Vol. 1 No. 1 June 2004.

Chapter 16

GENERAL CONCLUSIONS: ONE AFRICA, MANY DESTINIES?

Jideofor Adibe

We have seen from the various contributions in this volume that the notion of who is an African remains contested. Many of the contributors also implicitly suggest that the unresolved nature of African identity and levels of Africanity have implications for the various unity projects in the continent. This raises a fundamental question: If, as is commonly agreed, unity is very essential to the survival and development of any group, then the question of unity for what, and for whom, should equally be posed when talking about African unity. If the unity desired among Africans is to enable them withstand outside economic and political pressures and threats, then another related question must first of all be posed and resolved: Do Africans, sharing different levels of Africanity, and tied by various neo-colonial structures to different centres of power in the world, have a common perception of these threats? Do for instance those regarded as Arabs have a common perception of political threats with the Bantus of say, Nigeria? Do Francophone, Anglophone and Lusophone Africa have a common perception of political threat?

Answers to the above questions are obviously not straightforward and could be approached from different perspectives, with each perspective perhaps yielding a different answer. The point however is to show how complicated the forces pulling Africa and Africans in conflicting directions are. In other words, the problem of the different levels of Africanity borne by Africans appears to be complicated by the different regions of the continent being tied to different neo-colonial structures that approximate to spheres of influence of the former colonial powers: Thus Africa struggles not only with an identity issue but is also being pulled in different directions by the different neo-colonial structures to which they are tied. For instance through the notion of *la Francophonie*, the French-speaking Africans like Garbon, Burkina Faso often feel more attached to France, and French-speaking countries in much the same way that Malawians and Ghanaians for instance feel they have more in common with members of the British Commonwealth and

English-speaking countries than those grouped either around France or the Community of Portuguese Language Countries (CPLP). Clearly these structures seem to contribute to undermining a strong sense of African identity among Africans. As Issaka Souare (2005: 79-80) noted:

> Clearly, with one's hopes and all his aspirations focused on one entity, the devotion and significance that one attaches to this entity cannot be equated to what one may have in the case where you have split entities. Without doubt, as the conference of Berlin (1884 – 85) served to partition Africa, these different identities seem to be doing exactly the same. Africans are now divided between francophones, anglophones, lusophones and, to an extent, arabophones. Because of this, someone from southern Cameroon considers himself closer to Côte d'Ivoire than to his northern Cameroonian brethren just because they share French with the Ivorians and northern Cameroonians speak English... But it is not the psychological aspects and lack of attachment to, or consciousness about one's African identity, that is the only cause of worry here. The whole project of African unity could be unravelled if these divided allegiances were to continue to evolve at the pace they now seem to be doing.

Do the above problems mean that there is no hope for Africa? Do they mean that Africa will always remain without Africans, or at best with Africans who have different levels of Africanity or whose Africanness will remain contested? I do not think so. Despite the challenges, there is a lot of optimism about Africa and by Africans and recent developments in the world seem to favour the continent.

First, is that despite its numerous challenges, Africa holds the hope of turning its differences into advantages. The various levels of Africanity in Africa is a rich source material for turning the continent into a real melting point of culture pretty much the same way globalisation is turning the US and some European countries into real cultural melting pots. Africans have also shown that they could come together to fight against common threats. They did so during the struggle for independence, when liberated countries often aided those still under the yoke of colonialism, to free themselves. Arab Africa and non-Arab Africa also came together to impose sanctions against Apartheid South Africa and quite often take common positions in the United Nations. In addition, though globalisation will bring its own tensions, it also has within its bowels the seeds of unity as people will increasingly come to bond around common concerns such as whether they are getting their fair share of the fruits of technical progress, freedom, peace and security of life and property. These shared concerns and goals are truly capable of submerging the differences among Africans.

The rise of new economic powers – Brazil, China, India and Russia – is also likely to weaken the neo-colonial structures that tied different African countries to the former colonial powers, which, as we noted earlier, appear to contribute in undermining the various unity projects in Africa. As Howard W. French (2008) succinctly puts it:

> During the last decade of political neglect of Africa, China has made extraordinary inroads on the continent, eclipsing the commercial presence of Europe's old colonial masters, and lapping fast at the heels of the United States as Africa's most important trading partner. China's trade with Africa has more than doubled in the last two years alone, reaching roughly $120 billion this year. It is important to state that China is pushing into Africa not as some charity project, but because of two very carefully reasoned conclusions. China, for one, badly needs priority access to Africa's storehouse of minerals, petroleum and even farmland. Even more jarringly for Americans, who have embraced a deep and abiding bigotry of low expectations about the continent, though, China sees Africa as a frontier of opportunity; a place whose future is bright. (see also Adibe, 2008)

There is indeed evidence that other emerging powers, including South Africa, are increasingly looking towards Africa as the next big destination, not only for raw materials but also as a market for their goods. They also appear to be offering Africa and Africans new forms of relationship that is more respectful than what they were used to. Africa is therefore likely to have more choices, which will benefit it economically, and with it also politically. Based on these, Afro pessimism seems increasingly passé, despite the continent's current challenges, including with citizenship and identity.

There is also the apparent deepening of democratic ethos in Africa despite the reversals in Guinea Conakry and Mauritania. The successful civilian-to-civilian transitions in Ghana and Benin Republic, coupled with the rise in the use of the Internet and blogging, have raised hopes that the democratic project in Africa is deepening. Though there remain challenges in many countries, the increasing number of highly educated Africans in the West, with ready access to radical news websites and blogs, and challenging their governments on accountability and the rule of law, are all sources of hopes. As democracy deepens, the love of freedom that it brings in its wake is likely to supersede other fissiparous tendencies that underlie the various notions of Africanity.

Besides, as Africans – irrespective of the Africanity they bear - continue to do marginally worse than most parts of the world in terms of their share of the rewards from developments in technology and science, a common bond is created, a bond stronger, and deeper than any racial or political divisions that currently exist. It is a bond that makes people instinctively to seek to ally with others in similar positions, to improve their competitive ability, and maximise what they get from the global pool. The innate desire to better one's economic lot through alliance with fellow travellers is a bond that is stronger than the current centrifugal tendencies that make the notion of who is an African appear contestable.

The emergence of Barrack Obama, whose father is Kenyan, has also given a very powerful impetus to Africa's unity project. All over Africa during the presidential campaigns in the USA, Africans of various Africanities, race and religion, came together to pray for his success at the polls. Though no one knows yet how his regime will impact on Africa, the belief that he is an African - by the system of patriarchy dominant in Africa- appears to have unleashed a powerful can-do attitude. For many Africans therefore, Obama is both an African name they can relate to, and a metaphor expressing that anything is possible if you strive hard for it with the 'right attitude.' This 'right attitude' is an attitude that is post-chauvinism, for it is only by being post-racial and a reconciler that a Blackman, with an African Muslim father, who was not born into privilege, could emerge president of the most powerful country in the world. This lesson is not lost on Africans and it is a powerful boost to the African unity project.

References

Adibe, Jideofor (2008): "Winners and Losers From the Rise (or Recovery) of China" http://www.worldpress.org/Asia/3059.cfm January 7 (accessed February 3, 2009)

Howard W French (2008) "Obama and Africa: The Change We Have Been Waiting For?" http://www.huffingtonpost.com/howard-w-french/obama-and-africa-the-chan_b_141899.html November 28 (accessed February 3, 2009)

Issaka Souare (2005): "African Membership of the Arab League, Commonwealth, la Francophonie, and CPLP: Implications of Divided Allegiance for Regional Integration in Africa" in *African Renaissance,* January-February , pp79-80)

Afterword

BUILDING A POWERFUL AFRICA-NATION

Mammo Muchie

> "The future of blacks all over the world is interconnected. It was so in the past when black civilizations were under pressure. It is even more so at present... Black communities must find a way to articulate their historic unity." Diop, *Great African Thinkers*, p.246

When we say the diversity of Africans cannot be used to deny Africa's agency to a historic unity to valorize the dignity of the African people, to stand up on their feet rather than always kneeling before successive oppressors and tormentors, lots of people always smirk, and say this is a sort of pie in the sky thought.

Starting from the 15th century, African dignity has been violated, before the 15th century many flourishing African empires and communities existed. The pre-15th century situation can be a source of positive data to feed constructively the making of African unity. The history since the 15th century is also not all 'negative' in a sense, if we accept that hope could be found even a in worst situation. Africa's negative history is made of the shared experience of slavery, which provides the data for forging strong purpose for unity. The challenge of the European scramble for Africa also is another source to derive intellectual, political and moral energy and power to unite Africa. The arbitrary division of that period inherited largely by the post-colonial states has bequeathed a plethora of conflicts from which Africans have found it difficult to extricate themselves.

The more conflict persists, the more compelling the argument to create a broader framework of African unity to articulate an orientation where self-organizing communities that have necessary political will can grow and legitimately pursue local freedom and local governance.

Is it Africa must unite or perish or is it black people must unite or perish? Are we calling for a political unity of the continent of Africa, or for or all those that are racially African-black who have experienced a particularly uncongenial gaze from European and other communities? If we take the continent of Africa, how are those who are black Africans expected to relate with other communities, races, and peoples? Africa has been particularly hard hit by slavery, colonialism and the post-colonial international aid regime. These have created a situation where there is severe interference on the continent. Africa is the most violated and the most condemned continent in the world. No other place has been as violated as Africa mentally, physically and in terms of the plundering of its rich resources. This situation continues to this day without abetting.

Marcus Garvey is explicit in arguing strongly for the creation of a Black Super Power by uniting African Blacks the world over. He said that without a black super power that can provide the example for the rest of the world with concrete achievements, there will be no chance for black people to be seen as equal with other races. Garvey's Pan-Africanism can be seen as a pan-Africanism that privileges race and culture.

Dr. Kwame Nkrumah argued for the political unity of the African continent on the basis of the states just freed from the colonial yoke in the early 60s. His was a Pan-Africanism that privileged politics first and not race as in this unity are include Arabs who still today harbor primitive notions of the black African as an object to be bought and sold. This despicable practice, we are painfully reminded, still takes place in Sudan and Mauritania. In other places we still have millions of black maids and laborers for other races in Africa where the blacks have their original home.

Today we have the official AU/NEPAD processes to bring about painfully slow, and mostly unsatisfactory functional integration of African states and their activities. At a regional level, the regional communities like ECOWAS and SADC are trying to form regional mobility of factors of production such as investment and labour.

Even within the existing fragmented states we have potential super powers such as Nigeria in the Western part of Africa and South Africa in the South. To date no African Super power acknowledged and recognized by other Africans has emerged.

The question then is, if indeed for Africa to be seen as a player in world affairs, a black super power as Garvey said is a necessity, how is this super power to be created? If we disagree with Garvey, then there is no case to answer. If we agree that the rise of the black race is critical then a country, state or the collective unity of blacks – or any combination of these, need to be encouraged, to get the race to rise above the ugly gaze that others time and time again have relegated and degraded it through out the last 509 years, then we must act now and not tomorrow to redeem the race, and vindicate the long resistance by forging together Africa's bright future.

The Africa-Nation could be the answer to Garvey's Black Super power that also becomes the super example to future generations of Africans and others.

Africans did not surrender easily to slavery. They did not surrender to colonialism. The Zulus rebelled. The Ashanti fought. The Ethiopians can be regarded to have provided Africa's and indeed the black race's most potent resistance liberation logo that can serve very well to day's unfinished quest to unite Africa. When Emperor Haile Selassie led the Ethiopian-African anti-fascist resistance he was fully aware that he was fighting for the dignity of the black race and Africa

In the current post-colonial period the liberation and unity agenda is still open.

Talking about the inhibiting role of African diversity is not useful. We must understand a nation is more than a community of origin; it is a community of shared experience, globally shared history, a shared resistance-liberation logo, a shared project, opinion and purpose.

In Africa the blackness of Africans provide membership into a familiar group, regardless of how black Africans may use different differentiating identities, others' gaze see them without any distinction as black.

Africans both individually and collectively have the urge to be liberated from the colonial authorities and their oppressive power and the crippling and stifling gaze that has taken neo-colonial and patronising modes as time goes by even today and beyond.

In addition the African nation has the following attributes:

- A determined resistance against foreign domination until Blacks are fully sovereign and free,
- A mission for self-governance and independence,
- A struggle to preserve traditional values, indigenous structures, knowledge, and communitarian and rehabilitative justice from African tradition
- A common need to come together and become strong to overcome the condemnation of the gaze and belief that Africans are second-rate,
- The composition of an African personality from colonial mutilation;
- A shared project for achieving social, political, economic and cultural upliftment and enlistment,
- A shared approach to finding a pathway to taking Africa into the 21st Century;

These are necessary conditions to build both the black- nation and the black-super power that can be a super example to the rest of the world.

Let us build by any means possible the African black super example nation and leave open the options of how this could be done. It could be either South Africa or Nigeria, or the ECOWAS or SADAC, or it can be the unity of blacks the world over or it can be through the AU/NEPAD processes.

As we have no power to stop any of these processes, what we should aim at is to make sure that all these processes find meaningful synergies to forge the most enduring unity that inscribes as history and the future Africa's total emancipatory imagination, logo and liberation by finally ending the long resistance with full success by creating the Africa-nation that Africans build and the rest of the world respects. Africa must stand up on its feet, head high, and must never bow on its knees to any form of oppression ever again.

References

Diop: Great African Thinkers, p.246 quoted in Chinweizu, On Ubontology/Black Redemptionist Studies:Afrocentric Human Sciences for Black Redemption:Groundwork for the Intellectual Autonomy of the Black World, 2008, p.16

Muchie, M. (ed.) (2003) *The Making of Africa-Nation: Pan Africanism and the African Renaissance* (London, Adonis & Abbey Publishers)

Prah, Kwesi (2007), *The Africa Nation: the State of the Nation,* (Cape Town, CASASS),

NOTES ON THE AUTHORS

General Yakubu Gowon (Rtd) was Nigeria's Head of State from July 1966 to July 1975. After his regime was overthrown in 1975, he went into exile in the United Kingdom, where he acquired a Ph.D. in political science from Warwick University. In the 1990s he formed a non-denominational religious group, Nigeria Prays. He also establed the Gowon Centre for National Unity and International Co-operation in 1992, an NGO dedicated to furthering the cause of Nigerian unity. In his younger days, Dr. Gowon was a keen hockey player and took part in competitive sports, including soccer and boxing.

Jideofor Adibe studied political science at the University of Nigeria, Nsukka, and was the first to complete a doctorate degree in International Development Studies at Roskilde University, Denmark. He also studied the New Economic Powers at Oxford University, United Kingdom, and equally holds an LLM degree in Media Law from City University, London. He has been a guest research fellow in a number of institutes, including the Centre for Development Research, Copenhagen, Denmark, the Centre for Developing Area Studies, McGill University, Montreal, Canada, and the Scandinavian Institute of African Studies, Uppsala, Sweden. He is currently the editor of the multidisciplinary journal, African Renaissance, and the publisher, Adonis & Abbey Publishers Ltd. His books include The Loneliness of Exile (in Danish translation, 1995), Broken Dreams (2003) and Free Speech v Reputation: Public Interest Defence in American and English Law of Defamation (2009). He also writes a weekly for the Daily Independent, a leading national newspaper in Nigeria.

Professor Ali Mazrui needs no introduction to any student of African politics. Nominated as one of the 100 greatest living public intellectuals in the world by the Washington-based journal, Foreign Policy, Professor Mazrui is the author of more than twenty books and hundreds of articles published all over the world. He was the author and narrator of the highly regarded television series The Africans: A Triple Heritage (BBC/PBS, 1986). He is currently Director of the Institute of Global Cultural Studies and Albert Schweitzer Professor in the Humanities, State University of New York at Binghamton. He is also Andrew D. White Professor-at-Large Emeritus and Senior Scholar in Africana Studies, Cornell University, Ithaca, New York, USA; Chancellor, Jomo Kenyatta

University of Agriculture and Technology, Thika, Kenya as well as the Albert Luthuli Professor-at-Large at the University of Jos, Nigeria.

Kwesi Kwaa Prah is retired Professor of Sociology at the University of the Western Cape. He is currently Director of the Centre for Advanced Studies of African Society (CASAS) at Cape Town, South Africa. Educated in Ghana, he took university degrees in the Netherlands and has held research and teaching posts in Sociology and Anthropology in various universities across Africa as well as in Germany, the Netherlands, England and China. Prah has written many books including Beyond the Colour Line (1998), African Languages for the Mass Education of Africans (1995) and Capitein (1989). He also published A Critical Study of an 18th Century African (1992), The Bantustan Brain Gain (1989), African Languages for the Mass Education of Africans and Mother Tongue for Scientific and Technological Development in Africa (2000).

Mohamed A. Eno is a faculty at ADNOC Technical Institute. He holds a PhD in Social Studies Education and MA in TESOL. He has contributed chapters in a number of books. His volume The Bantu – Jareer Somalis: Unearthing Apartheid in the Horn of Africa is a major contribution to Somali studies. Mohamed is multilingual, poet and journalist. He is currently working on a major project on the theme of Somali Bantu literature. His interests are in oral traditions, oral literature, ethnic studies, sociolinguistics and teaching and learning.

Omar A. Eno is a PhD candidate (ABD) in History at York University, Canada, where he has taught History for several years. Currently he is faculty at Portland State University where he is also the Director of the US National Somali Bantu Project. He has contributed chapters in several books and presented extensively on issues relating to minorities and ethnic marginalization, peace and reconciliation, social development and refugee integration. Omar is a poet with interests in Diasporic studies, oral traditions and oral history.

Steven Friedman was a Senior Research Fellow at the Centre for Policy Studies, an independent policy research institute, in Johannesburg, South Africa. He is the author of Building Tomorrow Today (1986), a study of the South African trade union movement, and editor of two books on South Africa's transition - The Long Journey and The Small Miracle. He has also published widely on democratisation and related topics. He is currently a Research Fellow at the University of Johannesburg, South Africa.

Forster Bankie Forster was born in England, of Ghanaian and Gambian parentage. A lawyer by profession, his research interest is international relations, with emphasis on Africa and Asia. He has worked in a number of West and Southern African countries. He is a member of the General Council of the Sudan Commission for Human Rights (SCHR).

Garba Diallo was born in Mauritania, and is a specialist in international conflict management with special focus on Africa and the Middle East. Diallo is an experienced dialogue facilitator and lecturer working with youth, media people and educators in conflict zones in the Middle East, the Horn of Africa and Central Europe. He is the founding director of Crossing Borders and Garba Diallo of Crossing Borders Global at the Krogerup College in Denmark.

Franco Henwood is a London-based independent human rights commentator and analyst, with an interest in the relationship between armed conflict and human rights, ethnicity and human rights and economic, social and cultural rights.

Monique Theron teaches at the Department of Political Sciences, University of South Africa (UNISA), based in Pretoria.

Gerrie Swart teaches African Politics in the Department of political science at the University of Stellenbosch, South Africa.

Marcel Kitissou began teaching at the University of Benin (Togo), where he directed the Institut Superieur de Presse (du Conseil) de l'Entente (I.S.P.E.). He also served as Associate Director of the Ecole Nationale d'Administration (E.N.A) of Togo. In the US, he taught History, Political Science, and Public Administration at the State University of New York at Oswego where he later directed the Peace Education and Conflict Ethos (P.E.A.C.E.) Institute. Following his undergraduate studies in Togo and graduate studies in France and the US, he earned, among others, a doctoral degree in Contemporary History (University of Bordeaux) and a Ph.D. in Political Science (Maxwell School of Syracuse University). Kitissou was at various times the Executive Director of the Africa Faith and Justice Network (a Washington, DC-based NGO), and Faculty Director of the Global Humanitarian Action Program at George Mason University. He is Visiting Fellow with Cornell University's Institute for

African Development and professor of public policy at the Union Institute & University at Cincinnati, Ohio. His recent publications include Hydropolitics in Africa: A Contemporary Challenge (co-edited), and Africa in China's Global Strategy (edited).

Gamal Gorkeh Nkrumah is the eldest son of the first president of Ghana, Kwame Nkrumah and his Egyptian wife, Fathia Nkrumah. He received his Ph.D. in political science from the School of Oriental and African Studies, He worked as a political journalist in Al-Ahram Weekly, Egypt's leading English language newspaper, and is currently the editor of International Affairs section of the newspaper

Issaka K. Souaré is a Senior Researcher in the African Security Analysis Programme at the Tswhane (Pretoria) office of the Institute for Security Studies and PhD candidate in political science at the Université du Québec à Montréal, Canada. A Contributing Editor to the journal, African Renaissance, he is the author or co-editor of numerous publications relating to Africa, including Africa in the United Nations System, 1945-2005 (2006); Civil Wars and Coups d'État in West Africa (2006), the novel, Samassi (2004); and (co-editor) Somalia at the Crossroads: Challenges and Perspectives in Reconstituting a Failed State (2007).

Dossou David Zounmenou is a Senior Researcher in the African Security Analysis Programme at the Tshwane (Pretoria) office of the Institute for Security Studies (ISS). He holds a PhD in International Relations from the University of Witwatersrand, South Africa and is a regular speaker on African issues with many media organs. Dr Zounmenou lectured at both Wits University Walter Sisulu University in South Africa before joining the ISS.

Professor Helmy Sharawy is Director of the Arab & African Research Centre at Cairo, Egypt. He has published profusely on African political sociology and Arab-African relations.

Mammo Muchie is Research Professor at the National Research Foundation, South Africa, and also Research Professor at the Department of Science and Technology, Institute for Economic Research on Innovation, Tshwane University of Technology, Pretoria, South Africa He is equally the Chairperson of the Network of Ethiopian Scholars, and also a part time professor and coordinator of Research on Innovation and International Political Economy at Aalborg University , Denmark. His abiding research interest is to find conceptual tools for rethinking African unity, freedom and development.

INDEX

Z

www.ingramcontent.com/pod-product-compliance
Lightning Source LLC
Chambersburg PA
CBHW070405270326
41926CB00014B/2708

* 9 7 8 1 9 0 6 7 0 4 5 5 1 *